D0202858

Gated Communities

Gated Communities

Social Sustainability in Contemporary and Historical Gated Developments

Edited by
Samer Bagaeen and Ola Uduku

publishing for a sustainable future
London • Washington, DC

First published in 2010 by Earthscan

Earthscan Ltd, Dunstan House, 14a St Cross Street, London EC1N 8XA, UK
Earthscan LLC, 1616 P Street, NW, Washington, DC 20036, USA
Earthscan publishes in association with the International Institute for Environment and Development

For more information on Earthscan publications, see www.earthscan.co.uk or write to earthinfo@earthscan.co.uk

ISBN: 978-1-84407-519-5

Typeset by Domex e-Data, India
Cover design by Rogue Four Design, www.roguefour.co.uk

A catalogue record for this book is available from the British Library

Library of Congress Cataloging-in-Publication Data

Gated communities : social sustainability in contemporary and historical gated developments / edited by Samer Bagaeen and Ola Uduku.
    p. cm.
 Includes bibliographical references and index.
 ISBN 978-1-84407-519-5 (hardback)
 1. Gated communities. 2. Gated communities–History. I. Bagaeen, Samer. II. Uduku, Ola, 1963–
HT169.58.G374 2010
307.77–dc22

                                                                            2009021298

At Earthscan we strive to minimize our environmental impacts and carbon footprint through reducing waste, recycling and offsetting our CO_2 emissions, including those created through publication of this book. For more details of our environmental policy, see www.earthscan.co.uk.

This book was printed in the UK by the Cromwell Press Group.
The paper used in FSC certified.

This book is dedicated to both our families

particularly for

Victor and Olivia Bagaeen

and the late Dr W. C. Uduku

Contents

List of Figures and Tables

Figures

Tables

Acknowledgements

This book had a slow birth, evolving first in Glasgow late in 2005. It was eventually put together in Brighton, Edinburgh and London. The book features an international list of contributors, to whom we are grateful for their patience and cooperation. We would also like to acknowledge the comments sent by our anonymous reviewers; their constructive comments encouraged us to get it done. We are grateful to everyone at Earthscan who helped bring this book to life. Our respective institutions, the University of Brighton and the Edinburgh College of Art, have also been instrumental in the support given towards the completion of this book project. We give our particular thanks to Saskia Sassen and Ziauddin Sardar, who agreed to the task of reviewing the volume and contributed their thoughts on 'gating' as a global phenomenon. Finally we thank our families, who have had to put up with the endless nights of work put into this book.

Samer Bagaeen and Ola Uduku
Brighton and Edinburgh
December 2009

Foreword

Urban Gating:
One Instance of a Larger Development?

Saskia Sassen

This book opens up the question of gated communities at a time when its meaning has become fixed and narrow. In a major contribution, Samer Bagaeen and Ola Uduku, the book's editors, examine the long history of gated settlements, from walled hamlets to what we think of as today's American gated community and the new transformations of the gated concept in rapidly urbanizing settings in Asia and Latin America. As they traverse these diverse times and spaces in their examination they make legible the shifting meaning of gated settlements.

In this opening I find an invitation to shift from the familiar notion of gated community to a more generic notion of urban gating. Thus, several of these chapters give us the longer and the deeper history of urban gating, histories that show us that gated communities are one format that arises when urban areas expand. They 'belong' to urban sprawl and suburban space, here understood in a longer temporal frame. Yet they take on specific meanings across time and space. Thus, today's security-oriented urbanism is a core component of this global era, and it is so across the world, as we can see in the chapters on cities as diverse as Lagos, Buenos Aires or Johannesburg. At the same time, these authors show us that privately run and controlled residential developments were part of the *faubourgs* of early 19th-century Paris, a city much admired for its urbanity, and they were part of early Los Angeles development, a city whose urbanity is far less admired.

Conceptualizing and historicizing of this sort opens up the analytic terrain for understanding urban gating. And it has the effect of recoding what has become the standard meaning of gated communities since the 1980s. Gated communities, as these have been built and conceived of in large urban areas over the last 20 years, are but one of a range of instances of urban gating, one phase in a long history across time and space.

This, in turn, raises an interesting question. Does the fact that urban gating grew so sharply since the 1980s, at least compared with most of the 20th century, point to a foundational dynamic in the current global age, one that extends well beyond cities and urban communities? Armed with such an expansive meaning of gating, we can conceive of it as part of a foundational, though partial, disassembling of what were meant to be unitary systems: while urban gating has largely referred to the city as the unitary system it partly disassembles, I would like to extend the analysis to include non-urban unitary systems, notably nation states.

Urban gating can be conceived of as a particular type of assemblage of bits of territory, authority and rights once ensconced in the larger unit of the city. I find that a key, yet much overlooked, feature of the current global era is the proliferation of partial, often highly specialized, assemblages of bits of territory, authority and rights into novel formations where once those bits were firmly ensconced in national institutional frames. These assemblages can be internal to the nation state or cut across borders.

Mostly, gated communities have been seen as internal to an urban area. Yet it makes me think that especially in the case of the gated communities of the rich and the privileged, we may well have missed the fact of growing cross-border interactions among these increasingly global elites, not only through their workplaces, but increasingly perhaps also through their family and social life. This would mean that such elite gated communities are increasingly part of what I have elsewhere called geographies of centrality that connect the power centres of the world and cut across the old North–South divide. But this also raises a question as to the emergence of counter geographies of marginality and contestation that can connect the disadvantaged in major cities across the world. The global city is also a factor in the making of the global slum, a far more complex space, in my reading, than its poverty and miseries suggest. I find elements of this in some of these chapters: the poor also seek protected spaces.

Urban gating has never been seen through this lens; it is usually pigeonholed as an urban development and, hence, as somewhat epiphenomenal to the larger global arena. I have struggled to bring cities, especially global cities, into the conceptual frame of the global. And reading this book makes me think that perhaps urban gating in the current epoch is part of this larger foundational dynamic.

List of Contributors

Samer Bagaeen (www.samerbagaeen.net) is a self-styled socially responsible chartered town planner and senior lecturer and area leader for town planning at the University of Brighton, UK. Educated at the Bartlett and University College London, Samer also holds an MBA from the University of Strathclyde in Scotland. He has built a track record over 15 years in built environment education, community activism, international consultancy and policy-relevant research in the areas of ex-military sites conversion, urban power, urban conflict and sustainable regional development. He lives in a gated mews in Brighton's Kemptown.

Delphine Callen (callen@parisgeo.cnrs.fr) is a PhD student and lecturer at the Department of Geography of the University of Paris, 1 Pantheon-Sorbonne. She holds an MSc in regional planning and an MSc in theoretical geography. Her research focuses on the role of global property development firms in the production of suburban residential areas in the metropolitan region of Paris at the turn of the 1990s to 2000s. She also led research work on French gated communities.

Jennifer Dixon (j.dixon@auckland.ac.nz) is professor of planning in the Faculty of Creative Arts and Industries at the University of Auckland, New Zealand. Her research interests focus around issues of urban intensification and sustainability, private urban governance (including management of intensive housing), and the phenomenon of gated communities. Current projects include two multidisciplinary research programmes on sustainable water management and urban form.

Ann Dupuis (http://sscs.massey.ac.nz/dupuis.htm) is associate professor of sociology at Massey University's Albany Campus in Auckland, New Zealand. Her academic interests span two major areas: urban sociology and the sociology of work. She has published extensively in areas, including urban intensification, urban governance, gated communities, and housing wealth and inheritance; and sustainable employment and younger workers, labour market change and non-standard work and entrepreneurship.

Mónica Adriana Giglio (documentosgiglio@yahoo.com.ar) is an urban and regional planner based in Argentina. She holds DPhil in architecture from the Universidad Politécnica de Madrid and an MSc in urban and territorial politics, with a specialty in urban management from the Universidad Carlos Tercero in Madrid, Spain. She is also assistant professor of Planning at the University of Buenos Aires and environment adviser to the government of the city of Buenos Aires, Argentina.

Renaud Le Goix (http://rlg.free.fr) is an associate professor of urban geography at the University of Paris, 1 Pantheon-Sorbonne. He has a record of research on gated communities in the US (PhD thesis 2003), the outcomes of private urban governance on local and metro governance, spatial analysis of social segregation, and interactions between social patterns and morphological patterns in suburban areas.

Karina Landman (karina.landman@up.ac.za) is based at the Department of Town and Regional Planning at the University of Pretoria and was previously a principal researcher at the Council for Scientific and Industrial Research (CSIR) in the Built Environment Unit in South Africa. She is the author of several publications in the field of gated communities. Her main research interests are in housing, sustainable human settlements and urban design, spatial transformation in cities, crime prevention through environmental design, and gated communities.

Sonia Roitman (soniaroitman@yahoo.com) is a research associate at the Bartlett School of Planning, University College London (UCL), UK. Her background is in urban sociology with a PhD in planning from the Development

Planning Unit, UCL. Her research interests include urban social inequalities, especially processes of segregation and polarization and their impacts upon the urban space; edge cities, urban planning and economic growth; gated communities; and housing policies and micro-financing.

Ziauddin Sardar (ziauddin.sardar@btopenworld.com) is visiting professor at the School of Cultural Policy and Management, City University, London. He is the author of *Desperately Seeking Paradise* (Granta Books, 2004) and *Balti Britain: A Journey through the British Asian Experience* (Granta Books, 2008). A collection of his writings is available as *Islam, Postmodernism and Other Futures: A Ziauddin Sardar Reader* (Pluto Press, 2003). He is a commissioner for the Equality and Human Rights Commission, editor of *Futures*, and a columnist on the *New Statesman*.

Saskia Sassen (http://www.columbia.edu/~sjs2/) is the Lynd professor of sociology and member, the Committee on Global Thought, at Columbia University, New York. She is the author, among others, of *The Global City* (Princeton University Press, 1991/2001) and, most recently, *Territory, Authority, Rights: From Medieval to Global Assemblages* (Princeton University Press, 2008). She wrote a lead essay in the 2006 *Venice Biennale of Architecture Catalogue*.

Diana Sheinbaum (dianasheinbaum@yahoo.com.mx) is a researcher at the National University of Mexico. Fascinated by the development of her native Mexico City, she studied history and urban planning and combined these disciplines to better understand the historic and current dynamics that explain socio-spatial divisions in major metropolis. Her recent research interests focus on gated communities and the privatization of public space.

Luigi Tomba (luigi.tomba@anu.edu.au) is a political scientist with the Australian National University, Department of Political and Social Change. His research focuses on China's urban politics and governance, community-building, labour reform, social stratification, social conflicts and class. He is the co-editor of *The China Journal*, and his publications include *Paradoxes of Labour Reform: Chinese Labour Theory and Practice from Socialism to the Market* (Routledge, 2002) and *East Asian Capitalism: Conflicts, Growth and Crisis* (Feltrinelli, 2002).

Ola Uduku (o.uduku@eca.ac.uk) is senior lecturer in architecture and environmental design at Edinburgh School of Architecture and Landscape Architecture, Scotland. She wrote for and co-edited the text *Africa beyond the Post-Colonial* (Ashgate, 2002) with Professor Tunde Zack Williams, and she researches social infrastructure provision in Africa. Her other interest is the modernist movement architecture in Africa; she co-curated 'The AA in Africa' (2002) exhibition with Hannah Le Roux. She is completing a survey on school provision and education quality in South Africa and Ghana. She lives in a small gated community in Edinburgh.

List of Acronyms and Abbreviations

AGM	annual general meeting
ANC	African National Congress
ANR	French Agence Nationale pour la Recherche
CCTV	closed-circuit television
CEC	Commission of the European Communities
CEO	chief executive officer
CID	common interest development
CSIR	Council for Scientific and Industrial Research
CUBA	Club Universitario de Buenos Aires
DPMC	Sustainable Development Programme of Action
GDP	gross domestic product
GRA	government-reserved area
MABA	Metropolitan Area of Buenos Aires
MAM	Metropolitan Area of Mendoza
NSCC	North Shore City Council
POA	Property Owners' Association
SARS	severe acute respiratory syndrome
UCL	University College London
UK	United Kingdom
US	United States
VOC	Dutch East Indian Company
ZMVM	Metropolitan Zone of the Valley of Mexico

1

Gated Histories:
An Introduction to Themes and Concepts

Samer Bagaeen and Ola Uduku

Introduction

This book considers the genesis of gated communities in different areas of the world, offering both a historical and contemporary analysis of examples. In doing this, it seeks to respond to and engage with the ongoing debate surrounding the roots of gated communities. There is, at present, no unanimously agreed contemporary definition of what constitutes a gated community; however, the description of what constitutes 'gating' throughout urban history is extensive. Atkinson and Blandy (2005, p177), in the special issue on gated communities of *Housing Studies*, give their definition of the gated community as:

> ... a housing development that restricts public access, usually through the use of gates, booms, walls and fences ... residential areas may also employ security staff or CCTV [closed-circuit television] systems to monitor access ... [they may] include a variety of services such as shops or leisure facilities.

These building enclosures are usually governed by legal and social frameworks that form the statutory conditions that residents have to comply with. Blakely (2007, p475) further defines gated communities as:

> ... residential areas with restricted access, such that spaces normally considered public have been privatized. Physical barriers – walled or fenced perimeters – and gated or guarded entrances control access. Gated communities include both new housing developments and older residential areas retrofitted with barricades and fences.

From these two definitions, what is certain is that both the privatization of public space and the fortification of the urban realm, in response to the fear of crime, has contributed significantly to the rise of the contemporary gated community phenomena.

Despite the outpouring of literature and research on the subject, mainly from North America and more recently including authors from Western Europe, since the early 1990s, there is ample evidence to suggest that the phenomenon can also be linked to older historic patterns of enclosure found globally.

Recognition of this other 'strand' or notion enclosure, derived from more traditional housing and residence practices in the world, should equally inform the debate about the epistemology and nature of the gating phenomenon. This is important as the incorporation of 'gated communities', in one form or another, has influenced and had a bearing on the planning, design 'codes' and design guidelines in most contemporary urban areas, at both suburban and inner-city level today.

There is an ongoing discussion about the place of, infrastructure needs and spatial relationship of the gated community contextually within today's cities, both in the evolving and developed world. Much of the current analysis, and resultant planning guidance and codes assume that gated communities are simply a 'me too' reaction by the local elite in emulating the 'American' lifestyle within the local urban context.

Often, where gated housing enclaves of various forms have been incorporated within the city plan, the socio-economic and historic antecedents are assumed to be Western; links to earlier relevant historic fortified cities and enclosed forms of architecture from other parts of the world are rarely alluded to or incorporated within the new 'securitized' architecture of the contemporary 21st-century gated community.

In this chapter, we discuss the broad historic associations to contemporary gated communities, and then review current literature and research into these communities and linkages to social sustainability. Gated communities provide an example of a much wider rise in contractual governance resulting from the new relationship between the state, market and civil society designed to address concerns about social order. 'Gated living' often means that residents agree to sign up to communally agreed arrangements that allow for money to be charged for payments for services such as waste collection, snow ploughing, leaf clearing, street lighting and parks management. In light of this, Atkinson and Blandy (2005, p178) refine the definition of gated communities, noting that they are 'characterised by legal agreements which tie the residents to a common code of conduct and (usually) collective responsibility for management'.

Other attempts at creating defensible space are worthy of attention. Suburban areas with electronic bars across private access roads and housing estates with buffer zones of grass and cul-de-sacs are all also intentionally designed to exclude or deter non-residents from acquiring access. Thus, although not creating overtly physical barriers, these moderated forms of physical separation of space ensure *de facto* spatial segregation and separation.

Can we then justify the need to 'gate'? We surmise that in the predominantly neo-liberal, capitalist-oriented urban landscape that still characterizes most global cities, this has been the free choice of residents and estate developers who have been willing to pay the price and know the profit potential, respectively, of these communities. Davis (1992), in his polemic text *City of Quartz*, describes the ultra-gated suburbs of downtown America, as does Low (2003) in her academic study *Behind the gates: life, security, and the pursuit of happiness in fortress America*. Clearly, in the West, contemporary America leads the revolution as its spacious suburbs and traditional residents, who value the certainty and sense of shared community ascribed to gated communities, make their location and construction from small housing estate level to whole-town level relatively easy to achieve.

Europe and elsewhere in the world are not far behind this evolution since increasingly globalized work patterns and lifestyles have meant that real estate construction in Boston, the US, is similar to developments in Lagos, Nigeria, or Beijing, China. Thus, the gated community has now become an ubiquitous part of urban life. Contexts are similar in most cases as the emergent middle class or bourgeoisie acquire local affluence and with it a real, or perceived, fear of encroaching crime and 'contamination' from society not part of their socio-economic status.

Coupled with this fear is the ability and willingness to pay for the segregation and services that a gated community can provide. This has driven much of the market for the construction of new gated residences, condominiums and town/housing estates. In addition, a relatively ready supply of subsidized land for developers to create new estates and occasionally convert existing residential enclaves into gated communes is a contextual feature familiar in many developed countries. This 'conversion' possibility has meant that in the less real estate-abundant countries in Europe, such as the UK, the gated community phenomenon has still managed to spread and also become rooted in national urban planning debates.

What issues, then, must we consider as the 'global gated' phenomenon continues apace in some parts of the world more than others? Its sustainability, the authors in this book argue, both conceptually and physically is a crucial issue to consider. By this we mean how viable are gated communities in the current socio-economic environment? In addition, is the current Western-based gated model sustainable in non Western-based cultural contexts?

We suggest that the sustainability of the gated community, as a physical and ideological urban design concept, depends on the ability to maintain barriers between those within the gates and those without, both physically and psychologically. Effectively, the fortress created by gated communities suggests that the status quo can be sustained, and those outside the gates can remain permanently excluded as the 'others'. These 'others' outside the gates could therefore legitimately be demonized as the low life, criminals and undesirables from whom the deserving middle classes needed to protect themselves. Psychologically, therefore, as well as physically, today's gated residences are in place to protect residents from the fear of the outsiders, as well as from anxieties about privacy and social integration.

Determining and describing the gated community: Urban form

There are a myriad of typologies for gated developments, all with contextual relevance. A general discussion about the forms that these developments may take provides an introductory background to the volume.

Despite the recent outpouring of literature and research on the subject of gated communities since the early 1990s (Davis, 1992; Caldeira, 1996, 2000; Blakely and Snyder, 1997; Low, 1997; Leisch, 2002; Atkinson et al, 2004; Wu and Webber, 2004; McKenzie, 2005; Blandy, 2006; Le Goix and Webster, 2008) there is ample evidence to suggest that the phenomenon can be linked to historic patterns of enclosure, to be found globally. Denyer (1978, pp66–73) devoted an entire chapter on traditional African dwellings to 'defence', in which she asserts that:

> It is a truism to say that defences were only required by those who felt threatened by external aggression… Simple small-scale societies living at subsistence level tried to minimize serious conflict … but even in the absence of armed conflict some protection was needed almost everywhere from large mammals. The slave raiding which intensified from the 18th and the political upheavals of the 19th century meant that few people were immune from danger, and by 1900 nearly every village and town in sub-Saharan Africa had some form of defensive cordon.

Her text and Oliver's (1987) further give examples of historic 'fortress' settlements in locations as geographically diverse as Afghanistan (Oliver, 1987), Greater Zimbabwe and Benin (Denyer, 1978). Within current literature on gated communities, Wu and Webber (2004) describe the historic Chinese gated community in similar detail.

While these examples might be considered more anthropological in their description, their influence on Western planning should not be underplayed. British colonial planners often incorporated or adapted existing planned settlements; thus, in Kaduna, Nigeria, Max Locke's 1966 plan incorporates the old walled town into the new plan (Locke, 1966). Arguably, England's first colony in Ireland was also built as a walled citadel (Home, 1997).

McKenzie (1994) suggests that the American engagement with the gated community also has British origins; the cross-fertilization of Ebenezer Howard's garden city movement from the UK to the US, he feels, began this evolution. Of critical importance also is Olmsted's study of the British park and its associated housing, which he then developed into his planning of Central Park and other great American landscapes (Olmsted, 1967). In effect, McKenzie's thesis claims that the American version of Howard's Garden City was always essentially a privatized one, as opposed to the more benevolent public view of the early English versions (see Howard, 1945).

There is also no doubt, however, that there are South American origins to the gated citadel, as many of the pre-colonial settlements in this southern continent were also communities built with defences against the elements and hostile marauders. The thick adobe walled architecture can be seen as far north as New Mexico, US, and other southern parts of the US. It is no surprise, then, that the contemporary evolution of the fortress citadel, now termed gated community, is most associated with the US. However Caldeira's (2000) discussion of the phenomenon in Brazil, and the literature on the post-apartheid city, embodied by Landman (2004), and Wu and Webber's (2004) discussion about China are equally valid descriptions of today's translation of 'gatedness' across the world.

Davis's (1992) description of the Carceral city in the City of Quartz is the most quoted description of the ultimate horror of the fortress idea, while both Newman's (1972) 'defensible space' and Jacobs's (1964) *The Death and Life of Great American Cities* discussion of space are most often given as the theoretical reason for the move to the safer gated communities, while the New Urbanist movement comes close to endorsing this closed-community network.

However, there has been, in the last few years, a more critical analysis of gatedness, the gated community network being a forum for this. Soja (2000), McKenzie (1994) and others question the inevitability theory that all cities will become compositions of self-governing gated communities for the rich and ghettoes of despair, non-governance and zero services provision for the poor.

Engagement amongst academics in this critical discourse is furthered by the activities of the gated communities' network, which with its diverse membership of researchers has a global remit and audience in which to spread its findings.

With respect to the cultural determinants of urban form, in some countries it was residual habits and customs such as personal commitments, tribal solidarities and self-regulating social structures that had an influence on form. This is what Galantay (1987, p8) called the 'culture specific determinants' (in this case, religious practices and legal traditions of Islam) that have shaped the built environment in the historic Muslim city. The nature of the physical fabric, the importance of law, communal responsibility and local networks have all contributed to how the inhabitants of this traditional city have solved their housing problems in the past.

Akbar (1988), Hakim (1986), Bianca (2000) and Bagaeen (2003) all emphasize that historic Middle Eastern cities exhibit an urban form that can be attributed to a spiritual identity as materialized through ritualized, consistent daily practices which work contextually with their built environment. In an analysis of the Muslim city, Kostof (1991) points out that urban form was allowed to work itself out subject to the respect of custom, ownership and neighbourhood cohesion based on kinship, tribal affiliation or ethnicity.

Meanwhile Blandy (2006), in an analysis of historic gated communities in England, identifies similar patterns of economic and socio-legal relations – alongside developments in property law – that shaped urban form. In England, she argues, defended buildings, whether individual or collective, are not new. She adds that the country has amassed many fortified dwellings from previous eras, and that feudal castles and medieval walled towns are often mentioned as early examples of gated communities (Blandy, 2006, p16). Blandy does point out, though, that unlike contemporary gated communities, the fortified medieval town was a self-sufficient entity with a far wider range of residents than today's homogenous gated neighbourhoods (see also Marcuse, 1997, p106). One clear distinguishable difference between these communes and contemporary gated communities was that there was no legal framework of contractual self-governance.

Glasze (2006) goes further with his examination of 'cultural difference' in the city by his use of case study examples: the compounds for Western foreigner workers in Saudi Arabia. These are enclaves explicitly based on the idea of a spatial seclusion of social groups with different cultural backgrounds. Here, access is strictly restricted to residents and their visitors. Administration and maintenance are provided through an onsite management, and Saudi nationals are mostly excluded from residing in these communities. This replicates the historic foreigners' quarters to be found in Islamic cities in West Africa, called *Sabon Garis*. Islamic or *Shari'a* law historically has not applied to residents in this part of the city, which is separated from the walled 'traditional' city (Schwerdtfeger, 1982).

Social sustainability and urban form

Jenks et al (1996, p11) have described the relationship between urban form and sustainability as one of the 'most hotly debated issues on the international environmental agenda'. Much research has been conducted into urban models and the idea of 'sustainable urban form' as a design criterion for new developments. There has also been a move away from focusing solely on the environmental dimensions of sustainability to consider other dimensions such as 'urban sustainability' and 'social sustainability'.

It was the Commission of the European Communities (CEC, 1990) who first promoted sustainable development and endorsed the concept of the compact city. Proposals to increase the mix of uses within a city include the juxtaposition of residential and commercial uses within new developments and the siting of new development, retail and leisure facilities close to existing housing areas, at the same time as discouraging out-of-town developments. In this context, Elkin et al (1991) argue that the implications for design and planning are that high-density and integrated land use are needed not only to conserve resources, but also to provide for 'compactness' that encourages social interaction. In the US, higher densities are also seen to be an essential component of the 'walkable city' – the 'new urbanist' antidote to the car-dependent sprawling city promoted by Duany and Plater-Zyberk (1991) and Calthorpe (1993).

This takes on board social sustainability arguments – particularly those related to the quality of life in cities – and often revolves around the idea of traditional streets and 'urban villages', which provide the conditions for social interaction and community. A significant proportion of the debate surrounding sustainable development stresses the importance of social 'qualitative' aspects of sustainability. In spite of this, there appears to be little agreement in the literature as to what this comprises or what measure can be made of the value of social sustainability.

Various authors have attempted to define 'social sustainability'. Polese and Stren (2000, pp15–16) define it as:

> … development (and/or growth) that is compatible with harmonious evolution of civil society, fostering an environment conducive to the compatible cohabitation of culturally and socially diverse groups, while at the same time encouraging social integration, with improvements in the quality of life for all segments of the population.

In their view, social sustainability is a reflection of degree to which inequalities and social discontinuity are reduced; to be socially sustainable, cities must therefore reduce the level of segregation and marginalization amongst their populations.

The relationship between urban form and social sustainability was examined by Bramley et al (2006), where they point out that even though the social dimension to sustainability as outlined above is widely accepted, what it actually means is not. Burton (2003) also argues that this is a concept that is difficult to quantify. Bramley et al (2006) propose two main dimensions to the concept, relating to equity of access and the sustainability/quality of community.

Their definition of social sustainability incorporates both social equity issues, with a particular focus on access to services and facilities, and sustainability of community issues, essentially concerned with the continued viability, health and functioning of 'society' itself as a collective entity, generally under the heading of 'community'.

Bramley et al (2006) summarize the literature on the wider concepts around ideas of social sustainability (such as social capital, social cohesion and social exclusion), but also indicate that the following dimensions are also likely to be significant in helping to sustain local communities and neighbourhoods: interaction in the community/social networks; community participation; pride/sense of place; community stability; and security (crime).

Density is one of the key elements of sustainable urban form considered by the City Form Consortium, whose work draws together the various dimensions of sustainability – economic, social, transport, energy and ecological – to examine their relationships both to each other and to urban form (see Jenks and Jones, 2009). In addition, Bramley and Power (2009) use data from the Survey of English Housing; this paper analyses the relationship between key aspects of urban form, density and housing type, and selected social sustainability outcomes. They find trade-offs operating within the social dimensions of sustainability, as well as between the social, environmental, and economic dimensions.

Previous work has found that the density of urban development has the potential to impact upon all of the dimensions of social sustainability identified by Bramley et al (2006). For example, higher densities may make access to services and facilities both easier and more economically viable (Bunker, 1985; Haughton and Hunter, 1994; Breheny, 1997; Burton, 2000b). Williams (2000) found that access may vary for different services. The Office of the Deputy Prime Minister (ODPM, 2003) argues that particular densities are needed to support basic amenities in the neighbourhood and to minimize the use of resources such as land.

Bramley et al (2006) note that Burton (2000a, 2000b) has produced the most comprehensive work exploring the impact of urban form upon social equity focusing on whether higher density urban form promotes social equity (Burton, 2000a). Burton (2000b) found that nearly all of the 14 social equity effects that she identified are related in some way to urban compactness, job accessibility and wealth being the exceptions.

From this, it is clear that most gated communities conform to many of these sustainability criteria in their form, urban footprint and locational context.

Under the US and South African models, fear and privacy have heavily influenced the development of contemporary gated communities. In the Southern Africa context, however, there has also been an older history of fortified towns such as Great Zimbabwe, and a continuing fortification culture in homestead design in rural areas.

Also challenging the belief that gated communities in the US are exclusive developments with high-cost homes composed of mostly white homeowners, Sanchez et al (2005) have found a prevalence of low-income racial minority renters living in gated communities, reflecting a divide between these fortified residences based on status and others motivated by immediate security and safety concerns.

It is not, however, only the fear of crime that is ensuring the building of gated communities. There are also aspirational motives, such as the perceived exclusivity of gated communities, their 'condominium' rules and other effects – all are perceived as attributes of social status that gated community life can ascribe.

Why are these fortified enclaves growing in societies characterized by lower prevailing crime rates? In some of the country case studies examined within this book, the need for gated communities may be challenged given that present crime rates do not warrant fortress-style enclaves. Wu (2005) examines the club realm versus the discourse of fear. In the former, the gated community is perceived as an exclusive members only club, while in the latter it is perceived as a bastion to keep the 'barbarians' from the gate. Wu's field study description mirrors our theoretical analysis of the contextual dichotomy in meaning and symbolism, both physically and psychologically, of fortified residences, communities and towns.

In the British context, historically, according to Webster (2001), little had been written on gated communities. Another study by Atkinson et al (2004) found that there were more than 1000 gated communities in England alone. The Atkinson and Blandy (2005) gated community definition, used at this chapter's introduction, gives the contemporary Western experience of the gated community. These developments often also include a variety of services, such as shops and some leisure facilities.

Residents in gated communities, especially in the US, are often bound by legal conditions that control lifestyle and social conditions within the community. These communities provide an example of a much wider rise in contractual governance resulting from the new relationship between the state, market and civil society designed to address concerns about social order, highlighted by writers such as McKenzie (1994) and Soja (2000). This demonstrates clearly that there is a divide between gated communities based on status versus others motivated by concern for security.

Challenging the general belief that gated communities in the US solely comprise exclusive developments of designer homes for affluent, predominantly white, homeowners, Sanchez et al (2005) have found a prevalence of low-income racial minority renters living in gated communities, more for security reasons than prestige or affluence.

The various authors in this book all emphasize that self-segregation has deep historical roots that transcend the growth of gated communities over the past twenty years. In the Foreword, Sassen argues for a shift from the familiar notion of gated community to a more generic notion of urban gating and recoding what has become the standard meaning of gated communities since the 1980s. In his reflection, Sardar's comments (see Chapter 2) emphasize the importance of values and of recovering the lost ecological values of traditional lifestyles. The remaining chapters highlight a comparative narrative about the history of urban gating.

In Chapter 3, Bagaeen explores how traditional settlements in the Middle East incorporated climatic, cultural, social, economic and religious control mechanisms that manifested themselves in the way in which physical elements and barriers were in the built environment. In Chapter 4, Tomba argues that the gating and privatization of residential spaces are acts of political classification. Uduku, in Chapter 5, attempts to pinpoint the contemporary and historic origins of domestic fortification in Lagos. In Chapter 6, Landman focuses on the relationship between gated minds (social needs and ideas) and gated places (order and form) as they manifest themselves through different time periods. In Chapter 7, Roitman and Giglio take us on a journey of gating in Argentina from the past all the way through to the present. In Chapter 8, Sheinbaum examines historical forms of urban space production that have given place to different physical expressions of segregation in Mexico City. In Chapter 9, Le Goix and Callen demonstrate that gated communities, often presented as a recent unsustainable trend of security-oriented urbanism, are, indeed, a classical and generic form in urban sprawl and suburban landscape. In Chapter 10, Dupuis and Dixon show that while gated communities are recent developments, gates and the enclosure of land by fences, walls or planting have long been part of New Zealand's urban and rural landscapes.

In the Afterword, we reflect on some of the key themes offered in this book, including how sustainability takes on a new life when considered alongside a process of urban gating that is firmly rooted in urban history. We argue that the idea of the gated 'community' also has pragmatic benefits since self-selecting communities of interest, such as the ones found amongst gated developments, do develop deeper ties at local level. We believe that the need to make this a force for good and positive development and not the 'gated minds' enclave phenomenon is the way forward. After all, if 'every man's home is his castle', gated communities simply respond to this innate need. The jury remains divided on the efficacy of the outcomes. We offer in the following chapters a set of contextual readings from which to ponder this.

References

Akbar, J. (1988) *Crisis in the Built Environment: The Case of the Muslim City*, Concept Media, Singapore

Atkinson, R. and Blandy, S. (2005) 'Introduction: International perspectives on the new enclavism and the rise of gated communities', *Housing Studies*, vol 20, no 2, March, pp177–186

Atkinson, R., Blandy, S., Flint, J. and Lister, D. (2004) *Gated Communities in England*, ODPM, London

Bagaeen, S. (2003) *Understanding Deterioration in the Built Environment: The Palestinian Quarters of the Old City of Jerusalem since 1967 as a Case Study*, PhD thesis, University of London, London

Bianca, S. (2000) *Urban Form in the Arab World: Past and Present*, ORL-Schriften, Zurich

Blakely, E. (2007) 'Gated Communities for a Frayed and Afraid World', *Housing Policy Debate* vol 18, issue 3, pp475–480

Blakely, E.J. and Snyder, M.G. (1997) *Fortress America, gated communities in the United States*, Brookings Institution Press & Lincoln Institute of Land Policy, Washington, DC

Blandy, S. (2006) 'Gated communities in England: Historical perspectives and current developments', *GeoJournal*, vol 66, pp15–26

Bramley, G. and Power, S. (2009) 'Urban form and social sustainability: The role of density and housing type', *Environment and Planning B*, vol 36, no 1, pp30–48

Bramley, G., Dempsey, N., Power, S. and Brown, C. (2006) 'What is "social sustainability", and how do our existing urban forms perform in nurturing it?', Paper presented at the Planning Research Conference, Bartlett School of Planning, University College London, April

Breheny, M. (1997) 'Urban compaction: Feasible and acceptable?', *Cities*, vol 14, no 4, pp209–217

Bunker, R. (1985) 'Urban consolidation and Australian cities', *Built Environment*, vol 11, pp83–96

Burton, E. (2000a) 'The compact city: Just or just compact? A preliminary analysis', *Urban Studies*, vol 37, no 11, pp1969–2001

Burton, E. (2000b) 'The potential of the compact city for promoting social equity', in Williams, K., Burton, E. and Jenks, M. (eds) *Achieving Sustainable Urban Form*, E & F N Spon, London

Burton, E. (2003) 'Housing for an urban renaissance: Implications for social equity', *Housing Studies*, vol 18, no 4, pp537–562

Caldeira, T.P.R. (1996) 'Fortified enclaves: The new urban segregation', *Public Culture*, vol 8, pp303–328

Caldeira, T.P.R. (2000) *City of walls: crime, segregation, and citizenship in São Paulo*, University of California Press, Berkeley, CA

Calthorpe, P. (1993) *The Next American Metropolis: Ecology, Community and the American Dream*, Princeton Architectural Press, New York, NY

CEC (Commission of the European Communities) (1990) *Green Paper on the Urban Environment*, CEC, Brussels

Christopherson, S. (1994) 'The fortress city: Privatised spaces, consumer citizenship', in Amin, A. (ed) *Post-Fordism: A Reader*, Blackwell, Oxford

Davis, M. (1992) *City of Quartz: Excavating the Future in Los Angeles*, Verso, London

Denyer, S. (1978) *African Traditional Architecture*, Holmes & Meier Publishing, London

Duany, A. and Plater-Zyberk, E. (1991) *Towns and Town-Making Principles*, Rizzoli International, New York, NY

Elkin, T., McLaren, D. and Hillman, M. (1991) *Reviving the City: Towards Sustainable Urban Development*, Friends of the Earth, London

Galantay, E. Y. (1987) 'Islamic identity and the metropolis: Continuity and conflict', in Saqqaf, A. Y. (ed) *The Middle East City: Ancient Traditions Confront a Modern World*, Paragon House Publishers, New York, NY

Glazse, G. (2006) 'Segregation and seclusion: The case of compounds for western expatriates in Saudi Arabia', *GeoJournal*, vol 66, pp83–88

Hakim, B. S. (1986) *Arabic-Islamic Cities: Building and Planning Principles*, Routledge and Kegan Paul, London

Handy, S. (2005) *Does the Built Environment Influence Physical Activity: Examining the Evidence*, Transportation Research Board, Washington, DC

Haughton, G. and Hunter, C. (1994) *Sustainable Cities*, Jessica Kingsley, London

Home, R. K. (1997) *Of Planting and Planning: Making of British Colonial Cities*, Routledge, London

Howard, E. (1945) *Garden Cities of Tomorrow*, Faber and Faber, London

Jacobs, J. (1964) *The Death and Life of Great American Cities: the failure of planning*, Pelican

Jenks, M. and Jones, C. (eds) (2009) *Dimensions of the Sustainable City*, Springer Verlag, Heidelberg

Jenks, M., Burton, E., and Williams, K. (eds) (1996) *The Compact City: A Sustainable Urban Form?* E & F N Spon, London

Kostof, S. (1991) *The City Shaped: Urban Patterns and Meaning through History*, Thames and Hudson, London

Landman, K. (2004) 'Gated communities in South Africa. The challenge for spatial planning and land use management', *Town Planning Review*, 75(2), pp151–172

Le Goix, R. and Webster, C. (2008) 'Gated Communities', in *Geography Compass*, 2/4, pp1189–1214

Leisch, H. (2002) 'Gated Communities in Indonesia', *Cities*, vol 19, pp341–350

Locke, M. and Associates (1966) *Kaduna: 1917, 1967, 2017: A Survey and Plan of the Capital Territory for the Government of Northern Nigeria Plan*, Frederick A. Praeger, London

Low, S. (1997) 'Urban fear: building fortress America', *City and Society*, Annual Review, pp52–72

Low, S. (2001) 'The edge and the centre: Gated communities and the discourse of urban fear', *American Anthropologist*, vol 43, pp45–58

Low, S. (2003) *Behind the gates: life, security, and the pursuit of happiness in fortress America,* Routledge, New York

Marcuse, P. (1997) 'Walls of fear and walls of support', in Ellin, N. (ed) *Architecture of Fear*, Princeton Architectural Press, New York, NY, pp101–114

McKenzie, E. (1994) *Privatopia: Homeowner Associations and the Rise of Residential Private Government*, Yale University Press, New Haven, CT

McKenzie, E. (2005) 'Constructing the Pomerium in Las Vegas: a case study of emerging trends in American gated communities', *Housing Studies*, vol 20, pp187–203

Mitchell, D. (1995) 'The end of public space?', *Annals of the Association of American Geographers*, vol 85, pp108–133

Newman, O. (1972) *Defensible space: crime prevention through urban design*, Macmillan, New York

ODPM (Office of the Deputy Prime Minister) (2003) *Sustainable Communities: Building for the Future*, HMSO, London

Oliver, P. (1987) *Dwellings: The House across the World*, University of Texas Press, Texas

Olmsted, F.L. (1967) *Landscape into Cityscape*, Cornell University Press, New York, NY

Polese, M. and Stren, R. (2000) *The Social Sustainability of Cities: Diversity and the Management of Change*, University of Toronto Press, Toronto, Ontario

Sanchez, T. W., Lang, R. E., and Dhavale, D. (2005) 'Security versus status? A first look at the census's gated communities data', *Journal of Planning Education and Research*, vol 24, no 3, pp281–291

Schwerdtfeger, H. (1982) *Traditional Housing in African Cities: A Comparative Study of Houses in Zaria, Ibadan, and Marrakech*, Wiley, Chichester, UK

Scottish Executive (2004) *Scottish Index of Multiple Deprivation 2004: Summary Technical Report*, www.scotland.gov.uk/library5/society/siomd-00.asp

Social Exclusion Unit (2000) *National Strategy for Neighbourhood Renewal*, HMSO, London

Soja, E. (2000) *Postmodern Geographies: Reassertion of Space in Critical Social Theory*, Verso Books

Webster, C. (2001) 'Gated cities of tomorrow', *Town Planning Review*, vol 72, pp149–170

Williams, K. (2000) 'Does intensifying cities make them more sustainable', in Williams, K., Burton, E. and Jenks, M. (eds) *Achieving Sustainable Urban Forms*, E & F N Spon, London

Wu, F. (2005) 'Rediscovering the "gate" under market transition: from work-unit compounds to commodity housing enclaves', *Housing Studies*, 20(2), pp235–254

Wu, F. and Webber, K. (2004) 'The rise of foreign gated communities in Beijing: Between economic globalization and local institutions', *Cities*, vol 21, no 3, pp203–213

2
Opening the Gates:
An East–West Transmodern Discourse?

Ziauddin Sardar

Gated communities are the apotheosis of the lifestyle of *laissez faire* consumer capitalism. They are the physical embodiment of a wealth-driven, growth-oriented idyll of conspicuous consumption in which individuals indulge their own celebrity/designer-styled existence in enclaves protected from those less fortunate: the envious and excluded who can only continue to dream of somehow possessing the comforts enjoyed behind the security barriers. Now that the apocalypse is upon us, in the form of global financial meltdown, it is not merely the assumptions and practice of this economic dispensation which are ripe for re-evaluation. The gated community is a microcosm, a metaphor for the ideology and interlocking relationships, global in extent, of this bankrupt system. Unpicking the values and ideology of the gated community opens a discourse on the system which brought them into being. Examining the relationships within and beyond the gates, their meaning and implications, exposes the dysfunctions of the global system whose ethos it represents. Looking beyond the gated community points to the potential for realignment and mirrors the reorientation which is both necessary and inevitable at a global level.

The dominant paradigm that has fuelled the rise of gated communities, from the US to New Zealand, the Middle East to West Africa, China to Latin America, is growth, which is seen as synonymous with progress. Both growth and progress are conceptualized on the basis and benefit of the individual. Economic man, the atomistic construct and putative beneficiary, is the rational individual making personal choices for his own particular advantage. The hidden hand of market forces manipulates what in this worldview is a mere spectral entity: society as a whole. The entire focus of analysis is the individual, the location of all the values of liberty, freedom and the potential for self-expression through happiness, to borrow the most concise formulation of the entitlements sought. Both growth and progress are the bedrock of the ideology of modernity, which emerged through a specific historical process of global expansion achieved by means of colonization, empire and neo-imperialism to become a global dispensation. The prime directive of modernity was, and continues to be, perpetual economic growth, which through the market mechanism would eventually alleviate all problems that might accumulate along the way. But global statistics of ever-rising material and technological standards mask a more sanguine story. The dream of ever-rising standards of abundance has always been radically and persistently unequal. Degrees of inequity might vary, but they can never disappear. The ease and plenty of the few living in splendid isolation in gated communities is created by the dispossession, subjugation, exclusion, exploitation and long-term poverty and drudgery of the many – and that is as true within the wealthy beneficiary nations as between the centre and periphery of the post-colonial globalized world.

The gated community exemplifies the vision of islands of abundance floating in oceans of poverty, which, as Townsend (1979) pointed out, is always a comparative measure of social exclusion rather than an absolute lack of money and resources. The existence within the gated community is always febrile and fearful, obsessed with security: securing the privilege conferred by wealth, which is the sole selecting and sustaining criterion of membership of the community; securing privileged access to the resources required to maintain the lifestyle of conspicuous consumption; securing the living environment from the decay, inherent threat and hostile envy of those without and by exclusion of all undesirables; and securing all the social advantage that confers presumptive continuity of the privilege, ease and comfort within the confines of the gated community.

None of the usual definitional features advanced for the gated community are in themselves new. The practice of spatial segregation, of defensible settlements, of social legal arrangements particular to a community that demonstrate their ideals and expectations of behaviour amongst group members – all these have their precursors in earlier forms of communal living. And, of course, wealth has always conferred privilege and the wealthy have ever sought to secure and preserve the unequal advantages they have gained. What distinguishes the quintessential gated community is the particular set of relationships that it establishes. It is a view of the state, the market and civil society crystallized in the contractual governance of the gated community. As such, the gated community is not a neutral development. The implications of the set of relationships it enshrines are toxic; they are the reactor core of the dysfunctions of the dominant paradigm which must now be re-evaluated and realigned if a sustainable ethos, environment and lifestyle are to be wrested from the chaos of the global financial crisis, its economic consequences, and the life-threatening planetary challenges that they have brought to the fore.

The gated community is not neutral because it idealizes, incorporates and empowers a particular set of aspirations and the social and economic organization that they require. It is a value-laden system which imposes and maintains an ordered set of relationships with implications far beyond its own security barriers. The gated community is the realization of the commodification and monetarization of everything and their subordination to the ideology of free-market relations. Free markets, the deregulated operation of the profit motive, are not the classic theoretical formulation of 18th-century speculation. There was nothing particularly benign about how markets actually operated in the context of the 18th century – the high point of mercantilist empire building. The classical conditions of perfect markets where all conditions would and could be balanced (and through the mechanism of perfect knowledge provide a self-regulating win–win situation for all participants) is, and always has been, mere mental abstraction. Real

deregulated markets, as their current meltdown has shown, are founded on a partiality for power, a licensing of individual greed, a reification of selfishness and partiality to personal gain accompanied by profligacy in the consumption of resources to provide for the inordinate expansion of ever-more varied consumer goods and services at ever-more attractive (i.e. cost-effective) prices. When entrepreneurship and profit are the supreme values in an already unequal world, inequality proliferates with the proliferation of the wealth of the elite: the rich get richer, the middle classes find it harder and harder to maintain the lifestyle to which they aspire, and the poorest are more and more excluded as an enduring underclass with fewer and fewer opportunities to get a foot on the supposedly ever-open escalator of upward mobility for which the entire system allegedly exists.

Without the unequal sets of relationship of a global economic system devised and operated in favour of the wealthy, the gated community would not exist. Gated communities are premium enclaves that provide premium material standards and services at premium prices and which need premium use of social and material resources to maintain their status, which is their *raison d'être*. Gated communities are not the ultimate in the suburbanization of the lived environment with all that means for exorbitant use of natural resources. They are the antithesis of urbanism as a communal collective social existence. They are plutocratic ghettoes of superior entitlement garnered from the inequalities of the economic system. The essence of urbanism is plurality, the coming together of diverse classes, groups and identities to create a symbiotic heterogeneous community where mutual intercourse and exchange is the lifeblood of society. By its own selective means of admittance, disposable wealth and system of contractual governance social survival within, the gated community emphasizes if not perfect homogeneity, then certainly a social monolith of conformity. It is a segregated environment on every level being purely residential, segregating work from home as well as segregating its residents from the rest of society. The gated community gathers around itself segregated services for its educational and health services, as well as its infrastructural needs for sewage, cleaning and refuse removal, maintenance of landscape and, of course, the quintessential provision of private security services. The gated community is anti-urban in its abandonment of the central place of the city for all except work and occasional entertainment. It is an abandonment of any signs and symbols of collective inclusion in an overarching identity; the careful selection of a gated community defines the lack of interest in the welfare of society as a whole in preference for the protection of selective individual well-being. The attitude of those clustered within the gates to other people is evidenced by the existence of guard patrols and the need for visitors to report at the gates to be granted admittance. The limited range of social relations permitted by the lifestyle of the gated community – there are only people like me and those who serve my needs at my convenience – deconstructs the familiarity with, and fellow feeling for, those whose existence is beyond the gates. In a gated community the barbarians are always at the gates, ever ready to pounce.

The process of the accumulation of wealth and structural advantage, economic and social, inherent in the gated community mirrors the historic process by which the developed nations acquired their dominance and affluence. Colonization was a process of segregation and separation by which the rest of the world was reconstructed to provide the natural resources and captive markets for the metropolitan centres and their elites. Gated communities are the neo-imperialist colonization of society: they are like empires within a city that maintain the relationship of the colonizers and the colonized, albeit in an urban setting. In this neo-colonial process, it is both the city as central place and society as an inclusive unit that is being de/reconstructed.

The implosion of the global financial markets and the economic impact that it has produced as a consequence of deregulation has changed the agenda. The search for more sustainable means to secure the future taking full account of the challenges presented by climate change and environmental degradation has begun. If the gated community is a microcosm of the problems at the heart of the matter, finding a way to transcend what they represent is part of the discourse that is urgently needed. But gated communities are also a symbol of larger malaise: the crisis of modernity. The Enlightenment idea of modernity that sees progress both as perpetual and purely in economic terms, without regard to issues of equality, has now become dangerously obsolete. Modernity privileges extravagant consumer lifestyles because it has been attributed to a single Western paradigm, rooted in one-dimensional notion of progress and dedicated to a view of change that has no regard for other cultures. Not surprisingly, it has privileged liberalism and secularism and, hence, the

domination of Western culture. The process of globalization that the world has witnessed over the last two decades itself predicates modernity. Globalization conjures the illusion that modernity is inherent good; the only way to be human is the modern way and, as such, it is something that should be imposed on a willing or unwilling world. This is why globalization is largely seen as a one-way street where the flow of ideas is essentially from West to the rest, where Western culture, political institutions and 'free market' are seen as a panacea that has to be imposed on the rest of the world. As a consequence, living in isolated gated communities has become a sign of modernity, an embrace of all that is good and wholesome in this best of all globalized worlds.

To open the gates of gated communities, to transform them into inclusive urban spaces, we need to transcend modernity itself. In short, we need a new way of being, doing and knowing. That new way of shaping the world, I suggest, is transmodernity. *Trans* confirms the meaning of 'going beyond' the present situation in all its aspects – the way in which we live and structure our communities; the way in which we interact with our environment; the way in which we pursue our economic activities; the way in which we perceive progress; and the way in which we shape discourses of knowledge. Transmodernity is based on the assumption that cultures do not, and have never, existed in isolation. All cultures interact and all future actions are located in the interactions of cultures. In a world of deep interconnection, transmodernity emphasizes inclusiveness and equality and gives equal importance to knowledge systems of non-Western civilizations and cultures, including indigenous cultures. As a concept, transmodernity is designed to address the positive element of *self-renewal* and *self-reformation* in a world of difference – between rich and poor, as well as within and between cultures. It proposes to encourage change *transculturally*. In this change, tradition plays an important part. Modernity sees tradition almost exclusively in negative terms: as fixed and unchanging, defining it as inferior in reference to itself and demonizing it. Transmodernity, in contrast, sees tradition both as a positive and negative force, amenable to change (indeed, traditions remain traditions by reinventing themselves), and as an essential component of sustainable change. Moreover, traditional societies can be modern too – it is just that they define modernity in their own terms. Transmodernity thus seeks to move forward with tradition, and all that means in terms of identity and sanity, stability and sustainability.

If gated communities are a product of our skewed economic system, then we what we should be seeking is a transmodern economic dispensation. A transmodern economy would be a function of transmodernity itself: a more plural, diversified world where the examples, ideas, values, cultures and traditions of all can participate equitably in a dialogue about available solutions. Just as structural readjustment requires reorienting the global power balance, so we need to reorient our source of critique and ideas on how to transcend such phenomena as the gated community.

It was the late André Gunner Frank who first coined the term reorient, the title of his 1998 study subtitled *Global Economy in the Asian Age*. In the current context, developing an East–West discourse is all about broadening the terms of reference of the term 'reorient', for it requires a revision of our understanding of modernity and serves as the bedrock for developing a clearer understanding of transmodernity. In his study, Frank (1998) demonstrated that modernity, understood as the rise of the West, was a self-serving concept. The engine of the pre-modern global economy, he showed, was the productive capacity of China and India, with Islamic civilization providing the connective lubrication of long-distance trade. Reorient, he argued, was a once and future reality: the economies of China and India were destined to reclaim their natural position as engines of the global economy, and not merely as vast reservoirs of cheap labour subsidizing the more abundant lifestyles of more affluent nations. The rise of modernity included a deindustrialization of China and India; their reindustrialization, especially in the context of global financial crisis, opens a new era and requires new analytical tools, referents and ways of thinking about the future.

Reorienting our thinking towards transmodernity allows us to interrogate modernity from the perspective of the values and practice of diverse traditions and cultural repertoires. In relation to the problem of the gated community, I would argue, one option is to examine how other cultures and histories have operated the axis of public and private, both as values and responses to the built environment. The gated community is an abandonment of the public domain in preference for private provision of all services, from home and garden to schools and safety, to obtain security and exclusivity. It requires separation on the basis of wealth and disposable income into monolithic environments. How does this compare with the practice of traditional environments? The classic cities of Eastern cultures had disparities of wealth and were no strangers to the endemic problems of lawlessness. Their response can be seen in traditional medina or *casbahs* of Islamic cities, such as Fez: houses turned a blank face to the outside world. The public presentation, the outer face of the living space, did not distinguish between the wealth and paucity within. The private space within was at the disposal, and disposable income, of the family. The space within was arranged around courtyards, a common pattern among Asian cultures, allowing for both privacy and congeniality within the space usually shared by multigenerational families.

The lack of outward display, the non-advertising of economic distinctions, had important consequences for the public space and social attitudes within traditional urban environments. The private space was the place for display and indulgence of conspicuous consumption. The public space was the place for social and ritual interaction of the heterogeneous population, the place for public consciousness of mutual obligation. Wealth, hierarchy, rank and status are not self-evident segregating features of a society. There are many ways in which they can be organized and performed to incorporate different sets of values. In India, Nandy (2001) has argued, traditional rulers were not markedly distinguished and certainly not separated from the mass of the people. Hierarchy existed and rulers operated as the redistributive centre of society, with strong ritual functions, which emphasized the interaction of all classes of people to strengthen the bonds of social solidarity. Wealth was not a segregating principle; rather, the display of wealth in regular feasts, for example, operated to demonstrate the obligations of the rich and powerful to the less advantaged. In traditional societies the public space and public ritual occasions serve to provide interaction among the rich and the poor, cross-cutting division and distinctions, and thus demonstrate collective communal identity.

Traditional societies were no less interested in the accumulation of wealth. China, India and the Islamic civilizations all had industrial production and periods of economic growth with rising living standards. But the relentless pursuit of conspicuous consumption and its conversion into the commodification and monetarizing of all relationships, and private gain and personal wealth as the sole value and a basic principle of segregation within society were tempered by alternative sets of values embodied in aspects of both social organization and nature and character of the built environment. Just as traditional cities have been bulldozed and developed out of existence – to be replaced by poor copies of Western cities, complete with gated communities, as is so well illustrated by Kuala Lumpur – so these alternative values of social organization and urban planning have evaporated. Recovery of these alterative principles and sets of relationships is the nature of the East–West discourse we need to recover as we seek more sustainable paths of economic regeneration. A responsible sustainable future within the constraints of climate change and prudential husbanding of the natural environment cannot offer unlimited conspicuous consumption to all of the world's people. If the gated community, with all their attended problems of isolation and segregation, were to become the accepted vision of the human future at a global level, there can be little doubt we would be doomed to destruction. And there would still be no guarantee that we would be able to eradicate the scourge of poverty in either its absolute or comparative guises.

It is instructive to note that when East Asian economies began to undertake programmed action for industrial development, they managed growth with increasing equity, as a seminal report by the World Bank (1993) showed. Between 1965 and 1990, the 'tiger economics' achieved what was then seen as an 'economic miracle'. Employing unorthodox policies, Indonesia, Malaysia, North Korea, Singapore, Taiwan and Thailand all produce dramatic results with far-reaching improvements in human welfare, literacy and income distribution. There was no miracle involved: the special ingredient was said to be 'Asian values'. These values were not without their self-serving aspects, the bolstering of authoritarian government not least among them. Yet, in how East Asian economies grew and what they achieved there is clear evidence of the influence of tradition and precepts which allowed growth with increasing equity and social inclusion to be significant features of their experience. And this 15-year experiment is the only undisputable example we have of growth with equity in the history of 'development'.

An East–West discourse, a discourse of transmodernity, can never be solely about reorienting power relations and adjustment of unquestioned economic structures. It must also be a discourse about values, about the re-evaluation of tradition, about recovering the lost ecological values of traditional lifestyles. To get beyond the impasses and unsustainable features of rampant modernity, with the gated community as a notable example, we need to be able to see the past differently and more clearly, as well as to envisage the future in new and innovative ways. The gated community stands as an example of how untrammelled growth and accumulation of wealth in fewer and fewer hands is not progress but a model of how to deconstruct society from within. Gated communities are a shining example of not how to provide security to a community, but to enhance and spread total insecurity by generating dysfunctional relationships. Societies marked by increasing equity have less to fear from internal social tensions. True physical and social security is provided by empowering the poor and the marginalized and opening the gates of gated communities. Valuing society and equitable social provision can liberate the private space for families. It can also suggest alternatives and the more sustainable values of living cheek by jowl with the diversity of one's neighbours and fellow citizens that will be necessary if we are to combat the challenge of climate change and not overtax the natural environment. Beyond the gates of highly self-selecting communities of wealth, there exist a wealth of alternative ways of thinking about and planning for the human future, of transcending modernity and of shaping inclusive, viable and sustainable futures for all.

References

Burckhardt, T. and Stoddart, W. (1992) *Fez: City of Islam*, Islamic Texts Society, Cambridge, UK

Frank, A. G. (1998) *ReOrient: Global Economy in the Asian Age*, University of California Press, Berkeley, CA

Nandy, A. (2001) *An Ambiguous Journey to the City*, Oxford University Press, Delhi, India

Sardar, Z. (2000) *The Consumption of Kuala Lumpur*, Reaktion Books, London

Sardar, Z. (2006) 'Beyond difference: Cultural relations in a new century' in Masood, E. (ed) *How Do You Know: Reading Ziauddin Sardar on Islam, Science and Cultural Relations*, Pluto Press, London

Townsend, P. (1979) *Poverty in the United Kingdom*, Allan Lane, London

World Bank (1993) *The East Asian Miracle: Economic Growth and Public Policy*, World Bank Policy Research Reports, Washington, DC

3

Gated Urban Life versus Kinship and Social Solidarity in the Middle East

Samer Bagaeen

Introduction

Historically, traditional settlements in the Middle East have incorporated climatic, cultural, social, economic and religious control mechanisms that manifested themselves in the way in which physical elements, and barriers, were built in the environment. In the Old City of Jerusalem, for example, the urban morphology included quarters as a form of self-segregation on ethnic-religious reasons. Here, each quarter is made up of a number of neighbourhoods, each neighbourhood (or *hara*) is made up of a number of *ahwash* (singular *hosh* – or courtyard complex), and each *hosh* is made up of a number of flats and tightly packed interlocking houses. Although there is little data available regarding the division of Jerusalem into quarters prior to the Muslim conquest of the city, Hopkins (1971) points out that the mixture of races and languages in the city would have made such divisions likely; the Muslim quarter, for example, was subdivided into smaller groupings based on tribal, village origins or family groups.

This chapter argues that these laws, local traditions and contingencies have together over many years given birth to the distinct formal expression of the traditional Middle Eastern city and revealed the non-formal patterns that had shaped its built environment. In this city, concepts of public and community ownership and control, along with privacy and private governance, have always existed even though some writers (Sorkin, 1992) view them as part of a postmodern trend towards the commoditization of public space.

This chapter takes a close look at how form and access mechanisms in these traditional cities and settlements came about and the prevalence of what we have come to know as private urban governance. As a small case study, the chapter also considers the rise of modern-day residential sanctuaries and new settlements that offer somewhat different forms of access and control, including closed-circuit television (CCTV) security and card-controlled access for vehicles and pedestrians, secure parking, property management service and the like. Master-planned communities in Amman in Jordan (Andalucia), in Dubai (Emirates Hills) or in Riyadh in Saudi Arabia in appearing to offer the three Ps (prestige, peace and perfect vistas) are proving popular. Jordan's first planned gated community, Andalucia, dubbed by developers as 'everything you would need in a city', is being built 27km south-west of the capital.

These secure communities are proving popular in a changing Middle East, where a premium on security is higher than it used to be. Gated living is being advertised as offering the very best of city living, which is about connecting with family, friends and a 'life you've always dreamed about', offering urban life with all the amenities of a metropolitan centre, and the added comfort of security of an exclusive community. Although privacy and exclusivity feature prominently in the material advertising of these sites, there is no mention of the older mechanisms, such as kinship and social solidarity, which gave rise to the form of traditional cities historically associated with the Middle East. These are examined in this chapter, which will show how, in catering for a new but already saturated market, the roots of the modern gated community in the Middle East can be traced back to the formal and control mechanisms prevalent in these traditional settlements.

The formal aspects of the traditional Middle Eastern city

In a wide-ranging discussion of cities, Van Kempen and Marcuse (1997) refer to a 'new social order' reflecting socio-economic polarization and its influence on the division within cities and life within neighbourhoods. Two scenarios that they highlight include, first, a potential lack of social solidarity as a consequence of the ever-increasing process of globalization where elites become less dependent (economically and spatially) on the lower status groups (they refer to the work of Reich, 1991). The second scenario picks up the dependence argument, noting that globalization can lead to socio-economic symbiosis within an increasingly polarized society where one group has the money for products and services that the other group can provide (they refer to works by Sassen, 1988, 1991). More recently, in 'The right to the city', Harvey (2008, p23) notes that 'the kind of city we want cannot be divorced from that of what kind of social ties, relationships to nature, lifestyles, technologies and aesthetic values we desire'.

Spatially, the first scenario is likely to lead to the formation of enclaves, while the second could lead to neighbourhoods where people with different incomes, ethnicities, skills and education all live. The first can be seen as giving rise to gated communities, while the second facilitates a kinder type of city with sustainable neighbourhoods. This chapter will show how cities in the Middle East have been dropping the latter in favour of the former, in the words of Harvey (2008, p32), touting 'the sale of community and boutique lifestyles to fulfil urban dreams'.

In examining the formal aspects of the traditional Middle Eastern city, the nature of its physical fabric, the importance of law, communal responsibility and local networks, as well as the processes by which inhabitants have solved their past housing problems, this chapter takes on board a suggestion by Le Goix and Webster (2008, p1190) that the issue with gated communities is not whether there is a gate or not. The issue, they argue, is the 'fragmentation of the urban governance realm into micro-territories', sometimes called the 'medievalization of the modern city'. In fact, these processes predate the medieval city, with Blakely (2007, p475) noting that gated and walled cities or residential areas are 'as old as community

building itself', citing archaeological evidence that points out that settlements in the Nile River valleys were walled against the hunter-gatherer tribes, that early kingdoms in Mesopotamia were known for their walls, and that many Greek and Roman settlements were also walled.

The literature on this city suggests that laws, local traditions and contingencies had given birth to the city's distinct formal expression and revealed the non-formal patterns that had shaped its built environment and worked to sustain its urban form.[1] This same literature indicates that the building principles that are the result of applying the *Shari'a*, unlike current zoning laws that are created by a central government and applied to the local level without being responsive to specific micro-conditions, developed built-in mechanisms that were responsive to the particular conditions that occurred at the neighbourhood scale and functioned as a guide for decision-making in matters of building at that level.

Works by Akbar (1988, 1989a, 1989b, 1992), Hakim (1986) and Bianca (2000) have all emphasized that traditional Middle Eastern cities exhibit an 'unmistakably Muslim character that can only be attributed to a prevailing spiritual identity as materialized through a consistent daily practice and the corresponding built environment' (Bianca, 2000, p9). Furthermore, Akbar (1989a, p3) notes that in the traditional Muslim city, the built environment was shaped by 'agreements in which users had maximum control'.

Law and the built environment in the Middle East

The Middle East went through dramatic changes during the 19th and 20th centuries when it moved from decentralized traditional decision-making processes based on the Islamic legal system in which users had total control, to contemporary centralized patterns based on government regulations in which users have little or no control over the built environment.[2] The decentralized decision-making process was abandoned under the Ottomans, whose property laws were codified in 1869. Further erosion of community ownership, control and responsibility took hold with the introduction of modern town planning principles in the 20th century under colonial rule.

Bianca (2000, p195) looks closely at this process and analyses the structural conflicts between 'traditional Muslim' concepts of public and community ownership and the 'modern Western' planning methods. He examines the effect of the latter on traditional community structures and institutions that were previously enhanced by 'shared values and sustained by direct human relationships, such as kinship and neighbourhood solidarity'. These were replaced, he notes, by a costly and highly formalized administrative system imposed by a distant government authority (Bianca, 2000, pp195–197)[3] and had become a 'bureaucratic straitjacket inflicting previously unknown restrictions on human activities', paralysing the internal control mechanisms of the community. The importance of community networks in urban development was previously highlighted by Turner (1996, pp339–347). This is an area I will return to later in this chapter.

The traditional city as an inherently socially sustainable entity

The origins of the traditional city continue to stoke controversy, with the literature on the origins of the traditional Muslim city typically offering contrasting images of those origins. De Montequin (1983, p47) puts forward the argument for an 'organic city'. He examines cities in the context of Middle Eastern urbanization and describes what he refers to as 'the private Islamic city' in the following terms:

> The classical Islamic city, with its compact sets of buildings, its terraces, its courtyards as sole open spaces, with those narrow and tortuous thoroughfares, is similar to no other because it is not a 'rational' or planned type of structure, but rather a purely natural and 'biological' one.

The irrationality, irregularity and the lack of predetermined layout present in the traditional Muslim city he attributes to the crystallization of nomadic life within the format of an urban entity. The old town in Riyadh, for example, at least until the 1950s, with its physical layout of clusters of courtyard houses with communal urban spaces, is a good example of this. In this layout, De Montequin (1983, p49) notes that the dwelling has always been the dominant and prevailing urban element and the factor that, for example, 'has

forced the traffic ways to conform to its physical volume'. Abu-Lughod (1980, p7) also indicates that 'in Islam's empire, in marked contrast both to Western cities built under Roman law or to Hindu cities built according to Vedic principles, the public ways developed after the residential cells were allocated'. Another unique feature of the structure of the city contributed by Islam is the creation of 'male' and 'female' territory (Abu-Lughod, 1993). It was this separation that necessitated the protection of visual privacy, prevented physical contact, and regulated the placement of windows, the heights of adjacent buildings, and the mutual responsibilities of neighbours towards one another so as to guard visual privacy.

Kostof (1991, p52) disagrees with De Montequin's analysis that the Muslim city was an irrational and irregular entity and notes that:

> Beneath all twists and alleys lies an order which may belong to a prior occupation, to the features of the land, to long established conventions of the social contract or to a string of compromises between individual rights and the common will where traditional concepts of community ownership, control and community responsibility provided an egalitarian tradition of building.

This city, Kostof (1991) writes, was allowed to work itself out subject to the respect of custom, ownership and the Muslim's right to visual privacy as opposed to 'methodical supervision over the city form' because citizens were allowed 'considerable latitude to exercise their personal rights in the treatment of their property' (pp63–64). In a tight urban fabric such as this, it was the informally established and observed social conventions between neighbours that influenced piecemeal changes to the fabric, as was customary procedure depending on religious law. In this city, the residential fabric, where this kind of piecemeal action was possible, was of greater importance than the public space of streets because the former was continually negotiated and redefined as buildings pushed out, over, interlocked and diversified. This 'special relationship between proximate neighbours' was, Abu-Lughod (1980, p8) points out, 'the one fundamental characteristic of Islamic law' that she has found relevant to the creation of the concepts of the private and the semi-private space in Muslim cities.

Figure 3.1 *A complex under construction in Riyadh, Saudi Arabia*

Source: Samer Bagaeen

So strong was this neighbourhood 'social' cohesion based on kinship, tribal affiliation or ethnicity that it was able, according to Kostof (1991), to rearrange inherited pre-Muslim grids of Graeco-Roman origin, fusing and introverting aspects of it into what Abu-Lughod (1993, pp22–23) has called 'social boundary markers' that intensified the physical segregation between juridical classes in medieval Islamic cities. What we appear, therefore, to have is an urban form that accentuates processes of social cohesion, social capital formation and social exclusion at the same time.

Fast forward a few years, and in looking again at Riyadh (capital of Saudi Arabia), Glasze and Alkhayyal (2002) also classify gated developments in the city in a manner not too different from Kostof's: extended family compounds, cultural enclaves and, they add to these, governmental staff housing. In doing so, they provide a clear indication that the urban form surveyed continues to behave here in the same way that it has always done, at least in terms of the emphasis on aspects of social networks, social control and social order.

They argue that the extended family compounds could be seen as a sign of the revival of the traditional living environment which offers mutual social and economic benefits. In the modern gated developments, the traditional shared space, traditionally used for social activities, is reconfigured as the common space within the walls of extended family compounds. In social

terms, extended family compounds offer a solution for the fostering of extended family ties while maintaining the independence of the nuclear family. In addition, they add that these compounds not only offer a safe common space for children's play, but, in economic terms, reduce their cost.

Examples of such developments can include extended family compounds that consist of a group of villas surrounded by a common fence or wall. Since the 1980s, these have been designed and built to accommodate extended families. The physical layout of these complexes is composed of two or more architecturally identical houses built on the same block (see Figure 3.1). Usually, these complexes contain one larger unit – which accommodate the head of the extended family. This would have the grandest entrance off the street with the remaining units benefiting from their own entrance in most cases.

Building and planning principles in the Middle Eastern city

Hakim (1986, pp95, 138) demonstrates the importance of law (and, in some instances, what he calls the 'spirit of Islam') through building guidelines as a prime factor which shaped the traditional Middle Eastern city. He argues that this physical organizational pattern, based on

Islamic law and models of governance, necessitated the level of interdependence between neighbours referred to above with regard to site management, including the use of party walls, maintenance of cul-de-sacs and problems related to rain and wastewater, and had the primary impact. It is Hakim's view that Islamic law responded well in fulfilling the demand for building and urban design guidelines in the traditional city, where it acted as a framework for adjudicating related conflicts.

This discourse is picked up later by Bianca (2000, p142), who also finds that the morphology of traditional Islamic cities, from an urban design perspective, can be attributed to the strong social order of Islam practised in conjunction with strong customary laws; the conspicuous absence of formal civic institutions; and the empowerment of self-regulating private communities and social groups. Both authors are in agreement that it was these factors that brought about an urban form from within conditioned by incremental decisions at the grassroots level, rather than responding to imposed external schemes. This is not too dissimilar, perhaps, from what Le Goix and Webster (2008) describe when they note that in some common interest developments (CIDs) in the US, some residents vote to erect gates and some vote to take the ones built by developers down. In both, the role of the community is crucial.

This important role for the community stands in contrast to areas where the community has no voice. Let's take, for example, Harvey's (2008) call to arms for the 'construction of a broad social movement' to reclaim the city for the dispossessed from the hands of 'private and quasi-private' interests that are 'reshaping the city along lines favourable to developers'. He cites as examples how Michael Bloomberg is 'turning Manhattan into one vast gated community for the rich', how Yale University is redesigning large chunks of New Haven's urban fabric, and how Carlos Slim re-cobbled the streets of Mexico city to 'suit the tourist gaze' (Harvey, 2008, pp38–40).

These examples clearly show, as Harvey (2008) would have us believe, that the right to the city, in contrast to antecedents in the cities of the Middle East, is 'too narrowly confined' and 'restricted to a small political and economic elite who are in a position to shape cities'. In the traditional cities, the elite, the local judges and the master masons were only seen as expert arbiters rather than shapers in disputes that sought to address problems in the built environment. In effect, the only shaper in town was the community, broadly defined, of course.

Where gating is concerned, it is worth referring to what Le Goix and Webster (2008) call 'the fragmentation of urban governance' as seen from the perspective of writers in the West today. In the Middle Eastern city as described by Hakim (1986) and Bianca (2000), these were natural processes undertaken at the grassroots level and therefore were not necessarily fragmented.

The production of space in the traditional Middle Eastern city

Previous sections of this chapter have clarified the role of the community in giving form to the traditional city, and Harvey's (2008, p23) 'The right to the city', where he argues that 'the kind of city we want cannot be divorced from that of what kind of social ties, relationship to nature and lifestyles we desire', sets this in the context of a modern city. Another important concept is that of power. Harvey, like Soja (1989) before him, acknowledges the role of ideology and power in shaping a city. He uses the example of Haussmann in Paris when he 'deliberately engineered the removal of much of the working class and other unruly elements from the city centre' (Harvey, 2008, p33).

These power dynamics may not have always been quite obvious or may have even been 'subtle'. While this is not the place to identify trends, it suffices to say that manifestations of power in the traditional urban realm were prevalent. For example, Raymond (1984, pp16–17) explains how the intervention of medieval judges in the *Maghrib* (present-day Morocco) in urban matters ranged from building regulations, security and the protection of privacy. More recently, Natsheh (2000, pp610–611) highlights the importance of religious power and examines how in Ottoman Jerusalem the *Shari'a* court played a vital role in controlling many issues related to buildings and their maintenance. The court was the competent authority in Jerusalem to deal with what we now know as a 'planning objection'.

Decision-makers are also examined in Hakim's work (1986, pp18–19, 102), where he outlines two sets of decision-making dynamics operating in the traditional Islamic city that had an impact on societal values and related building guidelines. The first was based on decisions made by the rulers, was 'macro' in nature and involved creating a planned effect on the urban fabric (e.g. Harvey's Haussmann), while the second involved decisions made by citizens at a 'micro' level (Lefebvre's urban revolution). He points out that while the latter had less discernible effects than the decisions of the rulers, its aggregate impact was ultimately more significant and affected the lives of most people directly because it would have affected urban physical systems such as houses and quarters, the street network, open spaces and building heights.

Abu-Lughod (1993, p28) explained how Islamic property laws 'left to the residential areas a large measure of autonomy since many of the public functionaries operated largely in the commercial sections of the city'. Ideologically, in the early Muslim cities, the planning authority was delegated to individual social groups (the judges and the master masons) who were responsible for the management of space. According to Bianca (2000, p54), this authority was characterized by the relative lack of institutional control; the supremacy of private arrangements (read 'private governance' or CIDs for the modern city) over public regulations; and the reduction of the circulation network to a minimum. What may distinguish these mechanisms from those prevalent in modern-day gated communities or private governance arrangements is that in the latter, residents tend to be tied to the common interests by a legally binding contract as opposed to local autonomy, self-management and common law arrangements in the traditional city, as described below.

At the micro-level of management (and governance), Hakim (1986, pp19–22) outlines several principles and guidelines affecting urban decision-making:

- *Harm*, meaning that one should exercise one's full rights in what is rightfully his, providing the action will not generate harm to others.
- *Interdependence*. This principle is meant to generate building solutions by encouraging self-regulatory behaviour.
- *Privacy*. In physical terms, this refers to the private domain of the home. The privacy of others must be respected and its invasion, such as direct visual corridors into the private domain of others, is prohibited.
- *Rights of original (or earlier) usage*. Ownership pattern across time creates rights of earlier ownership or usage, in effect granting certain rights to older and established facts.
- *Rights of building higher within one's airspace* to maximize its utilization for personal benefit even if it excludes air and sun from others. Even though

this is the only exception to the principle of harm, its allowance was waived when there was evidence that the intent to build higher was to harm a specific neighbour.
- *Respect for the property of others*. The ownership and integrity of a property (land, building, etc.) must be respected and no action is allowed which will depress its value or usefulness or create nuisance to its owner.
- *Pre-emption*. Pre-emption is the right of a neighbour or partner to purchase an adjacent property or structure when offered for sale by another neighbour or partner.
- *Seven cubits* (a cubit is equal to 46cm to 50cm) *as the minimum width of public thoroughfares* (the basis for this width is to allow two fully loaded camels to pass).
- *Any public thoroughfare should not be obstructed* by temporary or permanent obstructions (excluding, of course, city gates that lie on thoroughfares into the city).

Akbar (1988, p13) takes a slice from this argument when he examines the aggregate decisions by users in the traditional city. He looks at the local traditions and contingencies that have given birth to the distinct formal expression of the traditional city in the Middle East and attempts to reveal the non-formal patterns that have shaped the built environment and worked to sustain its urban form. These contingencies include societal norms, public and private responsibilities, kinship, property rights, privacy regulations, and the customs for the mixing of activities in residential quarters which were reflected in the layout and design of the urban building fabric.

Akbar (1988) concludes that their disappearance in the modern era of town planning and city plans and the shift in responsibility (e.g. for maintenance) from the user (the 'micro' environment) to the authority (the 'macro' environment) has adversely affected the condition of the built environment in such cities. He delineates the principles that had shaped the built environment in traditional cities by investigating traditional and contemporary legal systems, decision-making processes, cases of disputes among neighbours, territorial structures and conventions. He uses these analyses to construct a model of responsibility that traces the claims of use, ownership and control to predict the quality of objects and structures in the built

Figure 3.2 *The Portland Mews gated compound in Kemptown, Brighton, UK*

Source: Samer Bagaeen

environment (Akbar, 1989b, pp28–29). He argues that the condition of any object is a reflection of the handling of that object by individuals, whether they are users, owners or visitors, and is therefore related to the responsibility of those who own, maintain or use it.

Rather than examine the power dynamic in this 'shift' and its implications in a certain socio-economic context, Akbar focuses on the changing patterns of governance and responsibility in the traditional environment, including diminished responsibility and changed conventions and social relationships between residents of the city and their physical environment. This area of diminished responsibility is one that private developers in the modern era flourished under as it allowed them to set the agenda, including the building of what we have come to know as gated communities.

Placing this argument in a modern and gated context, one would expect the privatization of governance in this instance to result in a better-quality urban environment. In fact, it was Newman (1972) who first linked the prevention of urban decay to gating as a device that gives social control to residents over their environment. Examples of this in the modern environment include retro-fitted and infill gating of the kind described by Le Goix and Webster (2008) and previously by Blandy (2006). This process of gating is a common type of gated communities in England that tend to be located in towns and cities. It comprises a small group of new dwellings set back from the street frontage, entered through a gate or archway (see Figure 3.2).

To sum up, in line with these guidelines, residents in the traditional city could exercise their full rights over their environment providing that their action did not generate harm to others. Significant changes in the traditional Middle Eastern city took place in the 19th and 20th centuries. In the post-Ottoman Middle East, civil codes regarding ownership stipulated that an owner could manipulate a property within the limits of the law as opposed to the traditional environment where the same owner would have had complete freedom as long as no harm was done to other adjoining parties; local agreements took precedence over government regulations.

Gated communities in a contemporary Middle East

Gated communities in the Middle East can refer to planned urban areas that are fenced (e.g. Israeli settlements in the West Bank that come with electrified fences) or ones that are walled off from their surroundings and where access is controlled by means of a gate or a barrier of some kind or other. In many cases the concept not only refers to residential areas with restricted access, it can also include controlled access government compounds (e.g. the Green Zone in the centre of Baghdad). Developers have also tended to market residential gated communities in the Middle East in terms of their design and architectural features, the facilities they provide, and on account of their ability to provide exclusive urban living. This section briefly examines some examples.

It is helpful, first, if Blakely's (2007, pp477–478) division of gated communities into three main types is highlighted. The first includes lifestyle communities where gates and walls mark off and protect an area where civil authorities were no longer able to adequately protect the population from armed and dangerous groups. The second is the prestige community which feeds on exclusionary popular aspirations and the desire to differentiate. The third includes security zones where community safety is the primary goal. In the absence of armed gangs and social unrest in most countries (see the reference to Turkey below), most gated communities in the Middle East fall into the third type, with type two developments being newcomers onto the market.

While some gating trends in the Middle East have existed for some time, as the earlier part of this chapter has shown, others are relatively recent trends. Saudi Arabia is a good example of a country where gating has existed as a tradition for expatriate professionals and their families for a number of years (type 3). These tend to live in generally well-maintained landscaped compounds that offer a range of support services, including kindergartens, clinics, health clubs and shopping malls (see Figure 3.3). These compounds tend to be guarded, with access restricted to residents and their guests. Administration and maintenance are, in the

Figure 3.3 *Government housing compound in Riyadh*

Source: Samer Bagaeen

main, provided through a management company. Saudi nationals also tend to be excluded from residing in these compounds. Bigger compounds make use of high-end security measures such as CCTV and concrete barricades (Glasze and Alkhayyal, 2002, p326). Glasze and Alkhayyal (2002, p331) also note two different gating conditions in Lebanon, where during the civil war (1975 to 1990) people were attracted to gated housing in search of safety, while in the post-war era, the focus was on gated estates providing a 'modern global environment'.

Blandy (2006) argues that changing social, economic and political conditions over a number of years have led to the emergence of a different type of defended collective housing. The Middle East is no exception, where these were aided to a certain extent by the economic and building boom (taking advantage of high oil prices) that most countries in the region enjoyed between 2002 and 2008. This process is very evident in the examples from Turkey, the United Arab Emirates and Jordan that follow.

In Turkey, Genis (2007) attributes the accelerated growth in gated communities (type 1) to a growing search for security associated with increasing fear of urban crime and violence. There is, of course, a consistent link in the literature between the fear of crime and gated communities. This view is developed in the work of Landman (see Chapter 6) and Lemanski (2004), who also views gated communities as a continuation of a form of apartheid.

Genis (2007, p776) identifies a typology of upper-class gated communities in Istanbul, which includes the genre the 'private town':

> Located at the fringes of the city on rural land and near the lakes and forests; large in size and a variety of housing types; high-technology security and large private security personnel; top notch communication, infrastructure and sport facilities; large variety of social services; private government.

A typical example of this, Genis argues, is Kemer Country. This is a 'pioneering' gated community in Istanbul that translates the concept of the private enclave into the local context by incorporating vernacular forms within the design, alongside discourses of community within its planning and marketing, where emphasis lies in the provision of a 'total living experience' rather than simply a 'suburban living in a gated community' (Genis, 2007, p782) that comes ready with premium services and infrastructure. It is helpful here to refer to Le Goix and Callen who, in Chapter 9 of this volume, note that these modern gated collectives can also be described as 'a generic form in urban sprawl and suburban landscape' where 'speculation and location rent are preeminent forces structuring the urban space'.

Exclusive suburbs in the metropolitan hinterland are nothing new. In fact, it's ten years since Connell

Figure 3.4 *Emirates Hills in Dubai, United Arab Emirates*

Source: Samer Bagaeen

Figure 3.5 *The Andalucia gated community, Jordan*

Source: courtesy of Taameer Jordan

(1999, p417) described 'enclosed homogenous suburbs, designed and marketed as fragments of Europe' mushrooming in the Manila metropolitan area, and outlined five themes that constituted the strategy for selling these new suburbs: value, security, exclusivity, escape and community. Similar strategies have recently marketed similar developments in the Emirate of Dubai and in Jordan.

Dubai, a city until recently engaged in a construction boom of tremendous proportions (an 'instant city'; see Bagaeen, 2007), is the product of a super-fast urbanism that builds shopping malls, luxury hotels, exclusive residential towers and gated communities as an example of 'demand-oriented' planning. One of the first so-called 'prestigious residential developments' and signature freehold projects by Emaar (a Dubai-based Public Joint Stock Company) is Emirates Hills, which features 24-hour security (guests have to be signed in) and includes a residential golf estate, parks, 20 lakes and an 18-hole championship golf course.

In Jordan, Taameer Jordan Holdings, a real estate developer established in 2005, has set out a vision for building a haven of luxurious living and a lifestyle synonymous with modernity and highest comfort building. One example of this is the Andalucia project, a residential district that covers an area nearly 1 million square metres in size at 20km south of the capital Amman. In addition to 582 luxury villas, Andalucia contains an entertainment centre incorporating a health club, gymnasium, tennis and basketball courts, walking tracks, kids' club and nursery, a clinic, cafés and restaurants. It also has its own water treatment plant and water reservoirs. More importantly, a marketing brochure boasts: 'For the purpose of enhancing the residents' privacy and the city's exclusivity, Andalucia is a "gated community" with a main entrance and enforced security 24/7'. The brochure also notes that Andalucia is the first project to bring the gated community concept to Jordan.

Conclusions

This chapter has explored how laws, local traditions and contingencies have together and over many years given birth to the distinct formal expression of the traditional Middle Eastern city, revealing in the process the non-formal patterns that had shaped its built environment. Over the years, and especially recently, a handful of planned and mostly gated urban and peri-urban enclaves have been built in response to various factors that include everything from the desire for safety and security to the desire to be different and to be seen as different.

In Jordan, these gated communities are being embraced by policy as outlined in the new Amman City Plan (2008), whose Outlying Settlements Policy was articulated as a response to increasing interest in residential developments, particularly large-scale compounds and gated communities beyond the Amman Development Corridor in Greater Amman Municipality's outlying areas. This policy designates four growth areas around existing villages where outlying settlement development will be consolidated.

With the rate of construction of luxury developments in the Middle East grinding to a halt as the financial crisis takes hold (Lewis, 2009), this aspect of consolidation in the Amman plan could perhaps go some way to addressing some of the concerns about the sustainability of outlying suburban gated communities. Hype aside, the number of gated communities in the Middle East (apart from the security compounds for expatriate workers) is not high and steps taken to better integrate these communities within the existing infrastructure and reflect more of the traditional climatic, cultural, social, economic and religious control mechanisms that manifested themselves in the traditional built environment are not too late. This chapter has shown that gated communities are not in themselves a new form of housing provision in the Middle East, but a product of their time and circumstances. The financial crisis has given the region a breathing space; but whether it takes advantage of this remains to be seen.

Notes

1   Hakim (1986) de-emphasizes climate as a major determining factor and highlights the importance of law, in this case Islamic *Shari'a* law, as a prime factor that shaped the traditional Arabic-Islamic city.
2   Akbar (1989a, p7) attributes environmental problems in the Middle East to 'centralization that eliminated user participation' and the 'moving of elements in the built environment away from their beneficiaries' (Akbar, 1989b, p28).
3   An administrative system which literature claims was weak, corrupt and incapable of delivering.

References

Abu-Lughod, J. (1980) 'Contemporary relevance of Islamic urban principles', *Ekistics*, vol 47, no 280, January/February, pp6–10

Abu-Lughod, J. (1993) 'The Islamic city: Historic myth, Islamic essence and contemporary relevance', in Amirahmadi, H. and El-Shakhs, S. S. (eds) *Urban Development in the Muslim World*, Rutgers, New Jersey

Akbar, J. (1988) *Crisis in the Built Environment: The Case of the Muslim City*, Concept Media, Singapore

Akbar, J. (1989a) 'Law and environment in the Middle East', *Open House International*, vol 14, no 2, pp3–8

Akbar, J. (1989b) 'Losing interest: Blight of the Muslim city', *Open House International*, vol 14, no 3, pp28–35

Akbar, J. (1992) *Amarat al-Ard fi al-Islam*, Dar al-Qibla lil-thaqafa al-Islamiyya, Jeddah

Bagaeen, S. (2007) 'Brand Dubai: The instant city; or, the instantly recognisable city', *International Planning Studies*, vol 12, no 2, pp173–197

Bianca, S. (2000) *Urban Form in the Arab World: Past and Present*, ORL-Schriften, Zurich

Blakely, E. J. (2007) 'Gated communities for a frayed and afraid world', *Housing Policy Debate*, vol 18, no 3, pp475–480

Blandy, S. (2006) 'Gated communities in England: Historical perspectives and current developments', *GeoJournal*, vol 66, pp15–26

Connell, J. (1999) 'Beyond Manila: Walls, malls and private spaces', *Environment and Planning A*, vol 31, pp417–439

De Montequin, F. (1983) 'The essence of urban existence in the world of Islam', in Germen, A. (ed) *Islamic Architecture and Urbanism*, King Faisal University, Dammam

Elisseeff, N. (1980) 'Physical layout', in Serjeant, R. B. (ed) *The Islamic City*, UNESCO, Paris

Genis, S. (2007) 'Producing elite localities: The rise of gated communities in Istanbul', *Urban Studies*, vol 44, no 4, pp771–798

Glasze, G. and Alkhayyal, A. (2002) 'Gated housing estates in the Arab World: Case studies from Lebanon and Riyadh, Saudi Arabia', *Environment and Planning B: Planning and Design*, vol 29, pp321–336

Greater Amman Municipality (2008) *The Amman Plan: Metropolitan Growth Summary Report*, Greater Amman Municipality

Hakim, B. S. (1986) *Arabic-Islamic Cities: Building and Planning Principles*, Routledge and Kegan Paul, London

Harvey, D. (2008) 'The right to the city', *New Left Review*, vol 53, September/October, pp23–40

Hopkins, I. W. J. (1971) 'The four quarters of Jerusalem', *Palestine Exploration Quarterly*, vol 103, January–June, pp68–84

Kostof, S. (1991) *The City Shaped: Urban Patterns and Meaning through History*, Thames and Hudson, London

Lefebvre, H. (1996) *The Urban Revolution*, University of Minnesota Press, Minnesota

Le Goix, R. and Webster, C. J. (2008) 'Gated communities', *Geography Compass*, vol 2, no 4, pp1189–1214

Lemanski, C. (2004) 'A new apartheid? The spatial implications of fear of crime in Cape Town, South Africa', *Environment and Urbanization*, vol 16, no 10, pp101–112

Lewis, P. (2009) 'Dubai's six-year building boom grinds to a halt as financial crisis takes hold', *The Guardian*, 16 February

Natsheh, Y. (2000) 'The architecture of Ottoman Jerusalem', in Auld, S. and Hillenbrand, R. (eds) *Ottoman Jerusalem: The Living City 1517–1917*, Altajir World of Islam Trust, London

Newman, O. (1972) *Defensible space: crime prevention through urban design*, Macmillan, New York

Raymond, A. (1984) *The Great Arab Cities in the 16th–18th Centuries: An Introduction*, New York University Press, New York, NY

Reich, R. (1991) *The World of Nations*, Random House, New York, NY

Sassen, S. (1988) *The Mobility of Labour and Capital*, Cambridge University Press, Cambridge, UK

Sassen, S. (1991) *The Global City: New York, London, Tokyo*, Princeton University Press, Princeton, NJ

Soja, E. (1989) *Postmodern Geographies: The Reassertion of Space in Critical Social Theory*, Verso Press, London

Sorkin, M. (1992) *Variations on a Theme Park: The New American City and the End of Public Space*, Hill and Wang, New York, NY

Turner, J. F. C. (1996) 'Tools for building community: An examination of 13 hypotheses', *Habitat International*, vol 20, no 3, pp339–347

Van Kempen, R. and Marcuse, P. (1997) 'A new spatial order in cities?', *American Behavioral Scientist*, vol 41, no 3, November–December, pp285–298

4

Gating Urban Spaces in China: Inclusion, Exclusion and Government

Luigi Tomba

Gates and the Chinese city

Large-sized, high-rise, privately managed gated residential developments have become a dominant feature of the built environment in China's growing metropolis during the last 15 years. After a substantial overhaul of the socialist system of housing distribution, gated residential communities marketed to different social groups and featuring different lifestyle options have rapidly replaced traditional residential compounds and led to a massive privatization of the housing stocks. This transition has been interpreted either, on the one hand, as a sign of the impact of global trends of modernity, with developments reproducing Western lifestyles as signifiers of forms of first-world modernity mimicked by the elites of the developing world (Webster et al, 2002; Giroir, 2006); or, on the other, as the result of the reproduction of cultural, social and political traditions of gated spaces visible along the history of China's urbanization (Bray, 2005). If the former interpretation emphasizes the subjugation of China's cities and its citizens to the homogenizing effects of marketization, social stratification and globalization, the latter seems to argue the opposite: that gated spaces are quintessentially an evolution of traditionally Chinese spatial patterns. To use Bray's (2005, p17) words, 'the walled compound as a technology of spatial demarcation transcends any simple historical divide between "traditional" and "modern" China'.

While in many ways both interpretations are supported by the daily observation of the changing built environment in China, I believe both need qualification: one assumes too much subjugation, while the other risks essentializing 'the Chinese' cultural proclivity to live behind gates and overemphasizing its genealogy over its contingent political and social meaning. In this chapter, I would like to suggest an alternative view – in particular, that the gating and privatization of residential spaces are acts of political classification that, while framed within existing traditions, are engineered with a purpose by the late socialist Chinese state, partly directly and partly through the action of new agents. Both the state and its agents – even when these operate under market conditions – are concerned with the fundamental issue of order and social stability; in line with both tradition and the rubric of modernity, the design of residential spaces constitutes an essential tool of social control and classification. Despite almost 30 years of economic reform, the state remains the only decision-maker in urban planning, maintains control over the land market (Yeh, 2005) and fosters a broad network of grassroots governance institutions organized in ward-like sub-districts (Read, 2000; Benewick and Takahara 2002, Benewick et al, 2004; He et al, 2007). With Blakely and Snyder (1997, p1), I believe that 'the setting of boundaries is always a political act... Boundaries delineate space to facilitate the activities and purposes of political, economic and social life'. Gating is, essentially, an exercise in classification. The ability to zone and classify the territory and its population still facilitates the activity of governing in an increasingly stratified and complex society.

In the debate about social sustainability of urban forms promoted by this volume, I therefore wish to suggest that, in the present situation where the Chinese state still maintains control of the land, the planning mechanisms and the provision of services, gates produce a more legible, orderly and easy-to-govern environment, mainly in three ways by:

1   reducing or containing the social conflicts expected in times of rapid urbanization;
2   classifying the population through a lifestyle-based segregation; and
3   facilitating the transition to private forms of service provision through the introduction of privately managed but politically reliable forms of urban self administration.

From cities of production to cities of gates

During the high tide of socialism, and well into the reform period in the late 1980s, Chinese cities have been inhabited by a small but privileged class of state workers. From the mid-1950s, rural–urban migration was kept in check through the Household Registration System (Wang, 2005) that made it impossible for ruralites to be admitted to the highly subsidized urban industrial system. In a rare case of industrialization without urbanization, the growth of urban population stalled during the 1960s and 1970s, and China prided itself with having stamped out the need for big and wasteful 'consumer' cities to the advantage of rational socialist 'cities of production' (*shengchan chengshi*) (Salaff, 1967; Schurmann, 1968). The consequence was that the urban population lived in a cellular structure, organized and administered through 'work units' (*danwei*) that reduced consumption and secured lifelong (and often multigenerational) employment. These industrial or service organizations took over the traditional productive, political, service and trading activities of the cities (Walder, 1986; Lü and Perry, 1999). In the work unit's residential compounds, housing distribution was relatively egalitarian; but workers and their families were assigned housing dependent on their family composition, work duties and political 'performance'.

The rapid demise of many work units during the 1990s and the rapid rise in rural–urban migration required by the new market economy radically transformed the built environment, but also the opportunity structure for urban residents and the

policy that the state had to put in place to govern urban areas. Housing was radically privatized, first through the sale of existing public and work unit stocks to employees, and then with an aggressive plan to subsidize homeownership among urban residents that led in a few years to a remarkably high rate of homeownership in China's cities (over 80 per cent in Beijing and similar percentages in other large cities) (Tomba, 2004). In addition, large industrial cities began to redefine their priorities from productive to service centres, with all provincial capitals today owing the lion's share of their gross domestic product (GDP) to tertiary activities. Industry was rapidly moved to either satellite cities or so-called 'development zones' created to attract foreign investment. The local municipal and provincial administration pursued this strategy aggressively by eating up more and more of the agricultural land at the margin of the city to develop industrial sites, while the traditional inner district of most cities became greatly sought-after development sites for new residential communities, which greatly increased the value of the land and the profits local governments and developers could reap from them. Even cities such as Shenyang in the north-eastern rustbelt aimed at a post-industrial image that meant privileging a residential and commercial (rather than industrial) use of the urban land (Tomba and Tang, 2008).

With the decline of state employment and, consequently, of the role played by employers in administering, servicing and controlling the urban population, and a progressive delinking of residence and employment (Wang and Murie, 1999), urban administrations gradually rediscovered the importance of 'territorial' units of governance and established a grassroots system based on the principle of *zizhi* ('self-governing', or as Bray, 2006, suggests: 'government of the self'). Such offices as the 'resident committees' (*jumin weiyuanhui*), or (as they are now called) 'communities' (*shequ*), had been under the work unit system a secondary line of administration in urban centres. At the end of the 1990s, faced with the disappearance of many work units, the government decided to revitalize and expanded them (Read, 2000), assigning them the task of service providers traditionally played by employers for that part of the urban population that was now being laid off by state enterprises. Today they play an important role in rebuilding community support and reducing the alienation of elderly people and the unemployed, while contributing to the control and management of the unregistered population. Concurrently, private players such as property managers who were administering and overseeing large numbers of private developments also became important players in the new urban governance arrangement to the point that they often performed functions traditionally in the hands of the state (security, assistance to the elderly, maintenance, even sometimes family planning).

As mentioned earlier, the tradition of gating residential spaces is not at all new to China, although the use of gates in the work unit era was not intended as a device for social and economic exclusion (Wu, 2005). Socialist cities' cellular structure (centred on the all-encompassing social role of the work unit system) embodied the idea of a scientific rationalization of the urban space, an aspect of the long-term anti-urban policies of the Chinese Communist party that greatly limited urban growth during the 1960s and 1970s. In that setting, walls produced communities entirely dependent on the enterprise. Their consumption patterns (as well as mobility, access to services, education and information) could easily be controlled through the redistributive nature of the Chinese socialist system, as worker/residents had no other access to consumption than that provided by the rationing system through their employer.

Today's privately owned compounds resemble more 'club realms of consumption' (Webster, 2001; Giroir, 2006), whose members share properties that are neither entirely private nor public (gardens, community club houses and sporting facilities). By concentrating consumers and limiting access to members, the club aims at stimulating and making consumption (as well as service provision) more efficient. With respect to the way in which they manage collectively owned resources, Webster (2001, p149) defines proprietary communities as 'privately owned and privately governed estates in which a group of households or firms share certain communal facilities which they pay for via ground-rent, service fee or some other device'.

The reasons for and effects of gating parts of the urban territory have been thoroughly investigated by a number of important studies (Blakely and Snyder, 1997; Blandy et al, 2003; Low, 2003) and comparatively in this volume. Among the most important determinants of the gating syndrome seems to be the fear of the challenges and degradation of modern urban life,

something that American and Chinese middle classes seemingly have in common.

According to Miao (2003), during the 1990s, 83 per cent of all residential communities in Shanghai (old or new) underwent some form of physical separation, while by the year 2000 there were already 54,000 gated residential communities in Guangdong Province. In 2005, and in Beijing alone, 72.2 million square metres of new private housing were under construction (*Xinhua*, 2006a), the majority behind gates. The impression of an army of new homeowners walled off from outside dangers in the new spaces of their private residence is reinforced by a visible presence of security guards. According to the Ministry of Public security, in 2006 over 2300 security guards companies with over 1.1 million employees were active in urban China, including over 100,000 in Beijing alone, where the two largest security guard companies are state owned (Wang, 2004). A 2005 survey published by the Chinese journal *Community*, reveals that only about one third of all residential neighbourhoods in urban areas allow free passage to non-residents, while about two-thirds require registration for guests and employ private security guards (Gu, 2006).

This 'forting-up' syndrome is publicly encouraged by local policies to foster security. The fear of disorder (*luan*) shared by bureaucracies and residents results in the marketing of *exclusive* lifestyles appealing to different social groups and at different prices. Gated developments have come in different packages and options, from the reclusive villas adjacent to a prestigious golf course, with tennis courts and swimming pools, to the high-rise apartment blocks sharing only gardens and basic facilities. Different from the exclusive American and European gated communities built for the rich and famous and to protect wealthy classes from the dangers of modern life, gates are an essential part of any new development in China. While the social spaces they include are, indeed, different, the spatial patterns of a delimited area shared by owners is replicated across a broad spectrum of housing facilities.

The classification of urban space that results from the erection of these gated spaces produces exclusionary, as well as inclusionary effects: typically, walls and fences are intended to prevent outsiders from accessing the privately shared goods, while those who are inside experience a stronger sense of communitarian belonging, one that emerges from common interests, similar experiences and collective conflicts in these places devoted exclusively to dwelling and consumption (Tomba, 2005).

Structural and political reasons behind the triumph of gates

Spatial segregation is the result of the converging interests of well-off citizens, developers, managers and the governing bureaucracies. A number of economic and political reasons can be identified for the success of this form of settlement in a country such as China. The first is a structural need for large-scale housing estates to rapidly curb chronic urban housing shortages. Under this condition, large new, concentrated and privately managed projects attracted more interest than small dispersed developments or renovations, and seemed to serve better the public need for new residential space, a lot of it and as quickly as possible. Despite a significant increase in population, the per capita living space in urban China quadrupled during the last 30 years (26 square metres in 2005, an average close to 80 square metres per household), and the floor space built in the same period is 12 times what communist China built in the previous three decades (Xinhua, 2006b).

Under the work unit system, housing had remained a component of the welfare attached to life-tenure employment. A real estate market did not develop fully until the second half of the 1990s, when work units began to reduce housing distribution and were eventually prevented by law (1998) from allocating free housing. At the same time, the sale of large quantities of housing stocks at highly subsidized prices was accompanied by policies favouring access to homeownership by public employees and urban professionals, while financial institutions have entered the equation by issuing housing loans (Gu, 1998; Li, 2002). With a growing demand for higher standards of housing, new developments were increasingly planned in newly reclaimed land in the suburbs and became enormous: in 2002, the average floor space per residential area under construction in Beijing was over 53,000 square metres (Beijing Municipal Bureau of Statistics, 2006). On average, these new residential areas occupy between 12ha and 20ha and house 2000 to 3000 families (Miao, 2003), requiring the presence of some form of private governance, mostly a management company. In Beijing, as much as in other cities, the monofunctional 'sealed neighbourhood' (*fengbi xiaoqu*) has become the architectural standard. Alternative ways of designing residential neighbourhoods have been almost entirely abandoned. While a theoretical discussion has, indeed, developed on the advantages and disadvantages offered by 'sealed' (*fengbi*) as opposed to 'open' (*kaifang*) neighbourhoods, planning practices and design standards are still privileging the efficiency of large gated developments over small open neighbourhoods.

The second reason is that the mingling interests of developers, local bureaucracies, financial institutions and large enterprises (what Li Zhang called urban China's 'pro-growth coalition'; Zhang, 2006) also favoured large high-quality and privately managed projects over scattered and small residential developments.

In some cities, and most prominently in Beijing, large developments have been supported by the local government. New projects during the 1990s typically included both commercial housing sold at market prices and housing built on subsidized rental land (so-called 'economy housing', or *jingji shiyong fang*) to be assigned, at a substantial discount, to middle-income families (lower than 60,000 yuan a year, already a rather high income level). The gated version of the residential compound became attractive for developers, who also saw large communities of several thousand families as opportunities for long-term and stable flows of management fees. In the overwhelming majority of cases, the management companies are fully owned subsidiaries of the developers,[1] or commercial appendixes of such public agencies as the *fangguansuo* (the housing maintenance bureau) taking advantage of privatization to establish profitable operations. Management companies in large compounds could yield profits of hundreds of thousands of yuan a year. Some of these earnings inevitably trickle into the hands of local bureaucrats, both in the form of land-use fees and bribes and kickbacks often connected to the issuance of construction licences and land leases (HRW, 2004).

The interests of state agencies entitled to use rights in prime location land also favour large centralized housing projects. A major university in Chengdu, for example, managed to profit from the availability of its unused land in the centre of the city. Its deal with a local developer included the building of residential housing that the university was able to sell to its employees at a considerable discount, while the developer was allocated use rights over a portion of the same land for a private commercial development.

Similarly, city and district governments exploited a regime of growing prices to increase the value of their land holdings. The marketing of certain dilapidated areas of the city as 'new middle-class paradises' produced a virtual increase in the value of the land (Tomba and Tang, 2008) and contributed to an excessive supply of unaffordable housing.

The dominance of the gated micro-district (*xiaoqu*)[2] form and of large projects requiring significant investments and a considerable amount of land over small projects and renovations produced an imbalance in the housing market in favour of high-quality building and contributed to boosting housing prices. Highly priced compounds with a better and more profitable market eventually outnumbered affordable housing projects. In several reported cases, developers obtained subsidized land but were left with a great deal of freedom on how to allocate apartments to entitled families. They often hijacked subsidized projects by building apartments of a much higher quality, size and, consequently, price than they were expected to in order to satisfy the growing demand of those who could afford to invest in real estate (Li, 2002). As a consequence, often with the collusion of complacent local authorities, low-income families were left out of the buying frenzy that touched professional and middle-income public employees. Public ownership of urban land facilitates local authorities' ability to plan cities, but, under partial market conditions, does not eradicate the competition and speculation. Developers purchase use rights from local government (at regulated prices) and often from other developers (at market prices) and compete for prime locations and access to credit from banks. This 'double' land market (one for the land assigned by the state and one for the land auctioned at market prices) produced a black market for land-use rights in the cities (Yeh, 2005), pushing prices of land developments higher and demand for credit even higher. Public ownership of the land has not resulted in this hybrid market situation in less speculation and lower prices, despite the high subsidies provided directly or indirectly by local authorities and inexpensive credit provided by some enterprises to their employees.

The third and most important reason behind the success of gating is the attempt by local administrations to maintain social order and to improve the governability of the urban population. Official discourse directly associates gated compounds to the improvement of social stability and to the creation of harmonious communities (Tomba, 2009). Forting-up Chinese cities is, for example, a response to the convergent concerns of homebuyers and local governments with security. Demand for secure spaces ranked highest among homebuyers' priorities (Wang and Li, 2002), while local bureaucracies are trying to ensure that as much urban land as possible is enclosed behind walls and patrolled by (private) security guards. To give but one Beijing example, the Public Security Bureau, the Bureau of Land, Resources and Housing, and the Civil Affairs Bureau issued a joint document in November 2001 (Beijing shi, 2001) explicitly requiring that residential communities be 'sealed'. Those communities who 'satisfy conditions for closed management' but have not established a patrol system were encouraged to take formal steps to hire a private security company (Article 7), while those without a wall were encouraged to 'raise capital from the owners to seal off (*fengbi*) their housing estate' (Article 8). Concerns by the authorities about the ability to intervene within a very large population in case of environmental or health crisis such as the severe acute respiratory syndrome (SARS) pandemic have also contributed to this policy. During the SARS pandemic, communities behind gates were able to enforce a very strict segregation with unmistakable success in preventing the spread of the virus.

This gated built environment did not simply 'happen'. Gated spaces are rapidly becoming discrete units of a new government rationale in the cities and their erection is welcomed by residents, private actors and the state. Walls enclosing relatively homogeneous clusters of the population in well defined spaces are, essentially, forms of classification which, in turn, are necessary to the successful administration of a complex population.

Arenas for private conflicts

The inclusive and private nature of these new gated communities also makes them susceptible to collective conflicts. Disputes over homeownership rights generally take place directly between *private* stakeholders. The commercial nature of these disputes, as well as the bounded nature of these residential spaces, ensures that conflicts at this level have a very limited impact upon social stability, governance and the political legitimacy of the present regime. In general, conflicts erupt, are negotiated and are resolved without a direct involvement of the traditional neighbourhood institutions, while arbitration committees and courts are sometimes called upon to say the final word on disputes.

Many of these conflicts are of an individual nature. Typically, they arise from commercial disputes and the non-compliance by the developer with the terms of the contract (land allocation, discrepancy between promised level of services and the reality, the quality of the buildings or of the environment, misleading advertisement, etc.). Sometimes they only originate in a lawsuit or such typical forms of individual resistance as the non-payment of the monthly management fees. These forms of resistance to power abuse by developers and management committees are very common: in 2002 the National Consumers Association handled over 53,000 housing-related disputes involving homeowners (Yin, 2004). Resistance to the tyranny of the management committees is so common that some companies have been forced to act to protect their right to be paid a fee for services. In one famous case in Beijing, a large developer, who built and manages 24 estates in the city, took 568 individual residents to court for not paying their fees, complaining about losses exceeding 30 million yuan over three years (Xiao, 2004).

Numerous collective conflicts begin with the misappropriation or embezzlement of land-use rights, which often change hands and, consequently, destination when projects are well under way, damaging the economic investment and lifestyle expectations of the owners.

In November 2003, a group of owners organized a public demonstration against the construction of a new gas station in a lot originally allocated to a recreation centre serving several neighbourhoods. An angry but well-organized crowd, including some people still wearing power suits and high heels after work, gathered at the scene, pulled down the walls of the building site and left it in rubble. Despite the destruction of private property involved, the developer's reaction was not to seek prosecution or compensation. Instead, the company obtained formal approval for the project, rebuilt the site and had it protected by private guards (not by the police) to prevent further destruction. The

residents' response was then to turn to what they called 'legal weapons' and to bring the developer to court.

In another dispute concerning a 30-storey building illegally erected by a state-owned developer, residents turned to a mix of legal and direct 'weapons'. They combined a class action with a series of demonstrations to expose the 'corruption' of the developer, a large state-owned enterprise, and to request the closure of the construction site. The same residents also picketed the entrance of the building site 24 hours a day for several months, and participated in large numbers in the public hearings of their case in front of the local court. Despite growing frustration over the issue, the demonstrations were widely publicized in the press and remained largely peaceful. Although no proper permission was ever granted (residents repeatedly applied at the local police station but never obtained a reply), law enforcement officers were unwilling to intervene to disperse what would formally be an unauthorized demonstration. They only intervened on one occasion, when residents tried to bring their banners outside the walls of their gated compound. Scuffles followed, and the bitter lesson of a spatially limited freedom of demonstration was rapidly learned. All neighbouring communities involved in similar conflicts have, since then, carefully avoided pushing demonstrations outside of their privately owned ground.

In a different 'economy housing'[3] estate in 2002, the developer sold on the flourishing black market the land-use rights of a portion of the land that it had obtained from the local land bureau at a subsidized price. Residents realized the swindle when a few buildings of highly priced apartments were already under construction on some of their own land. As a consequence, they found themselves deprived of all the wonderful services and public spaces originally included in the planning and advertised as the main feature of the community. Many months of collective standoff ensued and ended before the local court.

In Beijing's outer suburb of Chanping, in 2003, residents of a gated community organized numerous rounds of protest against a developer for changing the destination of a lot of land from a garden to a new high rise. During the long-lasting *querelle*, a group of 150 residents also protested at a local exhibition in front of the developer's stand. Later that day, some senior residents were attacked and beaten by a group of migrant workers employed at the building site, an action condemned by the residents as a developer's revenge for the public shame imposed on the company by the residents' initiative.

The list of this type of conflict is almost endless and almost none of the Beijing developments I visited in 2003 and 2004 were exempt from some kind of conflict with the development company.

Disputes with management companies are even more frequent. They generally do not go beyond the level of collective complaints about the services provided by the management committee costs of the parking facilities, excessive fees for essential services, the poor quality of security services, the appropriation of common spaces and buildings for commercial activity, safety of the common grounds, the state of the gardens. Nonetheless, these complaints are generally shared by large numbers of residents, are dealt with through the owners' associations and do affect the perception of a collective sense of responsibility in the community. One important characteristic of these conflicts is, in fact, that they stimulate collective discussions about the shared nature of ownership and the nature of the services provided by the management companies. Communities of homeowners and blogs are among the largest on the internet, and each conflict is generally discussed, analysed and argued about both on and offline. During this collective elaboration, actions to defend very specific economic interests are often described as courageous and ethical actions to defend interests higher than just one's own.

A rhetoric of the responsible, self-disciplined 'high-quality' citizens, whose actions in defence of consumer rights contributes to the advancement and modernization of the nation, is a central thrust of collective action in China's gated communities. Homeowners often 'frame' their collective actions with the ambition to contribute to building the nation and strengthening China, a claim that is fostered by the dominant rhetoric of the middle class being a 'high-quality' (*gao suzhi*) vanguard of modernization and nation-building. Thus, greedy developers, inefficient management companies and even uncooperative neighbours become the embodiment of what pulls the brakes of China's modernization, whereas harmonious communities acting collectively become fundamental forces in the advancement of the nation (Tomba, 2009).

The politics of gates: Classification, autonomy and governmentality

If the emergence of privately owned and privately managed compounds is becoming a catalyst for the organization of collective interests, why is the state actively encouraging gating and a privatization of governance against what common sense suggests should be its primary interests (accessibility of the built environment to administrators)? What is the governmental rationale that these gates serve? In this conclusion I would like to offer two tentative answers to this question:

1   Gates both encourage and constrain societal autonomy among new economic elites by producing an ethic of responsibility that is linked to recently acquired property rights.
2   Gating and zoning produce a form of contemporary social classification that fits service-intensive post-industrial cities better than the traditional system of work units that dominated socialist urbanism: as a 'zoning technology' (Ong, 2006) gates constitute a tool of government.

Limited autonomy

The development of government-sponsored forms of self-government at the community level and the emergence of collective interests has suggested to some analysts (e.g. Read, 2003) that private gated communities might become the harbinger of grassroots forms of democratization. In fact, private compounds are now required, for example, to elect a 'homeowner committee' that represents the interests of the homeowners in the community and *vis-à-vis* other players such as the management company and the developer (Read, 2003; Tomba, 2004). While these elections are often a hotly contested exercise and are lively examples of participation, the autonomy they engender, I argue, is limited. Conflicts within the gates (as we have seen) are very common; but they generally are contained by the physical and administrative boundaries of individual compounds. Law enforcement authorities allow forms of public protest that are shielded by the community's structure but, indeed, do not tolerate any attempt by different communities to coalesce around similar issues to lobby and force government intervention. The limits of the autonomy allowed to private gated community residents is therefore very narrow, and civic action is generally triggered by local and commercial issues. A clear delimitation of spaces contributes to maintaining this segregation of interests.

One important characteristic of the new commercial housing environment is that residential compounds house today a much more variegated population than the socialist work unit compounds used to. While in the latter co-workers would have shared both work and social activities, thus maintaining an 'organized dependency' (Walder, 1986) on the enterprise in all aspects of their lives, in the new compounds, populations are mixed, and the relationship between residence and employment has been severed. The interests that the co-residents share can only be organized around the private issues of co-habitation and ownership. Housing is no longer a welfare item and has become most families' greatest capital investment, source of debt and concern. Increasing amounts of resources and time are therefore mobilized to augment or protect the value of this investment and to reduce the magnitude of the concern. The increasing importance of housing property, as well as the appeal of certain compounds in terms of their *use values* (qualitative and not directly economic) embodied in the lifestyle that they foster, plays a role in motivating homeowners to search for specific lifestyles and to act to protect them when they are threatened. John Emmeus Davis included use values in his idea of a 'bundle of interests' (Davis, 1991; Purcell, 2001), encompassing interests of exchange and interests of use. The solidarities forged to protect these interests are based on 'the place where they have their homes, raise their children and relate to each other more as neighbours than as co-workers' (Davis, 1991, p6). In a similar fashion, conflicts in China's gated communities reveal the consolidation of localized interests that are becoming essential concerns for the livelihood and strategies of families and constitute a new avenue for status achievement, now separated from the employment situation.

Spatial/governmental classification

The almost obsessive reproduction of gated spaces is also contributing to a classification of the social spaces within the built environment and to define the spatiality of the social stratification experienced by modern Chinese cities. Today's difference in housing situations was exacerbated by the 1990s housing reform (Li, 2002; Li and Niu, 2003; Tomba, 2004). The sale of public housing has done much to consolidate the differences inherited from the socialist redistributive system. With the marketization of real estate property and the manipulation of land-use rights by local governments to favour homeownership among middle-class urban residents, this gap in favour of traditional urban residents and new professional elites has expanded further. Until today, the market has not been able to dissolve the impact of the socialist system of distribution: registered urban residents have, on average, better housing situations than migrants, while those who have enjoyed membership in the subsidized urban system are doing better than those who have not, and this difference does not always directly reflect differences in employment situations (Tomba and Tang, 2008). It is not infrequent to find public servants with meagre salaries enjoying high-class housing that they obtained at discounted prices from their employer or at a discount from the state. Also, those who successfully remained 'within the system' managed to get clear advantages over those who were laid off during China's industrial reform.

The potential for autonomy argued by some (Davis et al, 1995) produced by the privatization of residential housing is at least as great as the potential for improving governmental capacity. The gated community provides China's new elites with enough autonomy to participate in the market, while it requires from them enough responsibility to participate actively in legitimating the regime. By empowering private agents, such as management companies and developers, local administrations are able to contain the inevitable conflicts emerging from the privatization of spaces and forms of governance, while avoiding that consumers' anger threatens political legitimacy, social order and authority.

This differentiation of housing situations produced by the privatization of housing is also a policy incarnation of the 'civilizing' mission upon which the Chinese government has embarked to 'improve the quality of the population' (*tigao renkou suzhi*) (Yan, 2003; Anagnost, 2004; Jacka, 2006; Kipnis, 2006; Tomba, 2009). Higher-'quality' citizens (with better education, a better sense of responsibility towards the nation and the party, and with enough resources to take care of themselves) tend to be those who have been the beneficiary of housing policies and now live in higher-quality gated compounds. But those citizens who still have not achieved such level of 'quality' (the disgruntled unemployed, the migrants) will live at the margins or in older compounds and will be the object of civilizing campaigns and of a more direct social control through neighbourhood organizations. The classification provided by the gates serves, therefore, to make the city more legible (Scott, 1998) for the administrators, providing territorial markers that separate those who can be trusted to govern themselves from those who cannot, and should therefore be made the object of the direct action of government.

Ong's (2006) concept of graduated citizenship could be useful here to interpret this phenomenon. To Ong, the zoning of a sovereign territory to favour foreign investors (as in China's special economic zones) produces a loss of sovereignty and a graduation in citizenship aimed at maximizing economic return for global capital. This graduation is 'an effect of states moving from being an administrator of a watertight national entity to regulators of diverse spaces and populations that link with global markets'. The active classification that the state is favouring through the 'gating' of urban spaces serves the purpose of legitimating forms of government that can be different for citizens of higher or lower quality, and facilitates the activity of social control.

In conclusion, the gated communities' boom in China is the result of an adaptation of traditional forms of communal residence, residential segregation and social stratification and structural conditions, including state control over land and its continual intervention in the construction of housing. It also constitutes a tool for the renewal of the socialist tradition of governance, and reveals the project to maintain large Chinese cities legible to their rulers despite their increase in social complexity.

The sustainability of the Chinese cities and their post-industrial transition are partly dependent on the success of this strategy. With the state still holding onto the most important planning responsibilities and planning powers, gated communities need not be seen as a cultural specific trait of the Chinese urban form. While both traditional residential forms and the homogenizing effects of globalization might be used to explain the mystery of gate-dominated Chinese cities, it is, in fact, the governmental/classifying logic behind them that explains why cities remain governable places.

Notes

1 Interviews with private managers revealed that this situation is only now beginning to change in the direction of a more professional service under mounting pressure from owners and local authorities to split the two functions.

2 The term *xiaoqu* (micro-district) originates as the translation of the Russian *mikrorayon* – the Soviet residential compounds that inspired China's early socialist residential areas in the 1950 (see Lu, 2006).

3 Housing built on subsidized public land. Developers are supposed to use the land to build affordable houses for citizens with specific characteristics (urban registration, income below a certain level, no existing property, substandard housing situation).

References

Anagnost, A. (2004) 'The corporeal politics of aquality (*suzhi*),' *Public Culture*, 16 February, pp189–208

Beijing Municipal Bureau of Statistics (2006) *Beijing Statistical Yearbook 2005*, Beijing

Beijing shi (2001) *Beijing shi guotu fangguangju, beijing shi gong'an ju, beijing shi mingzhengju guanyu jiaqiang juzhu xiaoqu anquan fangfan guanli gongzuo de tongzhi*, Communiqué of the Beijing Land Bureau, Police Bureau, and Civil Affairs Bureau on Strengthening the Security Management in Residential Areas, 5 November 2001

Benewick, R. and Takahara, A. (2002) 'Eight grannies and nine teeth between them: Community construction in China', *Journal of Chinese Political Science*, vol 7, no 1–2, spring/fall, pp1–18

Benewick, R., Tong, I. and Howell, J. (2004) 'Self-governance and community: A preliminary comparison between villagers' committees and urban community councils', *China Information*, vol 18, no 1, pp11–28

Blakely, E. J. and Snyder, M. G. (1997) *Fortress America: Gated Communities in the United States*, Brookings Institution, Washington, DC

Blandy, S., Lister, D., Atkinson, R. and Flint, J. (2003) *Gated Community: A Systematic Review of the Research Evidence*, ESRC Centre for Neighbourhood Research Paper no 12, April

Bray, D. (2005) *Social Space and Governance in Urban China: The Danwei System from Origins to Reform*, Stanford University Press, Stanford, CA

Bray, D. (2006) 'Building communities: New strategies of governance in urban China', *Economy and Society*, vol 35 no 4, pp530–549

Davis, D., Kraus, R., Naughton, B. and Perry, E. J. (eds) (1995) *Urban Spaces in Contemporary China: The Potential for Autonomy and Community in Post-Mao China*, Cambridge University Press, Cambridge

Davis, J. E. (1991) *Contested Ground: Collective Action and the Urban Neighbourhood*, Cornell University Press, Ithaca, NY

Giroir, G. (2006) 'The purple jade villas (Beijing)', in Glasze, G., Webster, C. and Frantz, K. (eds) *Private Cities: Global and Local Perspectives*, Routledge, London

Gu, H. (1998) 'Gongzheng yunzuo haishi qianjiu jide liyi: zhongguo zhufang tizhi gaige zhengce de fansi' ['A fair process or the adjustment of vested interests: Considerations on the policies of housing reform in China'], *Dangdai zhongguo yanjiu* [*Research in Contemporary China*], no 63, www.chinayj.net/Stub Article.asp?issue=980405&total=63

Gu, L. (2006) 'Shequ: Fengbi haishi Kaifang' ['Communities: Gated or open?'], *Shequ*, no 4, available at http://qkzz.net/magazine/1617-0967/2006/04/331094.htm

He, Z., Heberer, T. and Schubert, G. (eds) (2007) *Chengxiang gongmin canyu he zhengzhi hefaxing* [*Citizen Participation in Rural and Urban Areas and Political Legitimacy*], Zhongyang bianyi chubanshe, Beijing

HRW (Human Rights Watch) (2004) 'Demolished: Forced evictions and the tenants' rights movement in China', *HRW*, vol 16, no 4, www.hrw.org/en/reports/2004/03/24/demolished

Jacka, T. (2006) *Rural Women in Urban China*, M E Sharpe, Armonk, NY

Kipnis, A. (2006) '*Suzhi*: A keyword approach', *The China Quarterly*, no 186, pp295–313

Li, B. (2002) 'Zhongguo zhufang gaige zhidu de fenge xing' ['The unequal nature of China's housing reform'], *Shehuixue yanjiu* [*Research in the Social Sciences*], no 2, pp80–87

Li, J. and Niu, X. (2003) 'The new middle clas(es) in Peking: A case study', *China Perspectives*, no 45, pp4–20

Logan, J. R. (ed) (2002) *The New Chinese City: Globalization and Reform*, Blackwell Publishers, Oxford

Low, S. (2003) *Behind the Gates: Life Security and the Pursuit of Happiness in Fortress America*, Routledge, New York and London

Lu, D. (2006) *Remaking Chinese Urban Form: Modernity, Scarcity and Space, 1949–2005*, Routledge, New York and London

Lü, X. and Perry, E. J. (eds) (1999) *Danwei: The Changing Chinese Workplace in Historical and Comparative Perspective*, M E Sharpe, Armonk, NY

Ma, L. J. C. and Wu, F. (eds) (2005) *Restructuring the Chinese City: Changing Society, Economy and Space*, Routledge, London and New York

Miao, P. (2003) 'Deserted streets in a jammed town: The gated communities in China's cities and its solution', *Journal of Urban Design*, vol 8, no 1, pp 45–66

Ong, A. (2006) *Neoliberalism as Exception: Mutations in Citizenship and Sovereignty*, Duke University Press, Durham and London

Purcell, M. (2001) 'Neighbourhood activism among homeowners as a politics of space', *Professional Geographer*, vol 53, no 2, pp178–194

Read, B. L. (2000) 'Revitalizing the state's urban "nerve tips"', *The China Quarterly*, no 163, pp806–820

Read, B. (2003) 'Democratizing the neighbourhood? New private housing and home-owner self-organization in urban China', *The China Journal*, no 49, January, pp31–60

Salaff, J. (1967) 'The urban communes and anti-city experiments in communist China', *The China Quarterly*, no 29, pp82–110

Schurmann, F. (1968) *Ideology and Organization in Communist China*, 2nd edition, University of California Press, Berkeley, CA

Scott, J. (1998) *Seeing Like a State: How Certain Schemes to Improve Human Condition Have Failed*, Yale University Press, New Haven and London

Sit, V. (1995) *The Nature and Planning of a Chinese Capital City*, Wiley, Chichester

Tomba, L. (2004) 'Creating an urban middle class: Social engineering in Beijing', *The China Journal*, no 51, January, pp1–26

Tomba, L. (2005) 'Residential space and collective interest formation in Beijing's housing disputes', *The China Quarterly*, no 184, December, pp934–951

Tomba, L. (2009) 'Of quality, harmony and community: Civilization and the middle class in urban China', in *Positions: East Asia Cultures Critiques*, vol 17, no 3, pp591–616

Tomba, L. and Tang, B. (2008) 'The forest city: Homeownership and new wealth in Shenyang', in Goodman, D. S. G. (ed) *The New Rich in China: Future Rulers, Present Lives*, Routledge, London, pp171–186

Walder, A. (1986) *Communist Neo Traditionalism: Work and Authority in Chinese Industry*, University of California Press, Berkeley, CA

Wang, D. and Li, S. (2002) 'Housing preferences in a transitional housing system: The case of Beijing, China', *The Centre for Urban and Regional Studies Occasional Paper* no 28, Hong Kong Baptist University, Hong Kong

Wang, F. (2005) *Organizing through Division and Exclusion: China's Hukou System* Stanford University Press, Stanford, CA

Wang, T. (2004) *Shei zai fenshi zhekuai dangao? Bufen shengshi bao'an fuwu gongsi zhanyou shichang fen'e de diaocha fenxi* [*Who Will Share This Cake? Research Report on the Market Share of Security Guard Companies in Some Cities and Provinces*], Zhongguo bao'an, Chinese Security, no 1, pp22–27

Wang, Y. and Murie, A. (1999) *Housing Policy and Practice in China*, Macmillan, London

Webster, C. J. (2001) 'Gated cities of tomorrow', *Town Planning Review*, vol 72, no 2, pp149–170

Webster, C. J., Glasze, G. and Frantz, K. (eds) (2002) 'The global spread of gated communities', Special issue in *Environment and Planning B*, vol 29 no 3

Wu, F. (2005) 'Rediscovering the "gate" under market transition: From work unit compounds to commodity housing enclaves', *Housing Studies*, no 20, pp235–254

Xiao, R. (2004) 'Jiannan de wuye guanli qiye weiquan zhilu'['Management companies' difficult road to protecting owners' interests'], *Chengshi kaifa* [*Urban Development*], no 9, pp12–13

Xinhua (2006a) *Xinhua*, 2 June 2006

Xinhua (2006b) *Xinhua*, 5 July 2006

Yan, H. (2003) 'Neoliberal governmentality and neohumanism: Organizing *suzhi*/value flow though labor recruitment networks,' *Cultural Anthropology*, 18 April, pp493–523

Yeh, A. G.-O. (2005) 'Dual land market and international spatial structure of Chinese cities', in Ma, L. J. C. and Wu, F. (eds) *Restructuring the Chinese City: Changing Society, Economy and Space*, Routledge, London and New York, pp59–79

Yin, S. (2004) *Chengshi shouxin, jin yi bu baohu xiaofeizhe quanyi* [*Be Honest and Trustworthy: One Step Further in the Protection of Consumer Rights*], in *Xiaofeizhe jingji* (Consumer Economy), vol 20, no 2, pp4–7

Zhang, L. (2006) 'Contesting spatial modernity in late socialist China', *Current Anthropology*, vol 47, no 3, pp461–484

5

Lagos: 'Urban Gating' as the Default Condition

Ola Uduku

Introduction

Nigeria's economic capital city Lagos has been described by various authors as one of the most dangerous cities in Africa. This is due to the violent crime, which its residents deal with daily: car theft, property break-ins, and random muggings are commonplace. Unlike its equally notorious sub-Saharan sibling, Johannesburg, in Lagos these crimes are generally not race-related; most are purely pursued for the economic gains to be made, although politics and ethnicity are often drivers for premeditated violent break-ins.

The Lagosian reaction has been similar to Johannesburg; the mushrooming of individually walled and gated houses, housing estates and, in a few exceptional cases, walled mini-cities has taken place over the last two decades. The security measures in place, aside from the physical fortification of households and estates, begins with large domestic Alsatian dogs and extends to small-scale armies of security personnel in charge of policing gated estates.

The physical and psychological concept of separation from society by creating barriers, specifically 'gates', is recent to southern Nigerian urban life. Although the palaces of rulers, such as the *Obas* in Lagos, have historically had gates, much of urban life in southern Nigeria has been predicated on the engagement and association of residents with each other, using the street as the site for these exchanges. With the introduction of gated neighbourhoods, it is argued that there has been a significant transformation of living space and work-life rituals for the city's residents.

This chapter describes and analyses the typical generic forms of gated housing at individual and residential estate levels in Lagos. This contemporary condition is considered within a historical analysis of the development of Lagos, from pre-colonial times to the 21st century. It seeks to use this analytical study to pinpoint the contemporary origins of domestic fortification in the city and to determine whether there are links between this phenomenon and the earlier, more uncertain, period of the city's birth as a contender city to Badagry, a major centre for slave trading until the 18th century, and therefore built as a fortified territory for the forthcoming British colonial presence in Nigeria.

The second section of the chapter deals with the description of the state of contemporary Lagos, drawing on field research material and recent publications that have researched the city. The third section draws on archival and historical sources to formulate a view of pre-colonial Lagos and compares its level of 'security' with current levels, gauging through the material available and conducted interviews what lifestyles were like in the pre-colonial period and how these compare to the present day. The fourth section draws on the information and research material described in the earlier sections in order to consider the 'ideal' living scenario for Lagos, taking into account the real security issues that beset the city, but rejecting the 'default' fortress planning that has become a standard feature of urban design and planning in Lagos and, increasingly, other Nigerian cities.

Urban gating in Lagos as the *default* position: A critique

Lagos, the former capital city of Nigeria and the prime commercial centre, has for long had the reputation of having an environment plagued with congestion with a highly differentiated residential population. This section seeks to contextualize the current spate of gated and, indeed, armoured housing and exclusive housing estates within the historical context of the colonial government-planned early town of Lagos. By drawing upon earlier planning, the historical layout of the city and traditional Yoruba housing styles, an appreciation of the current growth in security housing is presented within a wider socio-cultural historical frame and considered within this context.

The relative success of the new security housing is also considered through the case study neighbourhoods of Ikoyi and the Princes Estate, Amuwo Odofin, as is the Koolhaas Harvard Lagos project.[1] Material on Lagos is drawn from many sources, duly acknowledged at the end of the chapter: without this background, the chapter would miss its central theme – the reinterpretation of intentions, and the sustainability of interventions, within the 21st-century post-plan focused emergent city of 10 million inhabitants.

A short planning history of Lagos

The colony of Lagos was founded by the British relatively recently, in 1861, taking over in prominence from Badagry, the former administrative capital and major slave *entrepôt* in south-western Nigeria. Its elevation from a small fishing area to a major British colonial city brought with it both the trappings of colonial planning and the traditional residential patterns of the Yoruba villages in western Nigeria.

The small island which constitutes 'old' Lagos, or Isale Eko, was transformed from a collection of villages with a central chieftaincy structure to a planned colonial settlement with a clear separation of residential commercial and semi-industrial uses (Vaughan-Richards, 1977; see also Mann, 1985, and Peil, 1991). The effect of this mix of the colonial plan and the traditional residential settlement was the development of residential neighbourhoods, both in the European government-reserved areas and the 'native' residential estates that were effectively walled residences, for different reasons.

The 'native' city had walled and exclusive residences for the chief and other dignitaries in traditional society, as had always been the case amongst the Yoruba, who have lineage links with the ancient kingdom of Benin, noted for its walled city and residences. In the Lagos area, with the ravages of the slave trade from the mid-18th century, the need for security became more acute; thus, whole settlements were essentially fortified or walled, both by tradition and for protection.

The British colonial planning project, as discussed by Home (1997, Chapters 1 and 2) and others, on the other hand, had its own historical origins and had evolved through involvement with colonial and trade possessions throughout the world. In many ways the precursor to the classic 'apartheid' city, governed by the separation of residences and facilities for the different races, the government-reserved area (GRA), in effect, was, and to a large extent remains, a fortified enclave of residences for the rich elite who rule the city.

Despite the attainment of self-rule or 'independence' in 1960, the residential patterns in Lagos have not significantly changed in the ensuing post-independence years. In keeping with other cities such as Port Harcourt and Kaduna, new, more exclusive walled and gated estates for the nouveau elite, such as the Shonibare Estate in Ikeja (north Lagos) and the exclusive Embassy and Company residential estates to be found in Ikoyi and the newly reclaimed Victoria Island suburb of Lagos.

In parallel to these exclusive developments was the proliferation of the informal/semi-squatter developments for what now constitutes the majority of Lagos's inhabitants, in areas often adjacent to the salubrious estates of the rich, such as Ajegunle, which famously shares a creek with Apapa, a historically wealthy Lagos suburb. The settlement of Maroko, now demolished, was similarly part of the wealthy suburb of Victoria Island (see Peil, 1991).

Since the late 1970s, with the upsurge of urban violence and crime, there has been a similar increase in the design and development of walled and gated housing as both residential 'estates' and complexes, and as fortified individual dwellings (see Figure 5.1). Lagos, in particular, succumbed to significant periods of 'armed robbery', during the changing civilian and military regimes from the late 1970s until the present day (Fabiyi, 2004, 2008). This real threat, and also the influence of design subcultures from the US, helped develop the growth in and demand for gated 'fortified' housing.

Figure 5.1 *Typical gated 'fortified' upper middle-class residence in Lagos*

Source: Ola Uduku

Like Johannesburg and other cities throughout Africa and the developing world, exclusive Lagos residences today boast not only walling and gating, but also electrified fences, security dogs and armed response guards as a standard for the homes of the rich and powerful. This section seeks to examine a recently developed gated estate within greater Lagos and examines its success in delivering security, esteem and other services to its residents that might not have been available to housing in areas outside the estate.

As Lagos has begun to lose its 'danger ranking' to other African capitals, such as Johannesburg, Kinshasa and Mogadishu, there has yet to be a noticeable effect on the proliferation of the gated residence (Enwezor et al, 2002). Lagos has recently become the beneficiary of more estates as the oil service-related expatriate sector that resided in Nigerian cities (e.g. Port Harcourt and Warri) near the oil drilling areas to the south-east of Nigeria have begun to relocate their residential estates to the 'safer' exclusive (less kidnap target-prone) residential suburbs of Lagos.

In addition, at the middle to the lower end of the housing market, residential 'road blocks' that act as effective 'gates' which exclude undesirables and access to public thoroughfares remain in place and are of value to residents in these neighbourhoods. Will this mix of semi- to ultra-fortified communities stay together by default,

or should there be, or are there, other feasible alternatives to delivering perceived security and the resultant peace of mind that residents in Lagos and other cities in urban Africa crave? More importantly, is the gated fortified model of living really secure, and is there an inherent sustainability in the models of community living that gating a street or residential estate can provide?

Categories of gating

What does a gated residence mean in Lagos? The descriptor 'gated' could mean many different kinds of fortification to be found in a wide range of residences. Small housing estates are often developed with walls and a central gate entrance area; in other neighbourhoods the road block gantry system effectively 'gates' the street off. (see Figure 5.2)

The most affluent housing and most privately built housing are walled and secured with a gate. Often residences have the double fortification of a gate that has a road block and then individual housing that is also gated. The use of various forms of 'security' razor wire and different levels of security personnel correlates to wealth and income.

Using Glaze's (2005) terms, most of Nigeria's gated communities would be of *the club democracy type*; indeed, being part of an emerging developing world

Figure 5.2 *Informal gate or closing off part of Crystal Housing Estate, Lagos, Nigeria*

Source: Ola Uduku

country, the more organized and extensive that the gated residences are, the more autonomous they are from the strictures of local or national government service provision.

The Princes Estate Amuwo, Odofin

This estate gives a typical if unusually well illustrated example of forms of gating to be found in an 'average' Lagos suburb. The estate is built on land initially owned by a private individual who then sold on the freehold to the Lagos state government. The Princes Estate comprises a mix of residences for different income groups, from low-income flats to individual houses in their own grounds that are further walled and gated within the confines of the Princes Estate.

The Lagos state government has since sold 'land plots' on to private individuals, as well as semi-complete housing that owners can customize at will. The full freehold of the estate thus remains in the ownership of the Lagos state government, although house owners have rights over the plots of land and housing that they have completed on the estate. The estate is mostly residential but boasts a church, mosque, two nursery care institutions and a few small shops near its entrance.

The estate has poorly maintained roads; it is formally connected to the Lagos state municipal mains water supply and to the correspondent electricity grid for Lagos. Unusually, it also has its own small local police station (Figure 5.3).

This is assumed to exist due to the residence of some high-profile private individuals on the estate, who have links with the state security network. The main 'gates' of the estate are closed from the late evening to early morning, and there is a private estate security guard on duty at all times.

Figure 5.3 *Police station at Crystal Housing Estate, Lagos*

Source: Ola Uduku

The police station, roads and public utilities are, in essence, provided by the Lagos state government. In practice, however, the majority of residents rely on the use of private generators and boreholes to ensure regular domestic water and electricity supply. Furthermore, despite the police post within the estate, residents pay for the presence of the private security guard at the estate entrance and for their individual home security arrangements.

While the Princes Estate is unusual in having its own police station, the other characteristics of the estate are fairly commonplace for 'enclosed' residential estates within Lagos and Nigeria. The level of state government involvement with Nigerian estates is predicated on the exclusivity of its residents: the more exclusive are the residents, the higher profile is the security, although not necessarily the service provision.

In parallel with state or federal government residential estates, there are private estates that also have a long history of evolution in Nigeria. The large oil service sector in the country has evolved a series of residential estates for its workers since the 1960s when Shell had major estates built in Port Harcourt; similarly, private entrepreneurs such as the Shonibare family set up the Shonibare Estate in Lagos and the more recent internationally inspired and joint-funded condominium developments to be found in major cities in Nigeria. Private estates, then, generally, but not always, have more centralized utilities and security provision. With privacy, one buys exclusivity and a form of guaranteed service provision. Their continued proliferation and evolution suggests a continued local public demand and government acceptance of their existence in urban Nigeria.

The sustainable ecology of gates: A contemporary versus historical analysis

Are secure-enclosed estates sustainable in 21st-century Nigeria? Taking a purely philosophical stance, the answer has to be no. Effectively on grounds of public equity, the revenue to the government might be increased by service charges to these estates; but they are, by definition, exclusionary in conception and provision. However, on more cultural-anthropological grounds, could the enclosure simply be an extension of existing traditional settlement patterns? The city is not necessarily a traditional cultural organization in Nigeria; however, the western kingdoms of Benin, Oyo and Ife and the northern cities of Kano, Katsina and Zaria are all testament to this past historic connection with enclosure protection and fortification and the notion of the large enclosed settlement (city) in each region (see Schwerdtfeger, 1982, and Denyer, 1978).

These local 'neighbourhood' arrangements within historic settlements worked as micro-living units, with a symbiotic ecology that linked into the wider urban contexts of these traditional city states. Thus, Kano city in days gone by would run as a self-sustaining entity or city state with its own rulers and unique administrative, work and other skill groups. More importantly, housing was both enclosed for religio-cultural reasons and also for fortification.

This symbiotic work and living arrangement provided the model for these viable working city states that have essentially withstood centuries of change. Vestiges of this traditional urban set-up can be found both in northern Nigerian Islamic-focused cities and also in the more commercial-secular urban metropoles such as Lagos, Kumasi (Ghana) and Calabar (eastern Nigeria). These three cities, and many others in Africa, have achieved their current eminence through the incorporation of historic parts of old settlements, including, implicitly, the physical infrastructure of the historic fortified and sometimes walled compounds and villages into the make-up of the new city.

Colonial planners and also the later African planners and dwellers consciously (as in the case of Max Lock's plan for Kaduna) (Locke and Associates, 1966) and subconsciously (as is often the case in the 'native' residential areas in Calabar, Kumasi and elsewhere) incorporated ideas of the fortified/protected compound and local neighbourhoods. Since the mid-1970s, the transatlantic influence of residential design from the US has also played a large role in shaping the African city as global ties and connections with the US became more prevalent. In Nigeria, the temporary influx of capital from the emerging oil economy and the American oil city 24-hour lifestyle further fuelled the individualistic/capitalist cities which evolved.

Lagos was thus transformed from being an easygoing ex-colonial trading port commercial city to being the financial and commercial heart of the five largest oil-producing nations in the world. Earlier public housing projects rapidly gave way to private housing estates, with shanty/informal settlements emerging overnight and the new right-wing thinking favouring site and services schemes as a cure-all, at best, or trickle-down theories of economic development (Marris, 1961).

From the turn of the century to the current global credit crunch, Lagos and a few other choice global cities acquired a further reinvention of their global image. The Documenta third platform art and culture discourses focused on Lagos, Kinshasa and Johannesburg and gave a new post-modern cultural analysis of these metropoles and the issues that they now faced. Added to this have been in-depth documentary films of Lagos, Kinshasa, and, recently, Dar es Salaam, which give different perspectives on their city subjects.

Unsurprisingly, then, there are parts of modern Lagos that exhibit the same 'securitizing' tendencies as downtown Los Angeles. As Soja (1996) and others describe the shopping malls and exclusionary characteristics of US suburbia, so also are there emerging parallel narratives of the life, cultural lifestyles and possessions of the rich and nouveau riche in urban Africa. A homogeneous, interconnected urban ecology which promotes the securitized lifestyles of the West, superimposed on older traditional settlement patterns in cities across Asia, Africa and Australasia, is emerging. Like human behaviour, the concept of settlement is constantly fluid and changing; we are yet to see the final form of the gated enclave in spite of research on the factors that have shaped its emergence.

What next? The future of security town Lagos

The securitization complex that comforts Lagosians, Joburgers and other city dwellers in 'challenging, dangerous' urban areas is unlikely to diminish despite crime statistics that suggest that few gates and security blocks really provide a deterrent to crime. The perceived safety that residents feel from these visible forms of security overrides any reality which shows that crime levels do not lessen with increased street gating.

What has become clear is that the functioning and nature of contemporary gated and secure complexes in much of Africa and the developing world is different from the gated residential complexes which have become commonplace in parts of Europe and the Americas. While in both 'worlds' most gated communities are formed through the motivations of a self-selecting public, notions of class exclusivity are stronger in the West, where the social *caché* and exclusivity of living in a gated community is possibly of more importance than the 'security' that it accords residents.

Residents in cities such as Lagos and Johannesburg, on the other hand, are motivated to live in gated neighbourhoods for the pragmatic perceived reason of security, as well as the exclusivity and other class cultural benefits that such neighbourhoods may bring. There is also a traditional socio-cultural basis for much of the gating activity within the African building sector. The idea of the gated community, therefore, is neither new nor necessarily class exclusionary in the sense that there are self-selected suburbs or streets in lower- to upper-class neighbourhoods in urban Lagos that have some form of club democracy gating in place.

Thinking laterally, then, gating is not always an exclusionary class-dividing phenomenon; despite its preponderance amongst the richer populations in most countries, it does have clear benefits, especially in emerging cities, where micro-democracies have existed from pre-colonial times and have continued to proliferate since the colonial era. With increased globalization there is inevitably a merging or assimilation of ideas of the gated community from the MTV images of the gated West with the more traditional or culture-based fortifications common in parts of Africa. Truly hybrid or multi-layered cities, such as Lagos, are able to accommodate these diverse interpretations in their urban footprint, which has limited planning restrictions.

The resultant gated communities of the West and South may seem to have considerable diversity in their aims and objectives; but fortified communities on any continent and from whichever cultural context do have similarities. The quasi-autonomous organizational structure of these communities that operate in semi-independence of local (authority) governance is usually present.

Furthermore, many groups have had to develop innovative ways of avoiding censure from local authorities; this, in turn, has led to the evolution of cohesive, successful communities of interest, which in evolving cities such as Lagos are particularly successful in delivering a serviced lifestyle that others want to buy into – success breeding success. The Koolhaas Harvard project analysis on Lagos, although somewhat simplistic in judgement, can be applied to gated community groups – there is an order to the seeming anarchy of gates and fortification on Lagos streets (Koolhaas, 2000).

The future, then, of the phenomenon in Africa seems secure; a level of direction and development, however, could help this evolution further. The much-touted example of the foresight of Jamie Lerner's Curitiba transport and urban sustainability project has often been cited in the past. Similarly, the manifesto of the New Urbanists in developing town neighbourhoods has also been emphasized. For Lagos and other African cities, however, guidance would need to be home grown: there are enough examples of historic and contemporary gating scattered throughout the continent.

A tall order, it may seem; but the attention needed to focus on the evolution of workable cities is as important as the documentation of traditional vernacular settlements. Indeed, an understanding of the latter should inform the evolution of the former. The development of this distinction is important if we are not all to end up living in MTV-mediated street neighbourhoods in the future.

The 'miniaturization' of sustainable energy generation is one issue that is likely to help with this. In the South, solar energy generation and other forms of solar power servicing, such as hot water distribution, should reap gains for small mini-communities, who are able to generate all or the majority of their service needs. This can work through sustainable micro-environments within the larger urban city. In the West, this might turn to being more of a profitable situation where small groups could effectively 'sell' their micro-generated services to national grids and other national provision set-ups.

Liberalized governance structures at the local level, which are better able to allow creative micro-governance structures to exist within the local government framework, would also work in favour of creating sustainable fortified communities that might, in turn, evolve new ways of developing democratic administration at local sustainable levels. This harks back to the governance structures which were described in northern Nigerian Islamic caliphate cities such as Kano and Zaria in pre-colonial Nigeria and elsewhere in Africa (Lugard, 1923).

Finally, there is a need to encourage a public openness and debate of the demerits and merits of the gated community in order for the public and the media to enter into a non-skewed dialogue and debate about the issues that these communities face, the fairness of their existence and how they might better be integrated within, and contribute to, existing symbiotic sustainable urban networks in the city. This is likely to be a public–government initiative if it is to be successful.

The current onus on the developer to deliver a limited amount of information to the government planning office with little public consultation in much of Africa remains based in the imported UK planning law guidance that ex-British-ruled countries inherited during self-governance in the 1960s.

A more consultative and participatory approach to the planning process, and active attempts at local community education via local groups and local government initiatives, would also prove valuable if local residents are expected to contribute meaningfully to such proposed debates.

Conclusions

Despite the undeniably varied press information on the emergent gated and securitized housing estates in Lagos, this chapter has outlined a more positive contrary view to this received wisdom. While not denying the excluding capacity of the gated community and the possible inequities that can sometimes come about from their existence, the chapter has explored the successful attributes of the system. It has also highlighted its future potential as a sustainable micro-community model when sustainable energy sourcing becomes affordable and available at the micro-level.

What is being suggested is that a more neo-liberal view towards local networks of service provision and the resultant 'micro-governance' frameworks that this may engender might become the means by which local organizations bring about infrastructure provision and its organized management, which, in turn, using 'trickle-down' theories, might help to kick start development in parts of Africa's emerging urban suburban metropolis that have so far remained untouched by state provision.

This argument is not new, locals regularly have been known to organize, plan and, where successful, provide for themselves *in spite* of (or *despite*) the apathy or direct blocking influences of the state (Uduku 1994, 1996). The evolution and spread of the gated community, in both the 'club/condominium' high-end format or the 'road block/boom' low-income suburban format, have validity and fulfil local community needs, perceived or real, which beleaguered African state and local governments have not the wherewithal or ability to do.

In the emerging world, this phenomenon has arguably been the norm and is likely to attract more followers; with the uncertain economic climate, the state is likely to find it increasingly difficult to provide the bare level of infrastructural support it currently provides in these countries. The identified emerging middle class, it can be argued, has already acquired a taste for 'gating' that, although dependent on certain income profiles for its success at the exclusive club end, is unlikely to significantly diminish; for many, it already has become the status quo. At the other end, the make-do security gates are also likely to weather the economic storm through their semi-formality and links with employment opportunities for local and extended members of the community as 'security' personnel, often on a 24-hour basis.

Possibly, then, these two separate worlds of 'gating' will continue to run in parallel in the same manner as the segmented middle-class models in retail consumption and spending that have already been identified, each serving a different 'niche' purpose for each group.

Historic perspectives

Gating in Lagos and in much of sub-Saharan Africa, as examined here from a historical to a contemporary perspective, has similarities to cities elsewhere in Africa and in the South. The predominance of gating and its positive reception by local residents shows a pragmatic acceptance by most that gating, however unethical and imperfect a solution, does provide a way to 'control' the perceived, if not real, excesses of urban life in cities such as Lagos. This also has the historic precedent of past traditional settlement patterns (the fortified/gated palace of the Oba in Lagos) and colonial segregation (the GRA and 'native' town in cities such as Lagos, Calabar and Enugu) from which to base current planning and design decisions.

Legal imperatives

The legislative system in Lagos, like much of British West Africa, does not predate traditional customary laws, which often can take precedent in land issues even in metropolitan cities such as Lagos. This means that it is difficult to use current 'conventional' legislation or processes to find ways of improving upon or legitimating forms of informal gating processes. In other words, new 'blue sky' thinking is imperative to get new modes of legislation that are likely to be responsive to the evolving nature and perception of gating within Lagos, and have them respond with better ethical-moral, as well as socio-economic, sensitivity to the specificity of urban Lagos.

This, for example, might ensure that gated communities do have a relationship with the local police force and do not set up independent, near paramilitary, security personnel, who work outside of the law, however weak, to ensure the safety of residents. It may also mean having condominium-style rules for both the development and populating of such communities so as not to leave this to open-market *laissez faire* development and membership.

Final comments

Ultimately, then, there needs to be better engagement at all levels with the conception, planning and development of gated communities in Lagos, where they already proliferate and make up a significant proportion of new middle- to upper-class residential developments. This chapter has taken on a deliberately free market stance to their development, acknowledging that there must clearly be a positive public engagement with them which it is suggested has a pragmatic basis rooted in the need to find ways to ensure that infrastructure and services are provided in situations where the state or local government is unable or unwilling to do this.

To stigmatize the developments would be both foolhardy and near impossible in a metropolis the size of Lagos, therefore, the advocacy of the development of working relationships with gated communities in their different forms at legislative and government levels seems a more workable initiative. There needs, however, to be new legislative tools and instruments to have this take place as the traditional laws do not fit well into essentially individual autonomy within a structured administrative planning hierarchy.

Within a sustainability framework and ethos, however, the notion of the gated community or self-determining or semi-autonomous groups within cities makes good sense. Recent 'carrot-mob' developments in San Francisco and elsewhere in West Coast America have shown the power that such groups have in promoting and developing green infrastructure and services for their streets and neighbourhoods by directly challenging formal hierarchies of infrastructure distribution and, essentially, power (*The Economist*, 2009).

Gated Lagos may not, therefore, be a negative default condition, but rather a condition that could, with inspired future planning and management, become a micro-neighbourhood network condition which links into other livelihood ecosystems that create micro-communities who are able to self-determine and develop their own sustainable linkages into good practice governance and infrastructure networks within the wider Lagos metropolis.

Note

1   My thanks to Mrs N. Ubani for her first-hand information about the development of this housing estate.

References

Aderibigbe A. (1975) *Lagos: The Development of an African City*, Longman, Nigeria

Bienen, H. (1983) *Oil Revenues and Policy Choice in Nigeria*, World Bank Staff Working Paper no 592, Filecopy SWP592, World Bank, Washington, DC

Codesira (1993) *The State and Provision of Social Services in Sierra Leone since Independence: 1961–91*, Codesira, Dakar

Denyer, S. (1978) *African Traditional Architecture*, Heinemann, London

Echeruo, M. (1977) *Victorian Lagos*, Macmillan, London

Enwezor, O., Basualdo, C., Bauer, S. and Ghez, S. (eds) (2002) *Under Siege: Four African Cities – Freetown, Johannesburg, Kinshasa, Lagos*, Documenta 11, Ostfildern-Ruit, Hatje Cantz, Germany

Fabiyi, O. (2004) G*ated Neighbourhoods and Privatisation of Urban Security in Ibadan Metropolis Ibadan*, IFRA, University of Ibadan, Ibadan

Fabiyi, O. O. (2008) 'Space theft or space transfer: The nature of crime-induced spatial partitioning and control in enclosed neighborhoods in Ibadan and Johannesburg', *Space and Culture,* vol 11, no 4, pp361–382

Glasze, G. (2005) 'Some reflections on the economic and political organisation of private neighbourhoods', *Housing Studies*, vol 20, no 2, pp221–233

Home, R. K. (1997) *Of Planting and Planning: Making of British Colonial Cities*, Routledge, London

Koolhaas, R. (2000) *Mutations: Harvard Project on the City*, Actar, Barcelona

Locke M. and Associates, (1966) *Kaduna: 1917, 1967, 2017: A Survey and Plan of the Capital Territory for the Government of Northern Nigeria Plan*, Frederick A. Praeger, London

Lugard, F. (1923) *The Dual Mandate in Tropical Africa*, Blackwood, Edinburgh

Mann, E. (1985) *Marrying Well: Marriage Status and Social Change among the Educated Elite in Colonial Lagos*, Cambridge University Press, Cambridge, UK

Mann, K. (2009) *Slavery and the Birth of an African City*, Indiana University Press, Bloomington, IN

Marris, P. (1961) *Family and Social Change in an African City: A Study of Rehousing in Lagos*, Routledge and Kegan Paul, London

Montclos M.-A., de (1997) *Violence et sécurité urbaines en Afrique du Sud au Nigeria: Duban, Johannesburg, Kano, Lagos, Port Harcourt*, L'Harmattan, Paris

Olayiwola, L. Adeleye, O. and Oduwaye, A. (2005) 'Correlates of land value determinants in Lagos Metropolis, Nigeria', *Journal of Human Ecology*, vol 17, no 3, pp183–189

Peil, M. (1991) *Lagos: The City and Its People*, Belhaven, London

Schwerdtfeger, H. (1982*) Traditional Housing in African Cities: A Comparative Study of Houses in Zaria, Ibadan, and Marrakech*, Wiley, Chichester

Smith, R. (1978) *The Lagos Consulate, 1851–1861*, Macmillan, London

Soja, E. (1996) *Thirdspace: Journeys to Los Angeles and other Real or Imagined Places*, Blackwell, Oxford

The Economist (2009) 'Change we can profit from: Carrotmobbing', *The Economist*, London, 31 January, p71

Uduku, O. (1994) 'Promoting community based approaches to social infrastructure provision in urban areas in Nigeria', *Environment and Urbanisation*, vol 6 no 2, October, pp57–78

Uduku, O. (1996) 'Housing in south eastern Nigeria in the 1990s', *Habitat International*, vol 20, no2, pp191–202

Vaughan-Richards, A. with Akinsemoyin, K. (1977) *Building Lagos*, Afromedia, Lagos

6

Gated Minds, Gated Places:
The Impact and Meaning
of Hard Boundaries in South Africa

Karina Landman

Introduction

In August and September 2003, the City of Johannesburg engaged in public hearings on enclosed neighbourhoods, one type of gated community in South Africa, to obtain public input from a wide range of stakeholders. At the public hearings, one resident accused the city council of allowing the creation of 'luxury *laagers*' for the wealthy. This indicated that gated communities and, more specifically, physical intervention in the form of creating barriers is perceived as building '*laagers*' that will adversely affect those outside these closures. *Laagers* refer to the camps that were defended by a circular formation of wagons, created by the colonial settlers in Africa to defend themselves from attacks by the indigenous population. Given this, the word often has a negative connotation related to the history within the country. This raises several questions about the historical connections of certain forms of physical intervention and its linkages to the past. How far can some groups go to protect themselves and what memories does this reignite in a country with a long history of segregation?

Settlement and building fortification and segregation have a long history in South Africa, including interventions such as the building of the castle in Cape Town in 1666, building military forts in the 1700s, and building *laagers* to defend the moving settlers in the 1800s. However, fortification can also be achieved through laws that control access and restrict movement – for example, the infamous Group Areas Act, implemented during the height of apartheid. This raises questions about the relationship between older forms of fortification and contemporary gated communities in South Africa, as well as the meaning of settlement fortification within contemporary South African cities. Do gated places result from gated mindsets and can this become patterns over time?

Brunn (2006) started to address the first question and distinguished between three sets of maps: gated communities, gated lives and gated minds. *Gated communities* refer to physical areas that are protected by walls and gates and a range of other security measures aimed at restricting access into the area. *Gated lives* define those living in gated communities (i.e. behind walls), but may also include those who live separated or segregated lives based on fear or problems related to 'fitting in'. Finally, *gated minds* refer to individuals who portray minds or behaviours that are full of 'barriers and gates' that separate them from others around them, including characteristics such as dislike, hatred and contempt for others. Brunn (2006) also points out that the relationships between these three aspects are often not straightforward – for example, not all people residing in a gated community live a gated mind and life, while people can live a gated mind, but not life, or one can have a gated mind but not live a gated life and live in a gated community. This raises interesting questions about the relationship between social space (gated minds) and physical space (gated places) and their implications for urban living in contemporary South Africa, especially related to social sustainability.

The discussion also raises issues around the 'potentials of boundaries in South Africa' (Thornton, 2000) and the meaning of the constant remaking of boundaries throughout the country's history, both around and within settlements or cities. It is also concerned with the nature and multiplicity of boundaries in South Africa, both in terms of contemporary and historical boundaries.

This chapter focuses on the relationship between gated minds (social needs and ideas) and gated places (order and form) as they manifest themselves through different time, periods and the meaning thereof for social sustainability in South Africa. The following section presents a brief historical overview of gated minds and places in South Africa, while the third section highlights a number of patterns that emerge from the discussion. The penultimate section discusses the meaning of gated communities in South Africa.

Gated minds and places: A historical overview

For the purpose of this discussion, *gated minds* will refer to mindsets of people at a specific time, including various ideologies. *Gated places* will refer to physical areas that are characterized by physical elements such as walls and fences, gates and booms, signposts and a range of other security measures designed to control access into a demarcated area.

As mentioned in the 'Introduction', South Africa has a long history of fortification. This section will only deal with the prevalence of gated minds and places in three historical periods and common patterns emerging from these eras. The discussion primarily focuses on South Africa. While colonialism has a long tradition in many African countries,[1] the formal incorporation of the apartheid system was specific to South Africa.

Colonialism

Fortification started as far back as 1652 when Jan van Riebeeck took over control of the Cape in order to provide an outpost for the Dutch fleet. The Dutch East Indian Company (VOC) charged him with establishing a shipping station in the Cape of Good Hope. Immigration was encouraged for many years,

and in 1707 the European population of the Cape Colony stood at 1779 (Hatting, 1984; Fage, 1978). This was the first attempts at, or precursor to, colonialism in what later became South Africa.[2] The Castle of Good Hope was built by the VOC between 1666 and 1679. Its purpose was to act as replenishment station for ships passing the treacherous coast around the Cape on long voyages between The Netherlands and the Dutch East Indies and to protect the inhabitants. During 1664, tensions between Britain and The Netherlands rose, with rumours of war being imminent, and in the same year Commander Zacharius Wagenaer was instructed to build a pentagonal castle out of stone. The castle was built in the traditional Dutch star form (very characteristic of castles in Europe at that time) and included five bastions to protect the buildings on the inside. These buildings included a series of outlying buildings to act as the military storehouses and barracks for the solders and a line of buildings in the middle that originally housed the commanders, including the governor, admiral and food stores. Some of the moats were later destroyed to make way for modernization and infrastructure development (Hatting, 1984).

In 1795, Britain took over control of the Cape to pre-empt French intervention and gradually started to introduce cultural and legal changes that damaged the interests of the Boers.[3] This contributed to a growing divide between the British and the Boers. Comarof (1989) distinguishes between three models of colonialism as was evident in the 1800s – namely, state, settler and civilizing colonialism. *State colonialism* referred to the state model, according to which the colonial government was seen to oversee the territory, with its first priority 'Pax Britannica': the pacification of the 'tribes', under British law, in an ever-widening radius outwards from the Cape. To this end, the administration sponsored the exploration of the interior but did not impose direct rule on inland people. *Settler colonialism* (the Boer model) was revealed most clearly in and after, the Great Trek of the 1830s, when between 12,000 and 14,000 settlers or the so-called Boers left the colony for the interior. From the point of view of the British missioners, settler colonialism was seen to be founded on brute coercion and domination by force. Whether this was true or not, it did, however, serve to establish a new order of relations between these Europeans and the people from the interior. The encounter began with either war or alliance and ended, often, with the subordination of local communities to Boer control. The *civilizing colonialism* of the missioners was much more influenced by the Christians than the previous two models. They believed in the transformation of indigenous life to be more positive and uplifting. They therefore sought to cultivate the African 'desert' and its inhabitants by planting the seeds of the bourgeois individualism and the nuclear family, of private property and commerce, of rational minds and healthy clad bodies, of the practical arts of refined living and devotion to God (Comarof, 1989, p673).

In addition, Butler (2004) points out that by the 1870s, within the border of the yet to be created South Africa, three resilient groups of society were engaged in increasingly harsh competition for resources, but none achieving dominance. The first was the Bantu-speaking African peoples, including the Zulu, Xhosa, Tshwana and Sotho. African political kingdoms had been expanding into what is today known as South Africa from around the third century AD. The second group were the Boers, whose expansion north and east into areas occupied by the African polities began in the 1800s. The third group were the British Imperialists, interested in the advancement of the Empire.

These different models of colonialism and three distinctive groups in society therefore represented distinctive ideologies and specific mindsets, which often resulted in ensuing conflict over resources and need for protection. This had various implications for settlement formation, often including various types of fortification.[4] During the British expansion in the late 1700s and early 1800s, they erected numerous military camps and forts[5] to protect the British soldiers from the African people, especially along the Eastern Cape Frontier around the Great Fish River and in Grahamstown. However, constant conflicts with the Xhosa occurred in the border area at the Fish River, and the British government was neither willing nor able to give the Boers effective military protection. As a result of this and other factors, many Boers left the Cape Colony in the 1830s. Here they came face to face with the other African tribes, which resulted in further conflict and battles over resources (primarily land). After a few initial disasters, they evolved suitable tactics – the *laager*, or fortified wagon camp, for defence, and the swift mounted commando raid for attack (Fage,

1978). This approach was also used during the Battle of Blood River that ensued between the Boer settlers and the Zulus on 16 December 1838.

The growing tension between the Boer settlers and the British finally culminated in the Anglo Boer War (1899 to 1902), the grand finale of the colonial era and a major contributor to the establishment of the Union of South Africa in 1910. Prior to the Anglo Boer War the Boer settlers had built a number of forts – for example, in and around Pretoria, including Fort Klapperkop. During the Anglo Boer War, the British constructed numerous blockhouses in South Africa. These blockhouses were initially built to protect the railway, the main British supply route and lines of communication. The purpose was later extended, with blockhouses being built in a series of lines as obstacles against which pursuing British columns could literally fence in the Boers and trap them (Harold, 2004). The earliest blockhouses were constructed during the early months of the guerrilla phase of the war just after the fall of Pretoria on 5 June 1900. According to Tomlinson (1997), there were about 441 masonry blockhouses. These were distinct from corrugated iron blockhouses and engineering 'works'. A masonry blockhouse is defined as 'a structure of mortared stonework or concrete, one to three storeys in height, with a roof of timber and corrugated iron or concrete, with rifle ports, windows and doors protected by loop-holed steel plates and with or without steel machicouli galleries' (Tomlinson, 1997, p1). These blockhouses were mostly erected at prominent points such as railway bridges over rivers and were also found to guard railway stations (e.g. at Warmbaths), railway lines in open country (e.g. at Witkop and along the Vereniging line) and passes and high points in the Magaliesberg (e.g. at Hekpoort). There were a variety of blockhouse designs, including the most familiar square shape, measuring 6.1m externally and mostly two to three storeys high. Alternative forms included those that were T-shaped and L-shaped (e.g. Hekpoort), and hexagonal (e.g. at Aliwal North) (Tomlinson, 1997). According to Harold (2004), blockhouses were an important component of the success of the war.

In addition, the British also built several forts in the Eastern Cape for protection, including the Knysna Fort (1901), the Jansensville Fort (1901) and the Upper Van Standens Dam Fort in the Port Elizabeth area. The Knysna Fort comprised two lop-hold circular towers with vertical slits in the wall, connected by a perimeter wall enclosing an irregular area. Both the Jansenville and Upper Van Stadens Dam forts were constructed from un-mortared stone walls about 2m high, although the tapered loopholes occur at only one level (Tomlinson, 1996).

In summary, one can therefore broadly distinguish between four types of gated or fortified places that characterized the colonial period – namely, the castle, forts, *laagers* and blockhouses. Each of these came about as a result of specific needs for protection and ideas on how to address these needs through various physical forms in particular circumstances.

Post-colonialism and apartheid

According to Thornton (2000), apartheid is after the 'colonial' and one can therefore also reserve the label 'post-colonial' to apartheid. South Africa has a long history of racial segregation, which started during the time of Dutch and British colonialism (Beavon, 1992; Lemon, 1992; Badenhorst, 1999; Terreblanche, 2002) and later culminated in what has been commonly referred to as 'apartheid'. According to Butler (2004), the period between 1910 and 1960 can be referred to as 'early apartheid', characterized by the creation of native reserves, 'influx controls' and compliant 'traditional authorities', all of which became reliable mechanisms to control the labour force.[6] The African population was increasingly regulated where it remained on the land, and further forged into a working class through the migrant labour system (Butler, 2004). According to Thornton (2000), apartheid stands as a special form of modernism, with one of its key characteristics that of the rational 'progressive' bureaucratic administration.

The governments of the 1950s were in certain respects not that exceptional as white supremacy and the exclusion of Africans from participation in formal political activity were the norm in colonial Africa. However, the post-1960s, also referred to as 'high apartheid', brought a change in direction. Mass forced removals of 'incorrectly' located black people, newly created homelands and deliberate 're-tribalization' resulted in a new scale of socio-spatial engineering (Butler, 2004, p19). This was based on the so-called friction theory, which postulates that the physical, social, cultural and economic differences between people are fundamentally irreconcilable and lead to

friction upon contact. Harmonious relationships can therefore only be established if contact is limited to a minimum, especially in residential areas and as far as possible in places of work (Badenhorst, 1987, p220).

Given this, apartheid is synonymous with the meticulous making and marking of difference, especially that difference known as 'race, but also of space' (Christopher, 1994; Thornton, 2000). The apartheid policy was a social system based on 'setting apart' or dividing different race groups in space. This made the power of apartheid crucially dependent on spatiality (Robinson, 1996). Given this, apartheid resulted in a struggle for the control of urban space in South African cities:

> Black workers were also part of urban communities and so the struggle over time in the workplace came to be closely tied to the struggle over the nature and control of urban space. (Swilling, 1991, px)

Consequently, planners started to carve up society into racial categories (Swilling, 1991). The physical isolation of whites from other racial groups received great attention. Consequently, the racial dualism of 'whites' and 'non-whites' evident in apartheid were terms used widely in everything, from government notices to park benches and public toilets. Apartheid entailed the design of a multitude of laws preventing those who were not classified as white from occupying or using declared white space (Christopher, 1994). In this way, preferred social space was created and enforced through the nature of physical space.

Planners in South Africa very effectively made use of modern town planning ideas to assist with the creation of the apartheid city (Dewar et al, 1990; Dewar and Uytenbogaardt, 1991; Kotze, 1999). Numerous model neighbourhoods were laid out according to race groups. Well-developed traditionally white suburban areas developed around the central business districts, where most of the facilities and job opportunities were located. The African population were concentrated in townships on the urban periphery close to the main employment areas (Badenhorst, 1999). These areas were separated from the well-developed suburbs through buffer strips in the form of green belts, industrial zones and rapid transport routes (see Figure 6.1). Dewar (1992) identifies three spatial features that resulted from apartheid planning and characterized South African cities at the beginning of the 1990s: low-density sprawl, fragmentation and separation.

Apartheid was thus known for its totalizing system of social engineering in which the vision of 'apartness' was implemented through spatial dislocation in terms of a rationalized bureaucratic master plan of total differentiation. It was therefore based on a logic of difference that gave either 'race' or 'nation/nationality' a special place, and produced a set of practices concerned with boundaries between categories that it conceived. Thornton (2000, p142), however, further points out that there is an essential contradiction in the concept of totality based on disintegration of the polity, or of unity, based on the logic of division:

> Despite its remarkable longevity, apartheid (as concept), and Apartheid as a formal system of laws and practices failed because it constantly undermined the unity it sought through the implementation of difference.

Post-apartheid

Thornton (2000) asserts that South Africa is clearly post-apartheid and that the 'post-Apartheid condition' exists too. This condition emerges out of a special relationship between modernism, colonialism and apartheid. The end of apartheid is the end of 'modernism' and therefore may be either a new beginning or a return to the past, to tradition and to primitivism. The end of the rational modernizing order in South Africa, as in the rest of Africa, is seen as liberating and threatening, empowering and impoverishing. The condition in South Africa is therefore pre-future, a condition of the ante-tomorrow, of a new–old country that thought all along what would happen, and then did not know, and thus waits again for a regeneration of a past it has forgotten and the materialization of a future it does not know. What it therefore lacks is certainty (Thornton, 2000).

Although the infamous Group Areas Act was abolished in 1990 and many political parties, including the African National Congress (ANC) were unbanned, and although many negotiations were undertaken during the early 1990s, the actual transition from the apartheid regime to a democracy occurred only with the first all-inclusive elections held in April 1994. South Africa has undergone profound transformation after the transition to democracy. Despite many interventions, poverty became even more deeply entrenched in the poorest quarter of South Africans

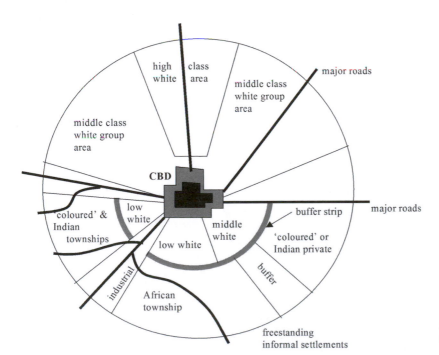

Figure 6.1 *The 'apartheid city'*

Source: adapted from Davies as cited in Napier et al (1999)

(Butler, 2004). Other social changes included increased urbanization, a decline of formal employment opportunities, high levels of crime and violence, and growing levels of fear of crime (Shaw, 2002; Smith, 2003; Butler, 2004).

The main impact of the 1990s, with respect to narrowing inequalities, has been the improvement of service infrastructure in poor parts of South African cities, most notably former black and coloured townships (Smith, 2003). However, for those left behind, without access to a subsidy house (mostly developed in peripheral locations) or with a need to be closer to the centre, informal settlements became the only option. Thus, one of the most dominant characteristics of the post-apartheid city is the random distribution of numerous informal settlements across the urban landscape. For some of the more affluent, these settlements became a threat to safety and order, leading to various responses in the built environment that involves many levels of fortification.

In essence, gated communities in South Africa refer to physical areas that are fenced or walled off from their surroundings, either prohibiting or controlling access to these areas by means of gates or booms. In many cases the concept can refer to a residential area with restricted access so that normal public spaces are privatized or their use is restricted. It does not, however, only refer to residential areas, but may also include controlled access areas for work (office parks), commercial (shopping malls) and/or recreational purposes. This chapter focuses on gated communities that are primarily residential with limited other uses. These gated communities in South Africa can broadly be categorized into two major types – namely, security estates and enclosed neighbourhoods. Security estates[7] are private developments (see Figure 6.2), while enclosed neighbourhoods[8] are concerned with restriction of access to existing public roads (see Figure 6.3).

With specific reference to South Africa, there are several factors that contribute to the growth of gated communities, including crime, the fear of crime and insecurity; the search for a greater sense of community identity, place and belonging in cities; the search for increased privacy and control, both economic and social; a specific lifestyle; status, prestige and elitism; and a growing lack of trust and confidence in the performance of local councils (Landman, 2006).

Consequently, in the post-apartheid city, the old patterns are reinforced by new patterns of segregation, such as different types of gated/walled communities (Bremner, 1999; Lipman and Harris, 1999; Vrodljak, 2002; Czégledy, 2003; Harrison, 2003). As such, Tomlinson (2003, p86), commenting on the sharp distinctions and inequalities between the wealthy and poor areas in Johannesburg, warns of the divide between 'the walled residential communities and secure office parks and malls in the north [which] will stand in sharp contrast to the desperation of the south'. Social justice remains a major challenge in South Africa's increasingly fragmented cities, especially for those subscribing to egalitarian ethics (liberal or social), which underpin much of the opposition to apartheid (Smith, 2003, p31).

Given the history of the country, it is therefore not strange that this is how contemporary 'gating' is interpreted. Some commentators even go beyond the

Figure 6.2 *Entrance to a security estate in Pretoria, South Africa*

Source: Karina Landman

Figure 6.3 *Entrance to an enclosed neighbourhood in Pretoria*

Source: Karina Landman

mere socio-spatial implications of segregation and fragmentation and start to link the establishment of gated communities and, especially, enclosed neighbourhoods more directly to past practices. At the public hearings in Johannesburg on access restriction for security purposes, a large group of residents perceived gated communities to be a mechanism of segregation and exclusion. This was constantly raised by many residents living outside closures who were concerned not only with the immediate but also the longer-term impact:

> Closures signal exclusion, separation. The explosive and exponentially negative effects of closure on nation building, on future perceptions and attitudes, cannot be more serious. We have barely stepped out of the *laager*. We must not step into a ghetto. (Pienaar, City of Johannesburg, 2003. Proceedings from the Public Hearings on Security Restrictions)

This excerpt specifically make reference to the '*laagers*' of the past and offers a warning not to replicate a similar type of action. A number of residents also pointed out that road closures were entrenching the apartheid city of the past:

> The areas where closures are being affected are all in suburbs previously restricted to whites by title deed and later by the Group Areas Act. A fundamental objective of the metro's planning has been to break down the racial divisions of the past. Permitting closures would be counter-productive. (Bird, City of Johannesburg, 2003. Proceedings from the Public Hearings on Security Restrictions)

In this way, security enclaves are perceived as being contradictory to the vision and goals of post-apartheid South Africa, which starts to point towards the nature of a future city as one that could become similar to the neighbourhoods established during apartheid. Another resident also raised the link between enclosed areas and the image of a new apartheid, making reference to a possible future format. He therefore requested the following:

> Please do not make Johannesburg a city of enclosed elite suburbs. We would soon degenerate into a system of economic apartheid, which has no place in a new and democratic South Africa. (Clayton, City of Johannesburg, 2003. Proceedings from the Public Hearings on Security Restrictions)

In this way, it is perceived as economic segregation, and not so much as racial exclusion. However, it is still perceived to be out of line in a new democratic environment and can have grave implications for the image of Johannesburg and that of 'the new South Africa'. Thus, as Thornton (2000, p142) maintains, and as illustrated above, in the aftermath of apartheid, 'the logic of difference remains, but it now lacks the political, philosophical and aesthetic image of unity of the (total) nation'.

What is interesting, however, is that in some of the cases studied, many of the residents remarked that the process of gating or moving into a gated place had contributed to an improved sense of community and social cohesion and in most cases to more effective maintenance of the neighbourhood. This excludes the cases where some of the inhabitants opposed the neighbourhood closure. This serves to highlight another contradiction – namely, a continuous logic of difference and consequent segregation manifesting on a larger scale (city), while simultaneously a greater form of integration emerging at a local scale (neighbourhood).

Emerging patterns: Boundaries, identities and their impact on social sustainability

According to Thornton (2000), one of the most remarkable things about South Africa is the multiplicity of boundaries that define it, divide it, and thereby give it shape. This making and remaking of boundaries serves to give shape to a variety of aspects, including the making and remaking of various groups and communities. Creating gated places and making use of various mechanisms to demarcate separate territories is all about establishing the boundaries and redefining the edges between the distinct spatial areas. It is, however, the nature of these boundaries and their implications in South Africa that deserve more attention:

> The South African boundaries are not mere edges; they are themselves the focus of attention and identity. Today these aesthetics and metaphysics of boundaries are under pressure in the changing South Africa. Boundaries are being manipulated 'rationally' by governing committees of well-intentioned people, but traditional values, practicalities, practices and habits all attach to the previous and long-standing multiple boundaries and borders… Boundaries themselves have a salience that surpass the merely practical. They are both political problem and political solution. They are entailed by the exercise of power, but undermine power and make possible the escape from it. The politics of boundaries, and the boundaries of the political, and of political community, all combine in South Africa to create a discourse that goes well beyond the political to the meta-political. (Thornton, 2000, p150)

This raises many questions about the nature of boundaries created by gated communities in contemporary South Africa and their purpose, as well as their link to similar responses in the past. Is the purpose of the boundaries to control space and behaviour inside or to escape the power from outside?

As Thornton (2000) maintains, all boundaries raise questions about who is 'inside' and who is 'outside', who is enemy and who is friend, etc. Given the history of the past, as well as the form and management of many present-day gated communities in the country, gated communities have raised serious concerns about the future in terms of the redefinition and control of space:

> Bluntly put, the major forms of private security that have been most active in policing the transition in South Africa have preserved, and in many ways extended, apartheid. They have done so through catering to public demands for security that are guided by old ideas for what security 'looks like', carving up the country's landscape into an archipelago of secure 'fortified fragments' from which 'undesirables' are barred entry or permitted to enter for circumspect sets of reasons. While this new apartheid bears a striking resemblance to the official governmental programme that preceded it, it has several qualities that make it distinct and even more worrisome in its implications than the hardships that have gone before. (Shearing and Kempa, 2000, p5)

The consequences for South African cities as a whole, or for large metropolitan areas, could be ominous: 'Those dynamics are producing an increasingly disparate, separate city. The gaps between the townships, the inner city and the suburb are widening. The chances that people of this city will develop a sense of shared space, of shared destiny, grow slimmer by the day' (Bremner, 1999, p10). Gated communities can therefore challenge the very existence of democracy in many cities and even more so in transitional countries where the practices of democracy are only being established after years of authoritarian rule.

However, on the other hand, it was pointed out that boundaries can also assist in bringing residents together in a geographical area as a result of a common purpose – to fight crime in the case of most gated communities. This, in turn, can contribute to the development of a shared identity and sense of community between those members who support the initiative. This raises interesting issues regarding the role of boundaries to facilitate social cohesion and a sense of identity. It also touches on the issue of the establishment of boundaries to mediate conflict and its consequences. To this regard it is very interesting to note that Thornton (2000) notes that according to

Gluckman, conflict itself becomes a mode of integration. This could therefore create a situation where boundaries are erected to mediate conflict and to foster integration and identity at a smaller scale (i.e. at the neighbourhood or community level).

It also highlights one of the great dilemmas related to the establishment of gated communities and their impact upon social sustainability. Gated communities often facilitate and promote a range of urban needs; but they do so only for those allowed access into the protected neighbourhood. As a result, many residents experienced an increased sense of community and quality of life inside the gated communities. These developments, however, exclude those outside from enjoying the benefits presented by these well-developed and maintained environments. The issue is therefore that gated communities effectively privatize urban space and limit public interaction between different groups and individuals within the city, which is a prerequisite for social cohesion and greater tolerance in cities, as pointed out by Madanipour (2001). There is an overemphasis on 'common interests' inside, linked to the internal community assets. The needs of the community are opposed to the needs of the broader society and support the notion that the implications of giving people the opportunity to withdraw from the surrounding community are serious (Wilson-Doenges, 2000, p608) since gated communities enforce and accentuate the different worlds within the city in an extreme way (Allen, 1999) instead of focusing on integration between these worlds. In this way, 'community-saving and forming drives' through the multiple partitioning of shared space (Horn, 2004) can directly oppose building the broader society, and may also contribute to the loss of citizenship in South African cities, as was the case in the US (Blakely and Snyder, 1997) and Brazil (Caldeira, 2000). This could have a negative impact upon social sustainability and at the level of the city and in terms of its overall contribution to urban sustainability (also see Landman and du Plessis, 2007).

The meaning of gated communities

The earlier discussions have referred to the work of Shearing and Kempa (2000), who pointed out that gated communities may, in fact, give rise or contribute to a new apartheid city in South Africa. This is based on three notions: a 'new text', created through the transformation of order and form; an emotionally loaded type of development in a specific place; and the symbolic meaning of these types within present historical realities, thus the relation to time. The meaning of gated communities in South Africa, therefore, revolves around the notions of terminology, typology and symbolism.

A sense of order and form: A new 'text'?

A number of theorists have pointed out that the city can be read as a text (including Short, 1996, and Ellin, 1997). Meaning in the built environment is conveyed by the physical elements constituting two- and three-dimensional space. These physical elements represent a specific text within the built environment, carrying with it the ability to convey a particular message. These messages are interpreted differently by different actors taking part in urban life (Short, 1996). This is especially the case with gated communities in South Africa. While some groups, considering gated communities as an effective response to crime prevention, focused on its perceived outcome, others, taking into account the consequences, focused on the impact.

This represents a formalistic approach to meaning in the built environment – that is, meaning based on form. The physical elements (form/morphology) arranged in a specific way (order/topology) perform the same function as words arranged in sentences and, therefore, represent a text. In the case of gated communities they address the meaning of walls and gates and, more specifically, the physical meaning or meaning related to physical space. A new text of closure is presented: neighbourhood walls, electric fences, booms, gates, security guard houses, warning signs, closed-circuit television (CCTV) cameras, sophisticated entry systems (intercom and PIN numbers) and various other access control measures. The collective meaning of these elements often translates into perceptions of separated spaces or new apartheid neighbourhoods. This is especially the case in South Africa where contemporary interventions are often judged in terms of the past. The following sub-section also raises the issue of place and type.

A sense of place: A 'new', 'old' or 'new–old' type?

The specific place in concern is post-apartheid South African cities. The mere wording suggests that one cannot consider the post-apartheid era without an understanding of, or some link to, colonialism and apartheid. It is also critical to consider the socio-spatial context or the specific place and time (Madanipour, 1996; Short, 1996). This raises the issue of space and society, or the relationship between physical and social space, which in turn establishes the preconditions for the development and experience of a sense of place.

Physical space often creates the preconditions for the experience of social space. In the case of the gated communities in South Africa, it translates into questions such as: what can 'we' or 'they' do 'here/there'? It becomes a question of 'ours' and 'theirs', or an issue of 'inside' and 'outside'. A sense of place, community and belonging relates directly to these issues and, more specifically, to the question of 'whose place'. It is also associated with the behaviour of people inside the gated communities and use of space. This creates the preconditions for a sense of identity, 'our people, group, and neighbourhood' or simply 'our place'. It is linked to access control and behavioural control enforced through rules and regulations, and/or community pressure. In this way it reflects Tuan's (1977) interpretation, where place is security and the protected space inside is freedom.

Such an interpretation represents a functional approach to meaning in the built environment – that is, meaning based on the use of space or what the physical space does or does not accommodate, what is allowed or not allowed inside closed-off spaces, and who may or may not enter. This is an especially loaded issue within the context of post-apartheid South Africa, given the legacy of colonialism and apartheid. Any form of restriction to space is often linked to the past and remembrance of the past invariably conjures up images of negativity and repression for many South Africans. It therefore raises the question of what gated communities represent related to different interpretations of place.

This chapter has indicated that gated communities encompass contested meanings based on different typologies. For some they become a reflection of *laagers* used by the settlers during the Great Trek: thus, an old type. For others, they become a new form of the old apartheid neighbourhoods or citadels of the elite where some race groups were prohibited and excluded: a new–old type. Yet, for others, gated communities represent an entirely new form of development particular to the late 20th century – a 'privatized' neighbourhood, thus a new type (e.g. as manifested through lifestyle estates, which represent the promise of an ideal lifestyle in an ideal place).

A sense of time: 'Gated' symbolic

Meaning is often attached to a particular typology – for example, a military fort, a church, a civic centre, a prison, and/or particular place. While this is true, the form and use of urban space change over time (Kostof, 1992). Meanings also change (Short, 1996). Therefore, while many perceive gated communities as a new form of the old apartheid neighbourhood, contributing to a new apartheid city due to their nature and extent, this symbolic connection may also change over time. History provides a case in point. The once majestic walls of medieval and baroque cities became obsolete with the invention of gunpowder and the expansion of cities far beyond the original boundaries. While remnants often remained, the gates were removed or opened and the walls were often taken down. As the threat of war subsided or the political climate changed, the purpose of physical elements to enforce control became unnecessary, as for example in the case of the Berlin Wall in Germany.

Transformation of post-apartheid cities through gated communities in South Africa is also part of a constant process of urban change. It should, therefore, be viewed as a circular process as opposed to a linear process where the end result is automatically presumed to be new apartheid cities. In the medium term, gated communities may be perceived to create new apartheid cities through socio-spatial and institutional fragmentation and exclusion. Yet, owing to the large number of variables that may influence future transition in South Africa, the long-term future is uncertain. A few academics and practitioners have alluded to the possibility that the walls may come down if there is a significant reduction in crime. This will show whether the main reason is related to crime.

Conclusions

Terreblanche (2002) maintains that it is important to remember the past in South Africa in order to understand the present. This is also true for urban studies and the comprehension of urban transformation of the South African city at the turn of the 20th century. According to Badenhorst (1999), those who study the relationships between social processes and spatial form are in agreement that social structure and, more particularly, the divisions in society are reflected in urban structure, and that urban residential patterns act as a mirror image of the relevant society. The South African city cannot, therefore, be viewed separately from the society in which it occurs and the history of that society where it still has an impact upon the present city. Therefore, in order to understand the post-apartheid city, one has to conceive of it as a product of large-scale socio-spatial engineering that goes as far back as 1656 when the Dutch settled in the Cape and culminated in 'high apartheid' in the second half of the 20th century.

This chapter has shown that South Africa has a long tradition of fortification and these forms were often the result of specific mindsets and ideologies that either necessitated the need for protection based on fear of others or because of the perceptions that the 'others' are different. Therefore, in some cases, gated places were the direct result of gated mindsets based on a logic of difference (social space) that manifested themselves in separated spaces in the built environment (physical space).

However, the impact of the physical separation of areas is not one sided. The multiplication of many gated communities on the urban landscape could have a negative impact upon social sustainability on a city level and, ultimately, urban sustainability through the exclusive use of local services, recreational opportunities and housing opportunities for those inside. On the other hand, the establishment of hard boundaries at a neighbourhood level could, in some cases, contribute to foster greater integration and a sense of community inside the gates. In this way, they could have a positive impact upon social sustainability in terms of greater pride and attachment to the neighbourhood, social interaction within the neighbourhood, greater safety and security and quality of the local environment, and stability and participation in neighbourhood activities. This highlights the dilemma for urban practitioners and decision-makers.

This is also further complicated by the dynamic nature of boundaries and the constant remaking of boundaries throughout various historical periods. It therefore makes it very difficult to attach a fixed meaning to gated communities in contemporary cities and one can at most reflect that its meaning relates to different interpretations from various stakeholders across time and place. What is certain, however, is that one cannot begin to understand the meaning of gated communities without an understanding of the mindsets and practices of the past. Therefore, at best, one can conclude that gated places are often influenced by gated minds and that in South Africa this spans across history and is likely to influence future development as a continuation of an old narrative.

Notes

1 Colonialism had a long tradition in Africa. British colonialism stretched from the Cape and Port Natal (later becoming part of the Union of South Africa), Rhodesia (currently Zimbabwe) and Bechuanaland (currently Botswana) to British East Africa (currently Kenya) in the north-east and the Gold Coast and Sierra Leone in the north-west (Fage, 1978)

2 The area that is formally known as South Africa today first came about with the declaration of the Union of South Africa in 1910.

3 'Boer' is a Dutch word, meaning 'farmer'. In this context it specifically refers to a South African of Dutch, German, or Huguenot descent, especially one of the early settlers of the Transvaal and Orange Free State. Today, descendants of the Boers are commonly referred to as Afrikaaners.

4 *Fortifications* are military constructions and buildings designed for defence in warfare. According to the *Collins English Dictionary* (1994, p328), it refers to 'walls, mounds, etc. used to fortify a place'.

5 Many military installations are known as *forts*, although they are not always fortified. A *fort* refers to a 'fortified enclosure, building or position' (*Collins English Dictionary*, 1994, p328).

6 The Union of South Africa was established in 1910 and the Republic of South Africa in 1961, which brought independence from British rule.

7 'Security villages' refer to private developments where the entire area is developed by a private developer. These areas/buildings are physically walled or fenced off and usually have a security gate or controlled access point, with or without a security guard. The roads within these developments are private and, in most cases, management and maintenance are carried out by a private management body. Security villages not only include residential areas (such as secure townhouse complexes and high-rise apartment blocks), but also controlled-access villages for

business purposes (office blocks) and mixed-use developments, such as large security estates.

8   'Enclosed neighbourhoods' refer to existing neighbourhoods that have controlled access through gates or booms across existing roads. Many are fenced or walled off, as well, with a limited number of controlled entrances/exits, and security guards at these points in some cases. The roads within these neighbourhoods were previously, or still are, public property, depending on the model used within different local authorities. The majority in the country are based on the public approach (where the roads remain public).

References

Allen, J. (1999). 'Worlds within cities', in Massey, D., Allen, J. and Pile, S. (eds) *City Worlds*, Routledge, London

Badenhorst, M. S. (1987) *Die residensiele struktuur van die metropool – 'n sosiaal ruimtelike vertolking van die Suid-Afrikaanse geval*, DPhil thesis, Rand Afrikaanse Universiteit, Johannesburg

Badenhorst, M. S. (1999) 'The South African City: A study in socio-spatial engineering', Paper presented at the Third International Urban Planning and Environment Association Symposium, Pretoria, 5–9 April

Beavon, K. S. O. (1992). 'The post-apartheid city: Hopes, possibilities, and harsh realities', in Smith, D. (ed) (1992) *The Apartheid City and Beyond: Urbanization and Social Change in South Africa*, Routledge, London and New York; Witwatersrand University Press, South Africa

Blakely, E. J. and Snyder, M. G. (1997) *Fortress America: Gated Communities in the United States*, Brookings Institution Press, Washington, DC

Bremner, L. (1999). 'Crime and the emerging landscape of post-apartheid Johannesburg' in Judin, H. and Vladislavic, I. (eds) *Blanc Architecture, Apartheid and After*, Nai Publishers, Rotterdam

Brunn, S. D. (2006) 'Gated minds and gated lives as worlds of exclusion and fear', *GeoJournal*, vol 66, pp5–13

Butler, A. (2004) *Contemporary South Africa*, Palgrave Macmillan, New York, NY

Caldeira, T. P. R. (2000) *City of Walls: Crime, Segregation and Citizenship in Sao Paulo*, University of California Press, Berkeley, CA

Christopher, A. J. (1994) *The Atlas of Apartheid Space*, Routledge, London

City of Johannesburg (2003) Proceedings from the Public Hearings on Security Restrictions, August to September. Unpublished document

Collins English Dictionary (1994) *Collins English Dictionary*, Harper Collins, Glasgow

Comarof, J. L. (1989) 'Images of Empire, contests of conscience: Models of colonial domination in South Africa', *American Ethnologist*, vol 16, no 4, pp661–685

Czégledy, A. (2003) 'Villas of the Highveld: A cultural perspective on Johannesburg and its "northern suburbs"', in Tomlinson, R., Beeauregard, R. A., Bremner, L. and Mangcu, X. (eds) *Emerging Johannesburg: Perspectives on the Post Apartheid City*, Routledge, London, pp21–42

Dewar, D. (1992). 'Urbanization and the South African city: A manifesto for change', in Smith, D. M. (ed) *The Apartheid City and Beyond: Urbanisation and Social Change in South Africa*, Routledge, London

Dewar, D. and Uytenbogaardt, R. (1991) *South African Cities: A Manifesto for change*, Urban Problems Research Unit and Urban Foundation, Cape Town

Dewar, D. and Uytenbogaardt, R. (1995) *Creating Vibrant Urban Places to Live*, Headstart Developments, Cape Town

Dewar, D., Watson, V., Bassios, A. and Dewar, D. (1990) *The Structure and Form of Metropolitan Cape Town: Its Origins, Influences and Performance*, Urban Problems Research Unit and Urban Foundation, Cape Town

Ellin, N. (1997) *Post Modern Urbanism*, Princeton University Press, New York, NY

Fage, J. D. (1978) *A History of Africa*, Hutchinson, London

Harold, E. R. Jr. (2004). *The Victorians at War, 1815–1914: An Encyclopedia of British Military History*, ABC-CLIO, Santa Barbara, CA

Harrison, P. (2003) 'Fragmentation and globalisation as the new meta-narrative', in Harrison, P., Huchzermeyer, M. and Mayekiso, M. (eds) *Confronting Urban Fragmentation: Housing and Urban Development in a Democratising Society*, University of Cape Town University Press, Cape Town, pp13–25

Hatting, A. S. J. (1984) *Kunswaardering*, Perskor, Pretoria

Horn, A. (2004) 'Reflections on the concept and conceptualisation of urban neighbourhood in societies in transition: The case of Pretoria (South Africa)', in Pak, M. and Rebernik, R. (eds) *Cities in Transition*, Strathclyde University Publishing, Glasgow, pp329–340

Kostof, S. (1992) *The City Assembled: The Elements of Urban Form through History*, Thames & Hudson, London

Kotze, C. P. (1999) 'The "Cape School": Towards the understanding and design of the South African City', *Open House International*, vol 24, no 4, pp21–35

Landman, K. (2006) *An Exploration of Urban Transformation in Post-Apartheid South Africa through Gated Communities, with a Focus on Its Relation to Crime and Impact on Socio-Spatial Integration*, PhD thesis, University of Newcastle upon Tyne, UK

Landman, K. and du Plessis, C. (2007) 'The impact of gated communities on urban sustainability: a difference of opinion or a matter of concern?', *SA Town and Regional Planning*, vol 51, May, pp16–25

Lemon, A. (1999) *Homes Apart: South Africa's Segregated Cities*, David Philip Publishers, Cape Town

Lipman, A. and Harris, H. (1999) 'Fortress Johannesburg', *Environment and Planning B: Planning and Design 1999*, vol 26, pp727–740

Madanipour, A. (1996) *Design of Urban Space: An Inquiry into a Socio-Spatial Process*, John Wiley, Chichester, UK

Madanipour, A. (2001) 'How relevant is "planning by neighbourhoods" today?', *Town Planning Review*, vol 72, no 2, pp171–191

Napier, M., du Plessis, C., Meiklejohn, C., Vosloo, L. and Lungu-Mulenga, A. (1999) *The State of Human Settlements Report: South Africa 1994–1998*, Contract report by the CSIR for the Department of Housing, South Africa

Robinson, J. (1996) *The Power of Apartheid: State, Power and Space in South African Cities*, Butterworth-Heinemann, Oxford, UK

Shaw, M. (2002) *Democracy's Disorder? Crime, Police and Citizen Responses in Transitional Societies*, SAIIA Publication, Johannesburg

Shearing, D. S. and Kempa, M. (2000) 'The role of "private security" in transitional democracies', Paper presented to the Crime and Policing in Transitional Societies: Comparative Perspectives Conference, SAIIA, 2000, Johannesburg

Short, J. R. (1996) *The Urban Order: An Introduction to Cities, Culture and Power*, Blackwell Publishers, Oxford

Smith, D. (2003) 'Urban fragmentation, inequality and social justice: Ethical perspectives', in Harrison, P., Huchzermeyer, M. and Mayekiso, M. (eds) *Confronting Urban Fragmentation: Housing and Urban Development in a Democratising Society*, University of Cape Town University Press, Cape Town

Swilling, M. (1991) 'Introduction', in Swilling, M., Humphries, R. and Shubane, K. (eds) (1991) *Apartheid City in Transition*, Oxford University Press, Cape Town

Terreblanche, S. (2002) *A History of Inequality in South Africa 1652–2002*, Natal University Press, Pietermaritzburg

Thornton, R. (2000) 'The potentials of boundaries in South Africa: Steps towards a theory of the social edge', in Werbner, R. and Rannger, T. (eds) *Postcolonial Identities in Africa*, Zed Books Ltd, London, pp136–161

Tomlinson, R. (1996) 'Anglo-Boer War town guard forts in the Eastern Cape, 1901–1902', *Military History Journal*, vol 10, no 2, pp69–72

Tomlinson, R. (1997) 'Britain's last castles: Masonry blockhouses of the South African War, 1899–1902', *Military History Journal*, vol 10, no 6, pp169–197

Tomlinson, R. (2003) 'HIV/AIDS and urban disintegration in Johannesburg', in Harrison, P., Huchzermeyer, M. and Mayekiso, M. (eds) *Confronting Urban Fragmentation: Housing and Urban Development in a Democratising Society*, University of Cape Town University Press, Cape Town

Tuan, Y. (1977) *Space and Place: The Perspective of Experience*, University of Minnesota Press, Minneapolis, MN

Vrodljak, M. (2002) *Place and the Politics of Subjectivity*, Thesis, University of Witwatersrand, South Africa

Wilson-Doenges, G. (2000) 'An exploration of sense of community and fear of crime in gated communities', *Environment and Behavior*, vol 32, no 5, September, pp597–611

7

Latin American Gated Communities: The Latest Symbol of Historic Social Segregation

Sonia Roitman and Mónica Adriana Giglio

Introduction

Gated communities are a worldwide urban phenomenon. However, their features vary within continents and countries. This chapter examines the development of gated communities in Latin America as the residential habitat for upper-class citizens, focusing on the analysis of Buenos Aires and Mendoza, two cities in Argentina. The following section of the chapter discusses the urban dynamic of residential settlements for affluent residents in Latin American countries. The third section concentrates on the historic evolution of gated communities in Argentina, considering the current typology of these closed and private residential compounds. Later, the situation of the Metropolitan Area of Buenos Aires is examined since it is the geographical area where they have developed most over the last decades. Finally, the evolution of gated communities in the Metropolitan Area of Mendoza, an intermediate city, is considered and compared to the situation in Buenos Aires.

Since the Spanish and Portuguese conquest at the end of the 15th century, an urban model of domination was created in Latin American cities. This model tried to override pre-Hispanic cities and created a safe environment for the conquerors and their allies, as explained by Sheinbaum in Chapter 8. Indigenous populations were displaced towards the periphery. The main square and its immediate surrounding buildings were used by the government and the Catholic Church or occupied by the most affluent citizens. After

independence in the 19th century, some privileges were abolished, but others continued. The access to urban land was still restricted to the most affluent social groups.

During the 20th century, industrialization processes led poor migrants from the countryside to settle in the periphery of medium-sized and large Latin American cities, while the upper and middle classes remained in central areas. Social segregation was a common feature of most Latin American cities that were neatly divided into poor, middle-class and affluent neighbourhoods. In the second half of that century, a process of suburbanization of affluent groups began. Housing units for upper middle-class families were built to be used as secondary residences, first, and later became primary residences. This flight to the suburbs was related to the command of private transportation by these social groups and the desire to move beyond the pollution and social turmoil of city centres (Fishman, 2003).

At the end of the 1980s and especially over the 1990s, the suburban housing model for middle-class and affluent families imported from the US expanded in many cities due to increasing urban crime and fear of crime, as well as the improvement and construction of motorways to link the periphery with the city centre by private transport. This process of 'suburbanization of the elites' (Torres, 1998) is still in progress and is likely to continue with a similar trend. It implies that social groups traditionally living separated from each other now share the same territory. Gated communities have developed accompanied by other private infrastructure, such as shopping centres, multiplex cinemas, super-stores, as well as offices and schools that have spread in the periphery to serve the new residents' needs. These new residential settlements might encourage urban sustainability since the 'original' population of the area gains access to new services and infrastructure that accompany gated communities. Nevertheless, the possibility of accessing these new services and infrastructure is strongly linked to the socio-economic level of the original residents since deprived groups cannot afford services targeted at middle-class and upper-class groups, and this creates the opposite effect, contributing to more visible social differences in the city.

Gated communities are residential areas closed by security devices (i.e. walls, fences, gates and barbed wire) with shared infrastructure and amenities, a code of behaviour and a residents' association. In Latin America, they are usually located in areas traditionally occupied by poor families since large extensions of land are available at affordable prices there. Sharing the same territory, however, does not mean social integration. On the contrary, there is hardly social contact between gated and non-gated residents. The use of security devices contributes to social separation (Roitman, 2008).

The occupation of the urban land through increasing gated communities characterizes Latin American countries in their globalization process. Within Latin America, Argentina stands out since it concentrates the highest growth of gated communities in the shortest time, as elaborated in the next sections. The late 1990s and early 2000s evidenced a spectacular multiplication of these settlements, especially in large and medium-sized Argentinean cities. Gated communities, considered as a very elitist housing option, became one of the most common housing supplies for affluent and upper middle-class groups, especially in the suburbs of Buenos Aires. They not only increased their target population, but also appeared in central areas of the city in addition to their expansion in the periphery.

Social segregation in the Latin American city

The Latin American city, as known today, appeared when the Hispanic city was created over the capital cities of the ancient civilizations, such as the Incas and Mayas. The Spanish conquerors created the 'Indies Code' (*Leyes de Indias*) in 1573 that gave new cities some design homogeneity distorting local differences. The Spanish strategy consisted of penetrating in a hostile environment to conquer, control and indoctrinate surrounding settlements (Morris, 1979).

The mercantilist and bourgeois pressure fostered economic development as well as social differentiation amongst groups. Cities, despite their political links, had actually increased their autonomy, which was evident throughout the 18th century with the constitution of local bourgeoisies. After independence in the 19th century, Latin American nations tried to differentiate themselves from colonial times. Urban models were imported from France, England and Italy. By the end of that century, cities attained a more cosmopolitan character due to urban transformations. The new image of the city was given by wide avenues and boulevards such as *Paseo de la Reforma* in Mexico, *Paulista* in São Paulo, *Alvear* in Buenos Aires and *Alameda* in Santiago de Chile (Gómez-Ferrer Bayo, 1992). Cities developed as a reflection of the countries that had a political, economic or cultural influence in Latin America. However, as mentioned by Ramón Gutiérrez (1992), this led to the contradiction between the models of those countries that had prosperity and endless progress and the reality of what Latin America was and still is.

The arrival of the railway and public transport, and the creation of new industrial centres, new settlements and new residential areas in the outskirts transformed cities at different times (Gómez-Ferrer Bayo, 1992). At the beginning of the 20th century, affluent families moved from the centre to other areas that became dominated by upper-class residents. Simultaneously, the inner city increasingly hosted poor residents who transformed old mansions and palaces into community homes (*vecindades* or *conventillos*) occupied by migrants from Europe and the countryside (Romero, 2005).

Not only the colonial style and the uniform layout made Latin American cities similar amongst themselves, but also the development of processes that enlarged cities over the 20th century. These processes included industrialization, foreign investments, trade of agricultural goods and the use of technology. The adoption of foreign cultural practices also gave similarity to particular social groups. English-style houses were built in affluent suburbs during the 1940s and Californian-style residences during the 1950s and 1960s (Gilbert, 1994). Social homogeneity, for example, was one of the main reasons for the creation of affluent neighbourhoods in the periphery of Guadalajara during the 1940s and 1950s (Ickx, 2002).

With the demographic explosion of the 1960s, the city was no longer considered by some social groups as a peaceful and placid place. These groups moved from the city centre to suburban areas, which imitated 'garden cities', such as *Ciudad Satélite* or *Lomas de Chapultepec* in Mexico (see Chapter 8), or *Ciudad Kennedy* in Bogotá. Garden cities also proliferated in cities such as São Paulo as a consequence of the new upper class benefiting from industrialization (Geraiges de Lemos et al, 2002). During that time, the wealthier groups of Montevideo moved towards the strip coast in the suburban areas (Alvarez, 2005). In Buenos Aires, affluent families built their secondary residences in gated communities located in the periphery, as explained later, where the practice of sports occupied a central role during weekends.

The development of gated communities in Latin America has been influenced by several drivers. Over the 1950s and 1960s, gated communities in Buenos Aires, for instance, responded to the need of exclusivity and status by affluent groups. Giving protection to particular groups was another reason for building these closed settlements, like the military neighbourhood (*colonia de los militares, Colonia General Arce*) in San Salvador, to protect them from guerrillas (Baires, 2003), and self-sufficient neighbourhoods for the staff of oil companies in Venezuela (Bracho de Machado et al, 2007).

During the 1980s, gated communities developed in Lima as a consequence of terrorism (Plöger, 2006) and due to increasing urban crime in Brazilian cities (Geraiges de Lemos et al, 2002). The expansion of motorways and increasing private transport along with urban insecurity and fear of crime contributed to the development of gated communities in Colombia over the 1990s. According to Ortiz-Gomez (2002), gated communities in Bogotá invest 60 per cent of their annual budgets in the provision of security and the acquisition of security devices.

Socio-economic changes have led to urban transformations in Latin America. In addition, urban societies have experienced increasing social problems related to the retreat of the state from security provision due to scarce resources, as well as the rise of urban crime and fear of crime. Social homogeneity, status, exclusivity, security protection from terrorism and urban crime, along with the development of private infrastructure in peripheral areas have all contributed to the expansion of this type of residential scheme in many Latin American cities, since the 1960s and especially over the 1990s. While in the 1960s and earlier, as in the case of Buenos Aires's country-clubs,[1] these settlements were considered very elitist, since the 1990s they increased their target population and emerged as a residential option for upper middle and sometimes even middle classes.

Gated communities with highly developed security devices have been 'justified' in countries where guerrilla and drug-dealing activities represent serious concerns. However, this type of extremely fortified settlement has been exported to other Latin American countries, insecurity being the most given justification for their development, although there are other relevant reasons, such as achieving a higher social status. In addition, in some countries such as Argentina, gated communities are clear objects of marketing campaigns led by the private sector. There are many unsuccessful projects due to an oversupply that did not consider the residents' needs but followed a process of real estate speculation. La Vacherie, a country club located in Mendoza, is an example of this. It was developed in the richest lands for growing fine grapes for the wine industry. The opening of the plots sale was done in 2000 by Menem, who was the president at that time. The gated community has 454 plots and very impressive sport amenities: two 9-hole golf courses, football pitches, tennis and volleyball courts, a swimming pool and a gym, in addition to a clubhouse with a bar and a restaurant. However, there were only five houses built in 2007 and therefore not all the sport amenities had been completed. This shows the strong influence of the private sector encouraging this type of residential habitat and the weak role of the state in the urban planning process. The private sector invests in the most profitable activities, although this means the destruction of agriculture and a particular industry, while the state allows for the construction of gated communities that will not necessarily have enough demand.

There are no official statistics of gated communities in Latin America since this type of housing has not been especially registered as such in most national censuses. Estimations of their numbers come mainly from field researches and are only for a few cities. Many Mexican cities have lately witnessed a spread of gated communities. In Mexico, there were 20 gated communities (see Figures 7.1 and 7.2) before 1994 in Guadalajara (Cabrales Barajas and Canosa Zamora, 2002), about 12 cases in Toluca and the same in Puebla (Rodríguez Chumillas and Mollá Ruiz-Gómez, 2002). They have since multiplied in most Mexican cities and have appeared as 'the only housing option' in some cities, as Enríquez Acosta (2007) mentioned, as in the case of the cities on the border with the US where this author identified at least 100 gated communities for upper-class and middle-class groups. Mexico City has also witnessed the expansion of closed and private settlements, as explained by Sheinbaum in Chapter 8.

There is no precise data about gated communities in San Salvador, although it is also an increasing phenomenon (Lungo and Baires, 2001). Gated communities are mainly targeted at upper social groups in Colombia and Ecuador. These are located in peripheral areas served by motorways and shopping centres. Borsdorf (2002) identified 27 gated communities in Quito in 2002 and Ortiz-Gomez (2002, p76) mentioned the spread of gated communities in Bogotá as a consequence of 'personal insecurity' and the 'entrepreneurial capacity of private

developers under conditions of market enablement'. There were about 300 gated communities in Lima in 2005 (Plöger, 2006). However, these included neighbourhoods formerly open that were informally closed off due to insecurity. Gated communities do not seem to be so significant in Bolivian cities, although there are a few examples.

The model has spread in Chile. However, gated communities have a smaller scale than gated communities in Mexico or Argentina and residential units are also smaller. Borsdorf and Hidalgo (2004) mention the existence of 763 condominiums of single houses (see Figure 7.3), comprising 17,542 residential units in Santiago de Chile in 2000 and 293 condominiums with a total of 9336 housing units in the Metropolitan Area of Valparaiso in 2007 (Borsdorf et al, 2007). However, not all of these condominiums would fit into the definition of gated communities since some of them could be considered simply as apartment blocks or social housing complexes.

There were ten gated communities in Montevideo in 2003. These residential schemes developed later, in smaller numbers and of smaller sizes than in Buenos Aires or São Paulo (Alvarez, 2005). There are no official estimations of gated communities in Brazil. However, a great number of researches carried out in large and

Figure 7.1 *Gated community in Guadalajara, Mexico*

Source: Sonia Roitman

Figure 7.2 *Gated community under construction in 2003 in Guadalajara, Mexico*

Source: Sonia Roitman

Figure 7.3 *Entrance to a gated community in Santiago de Chile*

Source: Sonia Roitman

medium-sized Brazilian cities (Caldeira, 2000; de Lima Ramirez and Ribeiro Soares, 2002; Geraiges de Lemos et al, 2002; Rodrígues Soares, 2002; Rodrígues, 2006) have emphasized the relevance of this type of residential settlements in the urban landscape.

The first gated communities in Brazil were located in rural areas and surrounded by fences that later became walls. They aimed at living in close contact with nature. Since the 1990s, gated communities have considerably multiplied and, similarly to what happened in other Latin American cities, this was a consequence of increasing urban crime and a solution to fear of crime. They are also related to the need for exclusivity and the predominance of individual values. Affluent residents were the target of these private settlements in their early stages of development, and later the target also included middle-class groups, diversifying the supply. Urban developers took advantage of increasing fear of crime in urban populations, as happened in Bogotá, to promote gated communities as secure places that also confer social status. There are two main types of gated communities in Brazil: condominiums, which are closed schemes with high-rise buildings that have controlled access, communal infrastructure and maintenance fees; and closed settlements of single houses where public streets have been closed off (Rodrígues, 2006). Brazil and Argentina are the countries where the model of gated communities has mostly developed. The following section examines the situation in Argentina.

Gated communities in Argentina

Over the first half of the 20th century there were only a handful of gated communities in Buenos Aires and none in other Argentinean cities. These were mainly related to sport practices and used as secondary residences. There were also a few open neighbourhoods with restricted access such as some military neighbourhoods as well as a few neighbourhoods with security devices for foreign skilled workers – for example, the neighbourhood for German employees working for Quilmes (a beer factory) located next to the industrial site in Buenos Aires Province.

It is only since the 1970s that gated communities began to grow in the Metropolitan Area of Buenos Aires (MABA).[2] During that time and later in the 1990s, Argentina went through processes of economy opening, privatization of public companies and foreign investments attraction. These processes led to changes in the urban landscape with the emergence of new shopping centres, private cemeteries, new motorways and the construction of gated communities, with private security and exclusive services for those who could afford them. At the same time, the remainder of the welfare state disappeared and large population groups lost their social benefits, while the quality of free-access social services such as education and health deteriorated in the extreme. Access to housing also became more restricted, leaving low- and lower middle-class families in precarious housing environmental conditions with overcrowding and substandard quality houses. This created economic growth without human development.

Gated communities created important transformations in the urban dynamic. The flight of affluent families to the periphery means that these areas now have most of the services and infrastructure provided by the city, such as schools, offices, and recreation and commercial areas, and the territory is shared between original (usually poorer) and new residents (usually more affluent). This implies urban sustainability in relation to the services provided and the available infrastructure, as already mentioned. However, socio-economic differences act as barriers to integration and social equality as poor residents cannot access services targeted at middle- or upper-class residents. In this sense, if social interaction is considered as one indicator for community and urban sustainability, this is missing in relation to the expansion of gated communities.[3]

Six types of gated communities can be identified in Argentina. The common features of all these types include a fenced perimeter, private security, restricted access, a code of conduct and shared facilities. These six types are as follows:

1   *Country clubs* (or '*countries*'). These are the oldest type. The first country club appeared during the 1930s in the MABA. Until the 1970s, they were used by the traditional elite as secondary residences. Houses were simple, modest and rustic. They were related to the practice of elitist sports such as golf and polo (with strong European influence); therefore, sport amenities were one of the attractions and extra-value of this type of gated community. Later, the suburban process of the upper classes intensified and houses lost their rustic features and became primary residences with more

comfort influenced by the US suburban model. Since the 1970s this type of residential settlement housed not only the traditional elite, but also a successful group of upper middle-class citizens, mainly business people and professionals, willing to assert their social status through the adoption of the 'country-club lifestyle'. Their surroundings are no longer rural areas, but poor neighbourhoods and security walls and fences in between them. The access to 'countries' has always been very selective.[4]

2 *Private (or closed) neighbourhoods.* These are residential settlements aimed at permanent residences. Their sizes vary, ranging from 1ha to 800ha. Their development occurred later than 'countries', and sport amenities are less important. Security is the main service provided. Plot sizes are smaller than in 'countries', making them more accessible to middle-class groups. Maintenance fees are also lower than in 'countries'.

3 *Garden towers (or vertical countries).* This type of gated community has recently spread as the most popular urban alternative within gated communities. These are residential towers of flats surrounded by green areas, with common amenities such as swimming pools and gyms. They are also fenced and have private security, and are usually located in central areas of the city.

4 *Farm clubs (or chacras)* appeared in the mid-1990s, but have had a restrictive spread. They are located in rural areas, mainly outside the city boundaries. This makes permanent residence difficult, yet gives a certain exclusivity to this type of gated community. They have large plots of over 1ha. Residents who choose this type of residence prefer to live in contact with nature. Due to their isolation from urban areas, they sometimes lack a fenced perimeter and sophisticated security measures, typical of other gated communities. They are aimed at upper-class citizens who can afford to maintain two or more properties.

5 *Nautical clubs (or 'marinas').* These are mainly located by the Río de la Plata, in the MABA, and appeared during the late 1990s. They are similar to 'countries', but with an emphasis on water sports, in addition to attractive landscapes. They can be used as a permanent or secondary residence.

6 *Mega-projects (or private cities)* are planned settlements made up of several gated communities, adding universities, schools, shopping centres, office buildings and health centres to the existing facilities of each settlement. They have had a promising development over recent years. The most famous example of this type is called Nordelta, located in the MABA, and comprises 1000 plots within 1600ha.[5]

The diversity of gated communities shows that they have become a common feature of large and medium-sized cities in Argentina over the last 20 years. Only 1450 families lived in gated communities during 1994 in the MABA and 4000 in 1996 (Svampa, 2001). By 2000 there were 350 gated communities comprising 13,000 houses and 50,000 residents in the MABA, scattered within 300 square kilometres (Thuillier, 2005). Rosario had about ten gated communities by that time (Bragos et al, 2002), while Córdoba had 13 'countries' and several closed neighbourhoods and farm clubs (Valdés, 1999). The Metropolitan Area of Mendoza (MAM) had about 45 gated communities during that time (Roitman, 2006), increasing to 70 in 2007 (Roitman, 2008). The situations of MABA and MAM are further explained in the following sections.

Gated communities in the Metropolitan Area of Buenos Aires (MABA)

Gated communities are not a new phenomenon in the Metropolitan Area of Buenos Aires. 'Countries', as previously explained, have existed since the second half of the 20th century. However, they became more significant over the 1990s when they rapidly expanded, leading to the isolation of some social groups through defensive walls and armed security guards. A brief historical revision identifies how social segregation processes, reflected in the urban segregation of gated community residents, have taken place in the MABA.

Buenos Aires was first founded in 1536 by Spanish conquerors; but this settlement was abandoned in 1541. The second foundation of the city took place in 1580. The city was designed according to the Indies Code and was surrounded by plots of land that could not be sold. These fields, both inside and outside the urban fabric, were distributed amongst the colonial landlords and did not comply with regulations establishing that paths had to be left between each property. This enabled landowners to control the circulation of wealth in the colonial economy by, amongst other things, not allowing the farmers to pass with their crops. There was restricted access to land because its distribution was made on behalf of the king and, consequently, the population was forced to invade fields to farm and build their dwellings. In 1744 there were 186 landlords and 6000 proletarians in Buenos Aires (Romero, 2005).

Buenos Aires had a slow growth until 1855. After that, it increased as a consequence of its integration within the world market. By 1875, about 60,000 people were living in the city and its boundaries had stretched to an area larger than Paris, with more than 1 million residents in 1906 (Romero, 2005). Buenos Aires was one of the most populated urban areas in the world, long before other Latin American cities, including Greater Mexico, Greater São Paulo and Greater Río de Janeiro (Vapñarsky, 2000). At the beginning of the 20th century, when only Greater London and Greater New York exceeded the 4 million inhabitants, Greater Buenos Aires was the largest city in Latin America with 2.5 million inhabitants (INDEC, undated) as a result of migrants coming from Europe and other Argentinean provinces.

Demographic growth increased the urban problems of poor groups, such as access to housing and infrastructure. The impact of the 1929 economic crisis accelerated change. The upper bourgeoisie joined the social consumption ideology, while in the cities, outcast crowds concentrated in *rancheríos* (informal settlements). Suburbs were usually occupied by poor families; yet 'aristocratic' suburbs also emerged in the form of holiday resorts. Different social classes only interacted at the marketplace (Romero, 2005).

The lifestyle of the new bourgeoisie began to change after World War I, while the *belle époque* also glimpsed its end in Latin America. Sport and open-air activities, influenced by the European elite, created a new lifestyle in which housing was related to the practice of sports. Following these ideas, Tortugas Country Club (known as Las Tortugas) was the first gated community built in Buenos Aires. It was created in 1930 surrounding an exclusive polo club, emphasizing its isolation rather than its gating (Verdecchia, 1995).

During the 1960s, the industrialization process led large industries seeking good locations and accessibility to occupy the metropolitan area. The need for a labour force created an internal migratory process from rural to urban areas. Cities could not cope with these new residents and migrants lived in extremely deficient situations, usually in the periphery.

Changes in the pattern of land occupation have accompanied the social polarization process experienced by the Argentinean social structure since the 1990s. Affluent groups have increased their incomes; but they have become smaller, concentrating wealth in the hands of a few citizens. During the 1990s, Argentina received major foreign investments that transformed the urban landscape. Buenos Aires, with more than 11 million inhabitants, attracted real estate products such as gated communities that did not emerge from a population's need, but were promoted as a consumption necessity by marketing operations carried out by the private sector. In 2000, US$4881 million were invested in gated communities, shopping centres and multiplex cinemas in 14 municipalities of the MABA, with more than 20 per cent of their population experiencing substandard living conditions (Vidal-Koppmann, 2008).

During the 1990s and early 2000s, although some upper-class and middle-class families moved to gated communities located in the periphery of Buenos Aires, unlike other cities in Latin America such as Lima, Santiago de Chile or Río de Janeiro, many upper- and middle-class families remained in the city centre. Therefore, the city centre maintained a life standard and an urban quality not common in big Latin American metropolises (Romero, 2005). At the same time, the periphery grew disorderly without clear planning guidelines. The supply of plots in gated communities increased because the target had been expanded to upper middle-class families. While there were about 29,000 plots in the real estate market in 1986, by 2000 the supply exceeded 78,000 in the MABA (Giglio, 2004).

Some of the municipalities of the MABA have considerably changed their urban landscape as a consequence of the expansion of gated communities in their territories – in particular, Pilar and Malvinas Argentinas. Pilar is located to the north-west of Buenos Aires, 58km away from the city centre, and had 226,000 inhabitants in 2001 (INDEC, undated). While in 1980 there were 20 of these settlements in Pilar, this number increased to 30 in 1991 and 115 in 2001 (Libertun de Duren, 2007). This significant number of gated communities brought new services and infrastructure to this municipality, such as shopping centres, office buildings, schools and universities. It also increased the revenues of the local government.

Malvinas Argentinas is another municipality of the MABA, also located to the north, 35km away from the city centre. It was created in 1995 from the division of a major municipality (Municipalidad de General Sarmiento), with over 1 million inhabitants. In 2001, Malvinas Argentinas had 290,000 inhabitants (INDEC, undated) and there were five gated communities. Although the number of gated communities is not large when compared to other municipalities, the relevance of Malvinas Argentinas is considerable since the state has played a significant role in allowing or preventing the building of this type of residential settlement and the closure of streets. This is a highly urbanized suburb and the creation of new gated communities (see Figure 7.4) has meant that these settlements co-exist in the same territory with old 'poor' neighbourhoods; as a result, social differences are more evident. The first gated communities in Malvinas Argentinas (formerly the municipality of General Sarmiento) were built during the 1950s. However, these settlements were initially built as open neighbourhoods with sport amenities (golf courses and rugby fields) in a rural environment, and in the 1990s they closed their perimeters with walls and hired private security guards to patrol the neighbourhoods. These neighbourhoods were created as secondary residences, only becoming primary residences later on.

San Carlos Country (see Figure 7.5) was built in 1956 in a 30ha plot, with sport facilities and 140 houses. The surroundings were rural, with easy access to the Panamericana motorway. Twenty years later this settlement was enlarged by 15ha, and 100 new houses were built. Shortly after, another 10ha were incorporated with a capacity of 70 more housing units, following a very speculative land division. None of these additions incorporated either green or common areas within the settlement. The increase in property values depended on the location. In 1995, when the municipality was created, the new mayor – who is still in office – encouraged the development of new regulations to control the expansion of these closed settlements. In 2007, this gated community was once again enlarged, adding new green areas and reaching a total of 70ha with about 400 houses.

The end of the 1980s saw the development of San Jorge Village (another country club) – the first gated community to be legally approved. It featured 110ha, with rugby fields and 350 houses. It is the most affluent neighbourhood in Malvinas Argentinas and by the time it was occupied, its area was already surrounded by poor neighbourhoods. Over the 1990s, four other gated communities with diverse characteristics were built. Their sizes range from 5ha to 50ha and the number of houses varies between 15 and 450. All of them are located in an urban environment, preferably near the motorway that leads to Buenos Aires City.

Another settlement called the Club Universitario de Buenos Aires (CUBA) was originally built as an open neighbourhood and was later closed off with walls and barriers. It comprises approximately 75ha, with sport facilities and about 500 houses. In 1995 when the municipality of Malvinas Argentinas was created, the new mayor abolished the municipal ordinance that authorized the closure of the settlement, arguing that the closure of the streets halted free circulation in the city. As a consequence, the neighbourhood became involved in a legal conflict that was taken to the national court of law and has not yet been resolved: it cannot be closed, but they are allowed to restrict access with barriers and security guards (see Figure 7.6). However, according to the law, all citizens have the right to access this gated community. This is one of the few cases where the local government has considered the interests of the majority of the population over the interests of a minority group living in this sort of gated community, which contributes to a more sustainable city.

The success of the 'gated communities business' consists of a good marketing operation, the existence of good security devices and a good accessibility to motorways to commute to the city centre. The internal landscape is carefully created and maintained, while the surroundings, which are usually occupied by poor families, decay and become 'remnant areas' (Torres, 1998). There is a remarkable contrast between the inside and the outside image of the gated community that degrades the surrounding environment and makes it less safe. This is part of the strategy of urban developers to promote their businesses and the idea that gated communities are the only residential option in a context of urban insecurity and deep social inequalities. In this context, gated communities appear as opposed to social sustainability since they create more unbalanced social situations where the interests of the few seem to prevail over the interest of the many.

Figure 7.4 *Fences and barriers at the entrance of a gated community in Malvinas Argentinas, Province of Buenos Aires*

Source: Mónica Giglio

Figure 7.5 *Entrance to San Carlos Country Club in Malvinas Argentinas (MABA)*

Source: Mónica Giglio

Figure 7.6 *Club Universitario de Buenos Aires (CUBA) gated community in Malvinas Argentinas (MABA)*

Source: Mónica Giglio

The use and appropriation of land for the construction of gated communities also shows great social inequalities and an unsustainable pattern of land acquisition. These closed settlements require large land extensions for housing, especially for the common infrastructure and amenities that can only be used by their residents. Thus, while the city of Buenos Aires houses 3 million residents in 200 square kilometres, gated communities of MABA occupy a territory equivalent to 50 per cent of the city's extension, with only 5 per cent of its population (Giglio, 2004). This also shows the concentration of wealth and the unequal access to economic, social and territorial resources.

This section has illustrated how the pattern of social segregation in the Metropolitan Area of Buenos Aires has spread with the development of gated communities. The latter appear as obstructing social sustainability: instead of supporting a more inclusive city, they respond to the interests of either the private sector or the privileged social groups who have managed to survive the economic and social crises faced by Argentina over the last decades. There are only a few cases where the government has taken a proactive role

opposed to gated communities or to its limitless growth without considering the interest of the whole social structure. This pattern of social differences in the urban landscape has also been replicated in Mendoza.

Gated communities in the Metropolitan Area of Mendoza (MAM)

In a similar fashion to Buenos Aires, the city of Mendoza has been a segregated city since its foundation by Spanish conquerors in 1561. It was one of the first Spanish settlements in the territory of what is now Argentina, but belonged to the *Reino de Chile* (Chilean Reign) until 1776, when the *Virreinato del Río de la Plata* (Río de la Plata sub-reign) was created, becoming part of it. The city followed a colonial urban grid, with most buildings and houses built around a main square.

Since 1776 the city has been strongly linked to Buenos Aires and has been the most important city in the road from Chile to the port of Buenos Aires. During the 18th century, there was a powerful bourgeoisie that managed agricultural activities, which were the core of the economy. The city was also favoured by commerce due to its location.

In 1861, 300 years after its foundation, an earthquake destroyed most of the city, killing 70 per cent of its population (Ponte, 1999). As a consequence, the city government was moved towards the south-west of the main square, and so did the affluent families. The 'new town' was created following a reticular layout around a new main square and the most affluent families built their houses around it. This new town rapidly gained water access and a sewage system, in addition to trees along the streets. Conversely, poor families were left in the debris and derelict 'old town' since they lacked the economic resources to build new houses in the 'new town'. Old and new towns were separated by San Martín Street, which became a successful commercial and social road serving both populations and working as a hinge. San Martín Street is still the main commercial road and crosses the Metropolitan Area of Mendoza (MAM)[6] from north to south.

The legacy of the earthquake was a divided city. The 'old town' became the poor district, with no water and sewage system and no trees, and debris accumulated for more than 20 years. This contributed to the poor health conditions of its population. Conversely, the 'new town' featured tree-lined squares, groves and boulevards, in addition to water access and a sewage system, and concentrated the affluent population and its government buildings. The media of the time highlighted the desire of affluent citizens to live away from poor residents who were excluded from the benefits of modernization such as access to services and better living conditions (Ponte, 1999).

The railway arrived in Mendoza in 1885. This brought European migrants and the expansion of the wine industry, which would later become the main economic activity. During the beginning of the 20th century, the western side of the 'new town' was developed, featuring top-quality houses for aristocratic families and a large public park designed by a French architect. This new residential area was served by public transport (trams) to increase house and land values, not to provide the service to a needy population (Ponte, 1999).

The growth of the city has followed a pattern of social differentiation. Although there are some mixed areas, there are also clearly delimited boundaries according to different socio-economic groups. The city centre and most of the municipality of Capital have been one of the most affluent, while Las Heras is the most deprived municipality of the MAM.

During the 20th century, affluent families were located in the city centre and the western side of the municipality of Capital. Later, during the 1970s, the suburb of Chacras de Coria was developed with affluent weekend houses. This area has been extended to its neighbouring district, Vistalba, both located in the municipality of Luján de Cuyo, which became part of the MAM in the early 1970s. Many families turned their weekend houses into primary residences over the 1990s due to a lack of economic resources to maintain two houses and to the desire to move away from the city centre to greener areas. As a consequence, real estate experienced a boost in Chacras de Coria, which is now one of the most affluent areas and concentrates a large number of gated communities.

The 'boom' of gated communities in the MAM occurred later than in the MABA. It was influenced by an increase of real estate credits for upper middle-class families, private investments in the real estate industry, and the search for more comfortable and spacious houses with a greener environment, a trend emanating from Buenos Aires and the US. Gated communities and investments in 'urban artefacts', such as shopping malls, multiplex cinemas, mega-stores and motorways, have changed the urban landscape of Mendoza over the last 20 years.

In 2007 there were more than 70 gated communities in the MAM (Roitman, 2008) (see Figure 7.7). The oldest settlement called *Dalvian* was built in 1976. The typology of gated communities in Argentina can be also applied to the MAM. The most common type is the closed neighbourhood; however, features vary according to plot size, the number of houses, the sophistication of security devices, management of the settlement and inside amenities. There are three country clubs (see Figure 7.8) that have important sport facilities (i.e. golf course, a polo course and a rugby field). There is only one vertical 'country' and one farm club. But more of these two types are under development, along with two mega-projects. No marinas have yet been developed, and there is no data on the number of residents living in gated communities. Residents are mainly middle upper-class and upper-class successful professionals working in the private sector in managerial positions. They are in their 30s and 40s and are mostly married with children.

Figure 7.7 *Houses in a gated community in Mendoza, Argentina*

Source: Sonia Roitman

Figure 7.8 *Entrance to a gated community in Mendoza, Argentina*

Source: Sonia Roitman

There is no legislation on gated communities at the provincial level in Mendoza. As a result, local governments issue their own regulations to rule the expansion of these closed settlements. This creates an array of different situations regarding how projects are treated according to each municipality. In addition to this, the local government usually faces three situations. First, it wants to attract investors and affluent taxpayers; therefore, gated communities appear as convenient projects to be encouraged in the territory. Second, and opposing the previous advantage, the local government is aware of some of the impacts of gated communities upon the built environment and the social fabric. Third, while some local governments have

a clear policy towards gated communities, the majority do not and this creates arbitrary decisions on whether to pass gated community projects or not. Many projects are approved after construction has begun, highlighting the different working times of local governments and private investors.

Gated communities usually improve the quality of the area in which they are located, attracting new investments on services and infrastructure and transforming neglected areas into strategic and highly valued spaces. Nevertheless, as in Buenos Aires, gated communities in Mendoza do not encourage urban social sustainability. There are four main reasons for this. First, gated communities are usually located in the peripheries where land is available at affordable prices, although this does not imply social interaction with the original residents of the periphery. On the contrary, the security devices used seem to make social differences more evident in these areas. Second, these settlements contribute to a very unbalanced appropriation of land as they require large extensions of land, while other residents cannot have access to this since they cannot afford it. Third, there is also an unequal access to services and infrastructure between gated community residents and non-residents. The latter are not allowed to use the inside amenities of these residential compounds and cannot afford most of the services located in the surrounding areas, which are particularly targeted at gated community residents. Finally, people living in gated communities do not usually become involved in the activities and events of their local areas. This does not favour social interaction between original and new residents.

Conclusions

This chapter has examined the evolution of the Latin American cities over the last centuries, focusing on processes of social segregation. The affluent and upper middle-class groups have always located in the best city areas, either in the city centre or the periphery. Over the past years, they have tried to distance themselves from city 'problems' such as epidemics, noise and waste contamination, or even traffic.

However, this flight to the suburbs is associated with the existence of good-quality services and infrastructure in this area that satisfy the needs and demands of these new residents. Motorways are one of these elements that are indispensable for everyday commuting to the centre by private transport since public transport is considered inefficient and uncomfortable. With some exceptions, these social groups have largely moved to the periphery in an attempt not only to avoid the city centre and to be in contact with nature, but also to avoid contact with some social groups and in order to claim social distinction. Gated communities are considered one of today's most relevant artefacts that highlight social segregation in the urban fabric. However, segregation is not new and has always been a central element in the historic development of Latin American cities.

The expansion of gated communities over fertile lands, as well as the growth of the urban fabric, in general, contributes to an unsustainable urban pattern that demands larger and costly networks of services and infrastructure to serve these new urban areas. This flight to the periphery also undermines protection of the environment and negatively contributes to climate change as a result of expanding motorways and the intensive use of private transport. In addition, gated communities oppose social sustainability as they do not encourage social interaction and integration between different social groups living inside and outside the walls of these protected residential settlements.

Despite these pitfalls, gated communities are likely to continue to develop; therefore, it should be the role of the state to find solutions to compensate for this trend with the aim of a more inclusive city. This trend will only be changed if society, as a whole, and especially governments and policy-makers become aware of its social, environmental and economic unsustainability.

Notes

1   Country clubs, or 'countries', are one type of gated community in Argentina and Mexico that feature important sports facilities, as is explained later in this chapter.
2   The Metropolitan Area of Buenos Aires (MABA) is formed by the Gobierno Autónomo de la Ciudad de Buenos Aires (Buenos Aires City) and 24 municipalities from Buenos Aires Province.
3   See Roitman (2008) for an analysis of the relationships between residents living inside and outside gated communities.
4   See Svampa (2001) and Rojas (2007) for more detail on this selection process.
5   For more information on this private city, see www.nordelta.com. Janoschka (2003) and Rojas (2007) have also analysed this case.
6   MAM is made up of six municipalities: Capital, Godoy Cruz, Las Heras, Guaymallén, Maipú and Luján de Cuyo. It had around 1 million inhabitants in 2001.

References

Alvarez, M. J. (2005) *Golden Ghettoes: Golden Communities and Class Residential Segregation in Montevideo, Uruguay*, Report no 02/2005, Research and Training Network, Urban Europe

Baires, S. (2003) *La Nueva Segregación Urbana en América Latina: Los barrios cerrados en el Area Metropolitana de San Salvador, El Salvador*, Universidad Centroamericana José Simeón Cañas, San Salvador, El Salvador

Borsdorf, A. (2002) 'Barrios cerrados en Santiago de Chile, Quito y Lima: tendencias de la segregación socio-espacial en capitales andinas', in Cabrales Barajas, L. F. (ed) *Latinoamérica: Países Abiertos, Ciudades Cerradas*, Universidad de Guadalajara–UNESCO, Guadalajara, Mexico, pp581–610

Borsdorf, A. and Hidalgo, D. R. (2004) 'Formas Tempranas de Exclusión Residencial y el Modelo de la Ciudad Cerrada en América Latina. El caso de Santiago', *Revista de Geografía Norte Grande*, vol 32, December, pp21–37

Borsdorf, A., Hidalgo, D. R. and Sánchez, R. (2007) 'A new model of urban development in Latin America: The gated communities and fenced cities in the Metropolitan Areas of Santiago de Chile and Valparaíso', *Cities*, vol 24, no 5, pp365–378

Bracho de Machado, D., Faría Larrazábal, C. and Paredes de López, M. (2007) 'Dos realidades: Dos maneras de habitar conviven hoy en la ciudad', *Revista INVI*, vol 22, no 60, pp37–58

Bragos, O., Mateos, A. and Pontoni, S. (2002) 'Nuevos desarrollos residenciales y procesos de segregación socio-espacial en la expansión oeste de Rosario', in Cabrales Barajas, L. F. (ed) *Latinoamérica: Países Abiertos, Ciudades Cerradas*, Universidad de Guadalajara–UNESCO, Guadalajara, Mexico, pp441–480

Cabrales Barajas, L. F. and Canosa Zamora, E. (2002) 'Nuevas formas y viejos valores: urbanizaciones cerradas de lujo en Guadalajara', in Cabrales Barajas, L. F. (ed) *Latinoamérica: Países Abiertos, Ciudades Cerradas*, Universidad de Guadalajara–UNESCO, Guadalajara, Mexico, pp93–116

Caldeira, T. P. D. R. (2000) *City of Walls: Crime, Segregation and Citizenship in São Paulo*, University of California Press, California

de Lima Ramirez, J. C. and Ribeiro Soares, B. (2002) 'Os condomínios horizontais fechados em cidades médias brasileiras', in Cabrales Barajas, L. F. (ed) *Latinoamérica: Países Abiertos, Ciudades Cerradas*, Universidad de Guadalajara–UNESCO, Guadalajara, Mexico *Latinoamérica: países abiertos, ciudades cerradas*, pp373–396

Enríquez Acosta, J. A. (2007) 'Ciudades de muros. Los fraccionamientos cerrados en la frontera noroeste de México', *Scripta Nova*, vol XI, no 230

Fishman, R. (2003) *Global Suburbs, Urban and Regional Research Collaborative*, 03-01, Working Paper Series, University of Michigan, Michigan

Geraiges de Lemos, A. I., Capuano Scarlato, F. and Pérez Machado, R. P. (2002) 'O retorno à cidade medieval: Os condomínios fechados da metrópole paulista', in Cabrales Barajas, L. F. (ed) *Latinoamérica: Países Abiertos, Ciudades Cerradas*, Universidad de Guadalajara–UNESCO, Guadalajara, Mexico, pp217–235

Giglio, M. A. (2004) *Bases Para la Construcción de Una Normativa Urbanística en la Región Metropolitana del Gran Buenos Aires*, PhD thesis, Universidad Politécnica de Madrid, Madrid

Gilbert, A. (1994) *The Latin American City*, Latin American Bureau, London

Gómez-Ferrer Bayo, A. (1992) 'La ciudad iberoamericana: Una encrucijada de nostalgias, una identidad perseguida', in Generalitat Valenciana (ed) *La Ciudad Iberoamericana*, Generalitat Valenciana, Valencia, Spain

Gutiérrez, R. (1992) 'La ciudad iberoamericana: La búsqueda de una modernidad apropiada', in AAVV (ed) *La Ciudad Iberoamericana*, Generalitat Valenciana, Valencia, Spain

Ickx, W. (2002) 'Los fraccionamientos cerrados en la Zona Metropolitana de Guadalajara', in Cabrales Barajas, L. F. (ed) *Latinoamérica: Países Abiertos, Ciudades Cerradas*, Universidad de Guadalajara–UNESCO, Guadalajara, Mexico, pp117–141

INDEC (Instituto Nacional de Estadísticas y Censos) (undated) *Argentina*, www.indec.gov.ar

Janoschka, M. (2003) 'Nordelta – Ciudad Cerrada. El análisis de un nuevo estilo de vida en el Gran Buenos Aires', Paper presented at the V Coloquio Internacional de Geocrítica: La vivienda y la construcción del espacio social de la ciudad, Barcelona, 26–30 May 2003

Libertun de Duren, N. R. (2007) 'Gated communities as a municipal development strategy', *Housing Policy Debate*, vol 18, no 3, pp607–626

Lungo, M. and Baires, S. (2001) 'Socio-spatial segregation and urban land regulation in Latin American cities', Paper presented at the International Seminar on Segregation in the City Lincoln Institute of Land Policy, Cambridge, MA, US, 25–28 July 2001

Morris, A. E. J. (1979) *Historia de la forma urbana: Desde sus orígenes hasta la revolución industrial*, 6th edition, Gustavo Gigli S. A., Barcelona

Ortiz-Gomez, A. (2002) 'Urban planning and the rationale of the market: The elimination of the intermediate urban level in Bogotá', in Zeter, R. and White, R. (eds) *Planning in Cities: Sustainability and Growth in the Developing World*, ITDG, London, pp71–92

Plöger, J. (2006) 'Practices of socio-spatial control in the marginal neighbourhoods of Lima, Perú', *Trialog*, vol 89, no 2, pp32–36

Ponte, J. R. (1999) *La Fragilidad de la Memoria: Representaciones, prensa y poder de una ciudad latinoamericana en tiempos del modernismo. Mendoza, 1885/1910*, Ediciones Fundación CRICYT, Mendoza

Rodrígues, S. (2006) *Loteamentos fechados e condomínios residenciais em São José do Rio Preto*, Pontificia Universidade Católica de Campinas, Campinas, Brazil

Rodrígues Soares, P. R. (2002) 'Fragmentación y segregación espacial en ciudades no metropolitanas: Las periferias urbanas del sur de Brasil', in Cabrales Barajas, L. F. (ed) *Latinoamérica: Países Abiertos, Ciudades Cerradas*,

Universidad de Guadalajara–UNESCO, Guadalajara, Mexico, pp549–580

Rodríguez Chumillas, I. and Mollá Ruiz-Gómez, M. (2002) 'Urbanizaciones cerradas en Puebla y Toluca', in Cabrales Barajas, L. F. (ed) *Latinoamérica: Países Abiertos, Ciudades Cerradas*, Universidad de Guadalajara–UNESCO, Guadalajara, Mexico, pp511–548

Roitman, S. (2006) 'Who segregates whom? The analysis of a gated community in Mendoza, Argentina', in Atkinson, R. and Blandy, S. (eds) *Gated Communities*, Routledge, Abingdon, UK, pp112–130

Roitman, S. (2008) *Urban Social Group Segregation: A Gated Community in Mendoza, Argentina*, PhD thesis, University College London, London

Rojas, P. (2007) *Mundo Privado: Historias de vida en countries, barrios y ciudades cerradas'*, Crónicas Planeta/Seix Barral, Buenos Aires, Argentina

Romero, J. L. (2005) *Latinoamérica: Las ciudades y las ideas*, 2nd edition, Siglo XXI, Buenos Aires, Argentina

Svampa, M. (2001) *Los que ganaron: La vida en los countries y barrios privados'*, Biblos, Buenos Aires, Argentina

Thuillier, G. (2005) 'Gated communities in the Metropolitan Area of Buenos Aires, Argentina: A challenge for town planning', *Housing Studies*, vol 20, no 2, pp255–271

Torres, H. (1998) 'Procesos recientes de fragmentación socioespacial en Buenos Aires: La suburbanización de las élites', Paper presented at the Seminario de Investigación Urbana 'El nuevo milenio y lo urbano', Instituto Gino Germani, UBA, November 1998

Valdés, E. (1999) 'La ciudad dual y los nuevos fragmentos urbanos: Los guetos de la riqueza', *Administración Pública y Sociedad*, vol 12, pp21–37

Vapñarsky, C. (2000) *La Aglomeración Gran Buenos Aires*, EUDEBA, Buenos Aires, Argentina

Verdecchia, C. R. (1995) 'Los Clubes de Campo', *Revista Arquis*, vol 5, pp26–28

Vidal-Koppmann, S. (2008). 'Mutaciones metropolitanas: De la construcción de barrios cerrados a la creación de ciudades privadas: Balance de una década de urbanización privada en la región metropolitana de Buenos Aires', *Scripta Nova*, vol XII, no 270

8

Gated Communities in Mexico City: A Historical Perspective[1]

Diana Sheinbaum

Introduction

This chapter looks at gated communities from a historical perspective. Its main objective is to go beyond the case study and offer a broader understanding of the development of segregation and privatization of public space in Mexico City. The history of this city suggests that fortified enclaves have existed since the first colonial urban grid was laid out. The chapter explores the historical forms of urban space production that have given place to different physical expressions of segregation in Mexico City. Finally, this study will try to answer whether contemporary gated developments constitute an expression of new patterns of urban segregation or, rather, are part of an ongoing historical process that reinforces existing urban and social inequalities, which have challenged the viability of creating a sustainable city.

Among academics, there is widespread acknowledgement that gated communities are a global phenomenon. Commonly defined as 'residential areas with restrictive entrances in which, normally, public spaces have been privatized' (Blakely and Snyder, 1997, p2), this type of housing development constitutes part of the contemporary urban landscape of many cities around the globe, and Mexico is no exception. The walls and fences, which characterized the physical dimension of gated communities, are more than ever present in the capital of this country. In wealthy and poor neighbourhoods, in the city and the suburbs, they are a prominent feature of what has been called a 'security-obsessed' urbanism (Peyroux, 2004).

The growing literature on this subject shows that gated projects have drawn attention from different disciplines. Anthropologists and sociologists, using oral testimonials, have examined the motivations, fears, desires and expectations that lie behind the decision to live in private enclaves (Svampa, 2001; Giglia, 2002; Low, 2004). Other scholars have concentrated on gated communities' governance and legal aspects, trying to understand the implications of the private provision of traditionally public goods and services (McKenzie, 1994; Chen and Webster, 2006; Blandy et al, 2006). Furthermore, some have explored the effects that enclosing neighbourhoods have had on property values and many others have examined their impact upon social dynamics such as integration and exclusion (Perfiles Latinoamericanos, 2001; Sabatini et al, 2001; Roitman, 2005; Le Goix, 2007).[2]

In any case, most scholars agree that 'enclosed communities are by no means new, nor are they the product of universal principles or circumstances' (Grant and Rosen, 2007). On the contrary, their characteristics and implications for space and society differ according to historical and cultural contexts.

Analysing gated communities from a historical perspective allows us to 'move beyond a focus of understanding basic causal relationships to understanding patterns and, ultimately, principles' (Landman, 2004). Therefore, the main objective of this chapter is to surpass the case study and to offer a broader perspective on the development of different forms of voluntary segregation in Mexico City. Although the proliferation of gated communities is typically linked to the transformations that took place after the implementation of neo-liberal policies in the 1980s, the history of the city suggests that fortified enclaves for the affluent classes have existed ever since the first colonial urban grid was laid out (Ayala, 1996).

As such, this chapter will attempt to provide an understanding of how gated housing has evolved from colonial times to the 21st century. Moving briskly through five centuries of history, from the founding of the city by Hernán Cortés and the construction of the first fortress houses to modern-day gated communities, we will try to show that self-segregation constitutes an integral part of Mexico City's urban structure. Historically, the city has been planned to satisfy the caprice of the most affluent groups over the needs of the many. The uneven distribution of goods and services, and the conflicts between social groups concerning the uses and modes of appropriation of urban space result in the lack of a sustainable model of development.

While we recognize the limitations of such a broad historical journey in which we must, undoubtedly, sacrifice depth into each of the historical periods under analysis, we consider this investigation important because it sheds light on the similarities and differences among new and old forms of residential arrangements and, in doing so, allows us to understand whether contemporary gated developments constitute an expression of new patterns of urban segregation or are part of an ongoing historical process that reinforces and consolidates existing urban and social inequalities.

The new city and its fortified enclaves

In 1521 when Hernán Cortés decided to build the capital of New Spain, he requested Alonso García Bravo and a group of specially trained men to design its urban grid. The new city, constructed over the vestiges of the conquered Tenochtitlan, ancient capital of the Mexica Empire, incorporated straight streets disposed at regular intervals in a large chequerboard configuration that acted as an extended centre.[3] Like many other Latin American towns, this area was reserved for the Spaniards and constituted what was considered as the city (see Chapter 7 in this volume; Sanchez de Carmona, 1989, p67).

The vast outskirts surrounding this area, which served as a reservoir of native inhabitants, were formed by four districts that corresponded to the former *calpullis* of the Indians: Zoquipan, Moyotlán, Cuepopan and Atzacualco.[4] After the conquest, these pre-Hispanic religious and territorial divisions were maintained; but catholic parishes and names were added: San Pablo, San Juan, Santa María la Redonda and San Sebastián, respectively.

This partition into two different residential areas demonstrates the policy of ethnic segregation that the conquerors imposed as early as the 16th century (O'Gorman, 1998). Spatial division was further reinforced by a political and judicial division into two 'republics', each with different laws, tribunals and civil and ecclesiastical authorities. The resulting juxtaposition in one territory of two different ethnic and legal spaces, the Spanish Republic located on the central grid and the Indian Republic situated on the outskirts, illustrates the extent to which socio-spatial segregation was part of the urban structure since its conception (Rubial, 1998). The severe spatial and political separation was additionally strengthened by disparities regarding architecture and infrastructure (Valero de García, 1991). While in the Indian quarters the casual dense agglomerations of adobe and cane-stalk huts were dispersed haphazardly on large tracts of land, the area reserved for the Spaniards received stunning buildings distributed systematically around large squares (Moreno Toscano, 1981, p347).

The first residential constructions built in Mexico City by the conquerors were fortress-like houses (see Figure 8.1). Its severe fortified look reflects the first settlers' fear of retribution after their victory over a powerful empire. In other words, their design was a response to the threat posed by Indian uprisings (Ayala, 1996).

In this sense, it can be said that the transformations of urban space during the first years of colonization reveal a process by which the Spaniards tried to insulate themselves from the natives by erecting physical and social boundaries. In this early stage, spatial segregation, indeed, responded to the dangers posed by a recently conquered empire. Yet, it is also true that it echoed a particular way of thinking closely linked to a culture in which racial distinctions and 'purity of blood' represented important aspects.

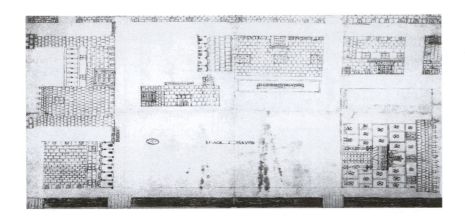

Figure 8.1 *Plaza Mayor de México*, circa *1562–1566. This image represents the central square of the city and the surrounding buildings with their fortified appearance*

Source: Lombardo de Ruiz (1996)

Opening windows and erecting spiritual walls

By the end of the 16th century the city had experienced important transformations. First, the devastation of the indigenous populations by diseases altered the built environment because the threat of being attacked disappeared. As a result, the fortified style of the first houses gave way to a more ornamental design.

Second, the arrival of different mendicant orders to New Spain and their significant role, both spiritual and secular, modified the urban landscape as the erection of physical walls was incompatible with the humanistic principles of Catholicism:

> As the Spaniards conceived it, America was to be a world without walls, a continent whose urban defences were to be less material than metaphysical, or to borrow a phrase from a 17th-century Mexican author, as spiritual walls. (Kagan, 2000, p119)

Along with the construction of elaborate churches, chapels, convents, palatial mansions and colleges that changed the physical aspect of the city came new ways of using public and private spaces. Soon, the original ethnic division between European and indigenous residential areas began to collapse as both groups invaded each other's boundaries. On the one hand, many of the second and third generations of Spaniards who arrived in Mexico City lacked the financial means of their predecessors and were forced to settle in the Indian quarters. On the other hand, a large number of natives began to inhabit the inner city because wealthier families increasingly required domestic labour. Moreover, the rapid growth of *mestizos* and the massive arrival of slaves from Africa and the Philippines created a multi-ethnic society that challenged

the spatial segregation the conquerors had tried to establish (González, 1993, p243).

During this period, the streets and plazas became the scene for intense cultural and social exchanges that characterized Mexican *mestizo* society. During the 17th century, civil and religious festivals were a defining feature of life in the capital. The largest of these events, sponsored by the Crown and the Church, were crucial means of embodying political and religious power. The victorious entrance of a new viceroy, or archbishop, the celebration of royal weddings and baptisms, and the religious festival of Corpus Christi, among many other public spectacles, functioned, from the authorities' perspective, as a way of maintaining the status quo and consolidating their hegemony.

In such special occasions, the guilds, religious orders, government employees, nobles, Indians and casts occupied a precise place, which accounted for their standing within the proper social hierarchy. For the elite, ceremonies and processions provided an opportunity to reiterate the values and norms on which their authority rested. However, from the popular classes' perspective, these festivities afforded a space for gluttony, lust and drunkenness in which routine and control gave way to excess and revelry. In this sense, public spectacles had different meanings to different participants; but, in any case, they constituted a unique tradition in which the barriers that defined the social hierarchy and symbolically weakened and separate groups came together to form a larger collective (Beezley et al, 1994).

A painting by Cristobal de Villalpando dating from 1695 shows the human dimension of the colonial plaza as a symbol of the urban crucible where all castes and social classes mixed: Spaniards, creoles, half-castes, Indians, blacks, and all the possible combinations in between are there (Monnet, 2006) (see Figure 8.2).

Figure 8.2 *Cristobal de Villalpando, Vista de la Plaza Mayor, 1695. Through this panoramic view of the central square it is possible to imagine the hectic life of Mexico City. The plaza and the streets were the stage where different social groups interacted: the nobility in elegant carriages mingling with half-naked Indians.*

Source: Lombardo de Ruiz (1996)

The city's openness certainly surprised Thomas Gage, an English traveller who was in Mexico in 1623. His diary reads: all arms are forgotten, and the Spaniards live so secure from enemies that there is neither gate, wall, bulwark, platform, tower, armoury, ammunition [nor] ordinance to secure and defend the city from domestic or foreign enemy. (Kagan, 2000, p130)

The flourishing social life found on the streets had its counterpart in the architecture of private dwellings. Renouncing the military style, the baroque residences of this period expressed the desire to establish a connection with the public space. With a façade littered with windows and balconies facing the street and built around a central quadrangular patio, this residential scheme very much favoured social interaction. The central patio itself became an increasingly important part of domestic life where many of the principal activities took place and where both labourers and their employees mingled.

In other words, during the 17th century, the houses of the affluent classes constituted spaces that reinforced the processes of syncretism and spatial proximity between different social classes.

Law and control: Strengthening social boundaries

The ascendance of the Bourbons to the Spanish throne in 1700 brought new changes. The programme of reforms that was implemented sought to increase the political and economic control of the monarchy over its colonies and at the same time to reduce the privileges that the Church, the mendicant orders and other corporations had accumulated over the years. In other words, its main objective was to weaken the local and regional networks of power, interests and influences.

As part of this initiative, laws prohibiting the foundation of convents were enacted. A 1734 decree established that for a period of ten years the mendicant orders were not allowed to admit new members. Three decades later, Jesuits were expelled from the territory and soon an edict was passed to weaken the economic assets of the Church (Florescando and Gil, 1981).

Along with these reforms came regulations concerning the order and control of the city. The general objective was to modernize and beautify urban space by improving its infrastructure. This included widening the streets, reorganizing civil and ecclesiastical jurisdictions, installing street lighting, and improving the cleanliness of the city, among others.

The multiplication of decrees and ordinances also attempt to prohibit certain popular diversions such as bull fighting, public inebriation, street performances and gambling. The idea behind these initiatives was that by controlling the errant behaviour of the masses, law and order could be enforced. As a result, festivities were brought into the private sphere, into houses and patios (Fernández, 1992, p60):

> Horrified by what colonial authorities and elites perceived to be the degeneration in the customs of the common people, the latter became the focus of reforms designed to reclaim the streets from the disorderly rabble and replace unwieldy baroque sensibilities with new (bourgeois) values that stressed moderation. (Deans-Smith, 2001)

Bourbons changed the character of New Spain's capital by implementing policies that sought to strengthen social divisions. From a culture in which ceremony and diversion helped to establish the hierarchical nature of society, the new conception of space once again worked to separate the elite from the masses:

> Instead of Baroque inclusiveness, the Bourbons Gallicized the culture of the elite and denigrated that of the masses. Against a backdrop of the growth of Enlightened despotism and Enlightened intolerance, government officials, purveyors of elitist ideas of rationalism, order and the new decorum, showed themselves committed to stamping out traditional social practices. (Socolow, 2000)

While Bourbon administrators did not succeed in eradicating the popular traditions that their enlightened mindset found so distasteful, Viqueira argues that the latter half of the 18th century can be seen as an indication of the new spatial order to come, in which the activities of the upper and lower classes would become segregated and the former sociability among different social groups end (Viqueira, 1987).

This turnabout brought with it alterations in residential architecture as well. The colonial aristocracy that used to build magnificent baroque residences as symbols of prestige and nobility was soon demanding modifications in order to fulfil new requirements of intimacy and privacy (Ayala, 1996, pp63–64). Although the central-patio residential scheme was still current, the

Enlightenment introduced changes in the use and distribution of spaces inside the house and also in the way in which its inhabitants socialized (Jaiven, 2003). The idea of a nuclear family, perfectly distinguishable, gained strength during this period and led to an increased importance in intimate spaces designed for private use. As such, the functional ambiguity of some areas, which was a characteristic feature of past centuries, experienced a process of specialization. For example, kitchens lost their meaning as places where social interaction occurred and transitioned into purely functional spaces. In substitution, dining rooms, specifically reserved for the family, emerged (Ortiz, 1994).

Furthermore, the affluent began to feel the need for new forms of domestic life that would strengthen the boundaries between social classes. This probably explains why Japanese folding screens became popular among the Spanish and Creole elite of New Spain. Besides their decorative functions, they were mainly used to divide space and to distinguish between the public and private spheres inside the houses.

Another important transformation targeted economic activities that took place in the mansions. While in the 17th century the ground floors of colonial palaces were used as stores, workshops, warehouses or other commercial spaces, the end of the 18th century saw a zoning process which relocated these establishments to other parts of the city (Loreto López, 2001)

In sum, Bourbon reforms reinforced social and physical barriers within society. Rather than expanding the benefits of urban modernization to all social strata, these ordinances and decrees constituted a systematic policy of socio-spatial segregation, which entailed an unequal distribution of services and resources along socio-economic lines.

Order and progress: Segregation by class

In the years that followed Mexico's independence from Spain and throughout the next half of the 19th century, the city remained virtually unchanged, particularly regarding its extension. Nevertheless, by 1859 the application of the Liberals' *Reforma* laws allowed the nationalization and later privatization of ecclesiastical and Indians' communal lands, making possible the development of a rapidly expanding real estate market, which promoted as never before urban expansion and growth.[5]

Figure 8.3 *New neighbourhoods of the elite, 19th century. The photograph shows the mansions that were built using different European styles during the Porfirian regime.*

Source: Ayala (1996)

However, it was mainly during Porfirio Díaz's regime, from 1876 until 1910, when the city oversaw a renaissance in terms of economic stability and prosperity, reflected in the proliferation of a large number of new neighbourhoods, many developed on lands previously confiscated from the Church (Hernández, 1981). At first, the growth was internal and focused primarily on the demolition and rebuilding of former Church property; but a second wave, after 1880, took place beyond the city's limits, pushing outward and westward where rural lands were transformed into residential plots (Lear, 1996, pp454–492).

Díaz's government embarked on a programme of modernization, attempting to bridge the gap between Mexico and other more developed nations. It established a stable environment that attracted foreign capital investment at a time when US and European governments, banks, and corporations were eager to expand their worldwide holdings:

> In this period of dependent capitalism, the Mexican government granted numerous concessions to encourage industrialization and to shift the national economy away from its agricultural base. The combination of peace, growing mineral exploitation, industrial development, the beginnings of a national railroad system, and rising exports and imports led to a predictably sharp boost to urbanization. (Kemper and Royce, 1979, pp267–289).

The economic modernization and the improvement of the communication network transformed the city into a magnet for migrant workers. From 1858 to 1910, the population increased from 200,000 to more than 470,000 inhabitants, and the city grew from 8.5 to 40.5 square kilometres (Morales, 1978).

As demand for urban land increased, private developers who had purchased vast plots from the government flourished. Unfortunately, the economic elite who willed, financed and profited from the transformation of Mexico City was limited to a small group of powerful merchant financers. Primarily European and American born, they controlled much of the industry, commerce and real estate of Mexico City and they created a type of oligopoly supported by the political elite that allowed them to control the urbanization process according to their best interests (Jiménez, 1993; Lear, 1996).

The new neighbourhoods, known as *colonias*, were designed to accommodate different sectors of society. In this period, the aristocracy struggled to prove their wealth by moving away from the traditional multiclass downtown to the western periphery of the city, primarily to the area bordering the new grandiose avenue Paseo de la Reforma, inspired by the French Champs-Elysées. The *Juárez* and *Roma* neighbourhoods were the best examples of this opulence, where vast mansions in different European styles flanked wide avenues (Hernández, 1981; De Gortari, 1987) (see Figure 8.3). As explained in Chapter 7, by the beginning of the 20th century, Latin American cities developed as a reflection of countries that had a political, economic or cultural influence in this region.

Affluent groups decided to abandon the city centre because the demographic growth caused by massive migration from the countryside intensified the already serious problems regarding public health and sanitation. Getting away from diseases was an important concern for the Porfirian aristocracy (Agostini, 2003). On the other hand, there was an explicit desire to leave behind former lifestyles and imitate the customs and habits of European, and particularly French, bourgeoisie, which was considered an archetype of refinement and good taste.

The greatest contrast with the old city centre was in residential architecture. The new mansions were quite different from the former traditional patio configurations. Fenced-in houses were moved away from the street fronts and adjoining boundaries, providing families with one further degree of separation from the crowded buildings and neighbourhoods, as well as from the sociability of streets and sidewalks.

The differences between rich and poor neighbourhoods grew deeper as the government provided services and urban infrastructure to those who could afford the costs. This condition of serving primarily those areas of greatest visibility and tax revenue led to a pattern of great inequality between the 'modern' and the disenfranchised sections of the city (Lear, 1996).

The 1910 Mexican Revolution brought about a temporary halt to urban development as Mexico City became a refuge for both peasants and elites fleeing violence in the countryside. In 1921, when the armed movement ended, the capital population was 662,000. Ten years later it topped 1 million (González, 1993). Despite the new concerns for removing social inequalities, the post-revolutionary governments maintained former urban policies. This led to a further chaotic, uneven and fragmented development.

As the population increased, the lower classes crowded into downtown tenements called *casas de vecindad*, while the upper and middle classes persisted on their flight from the city centre to the western suburbs looking for a quiet and calm location close to nature (Kemper and Royce, 1979).

Around the 1930s a paradigmatic example of a new type of housing development for the affluent classes was built in Mexico City. *Lomas de Chapultepec*, promoted as 'the first Garden City', attempted to imitate the Anglo-Saxon model developed at the end of the 19th century in the writings of Ebenezer Howard.

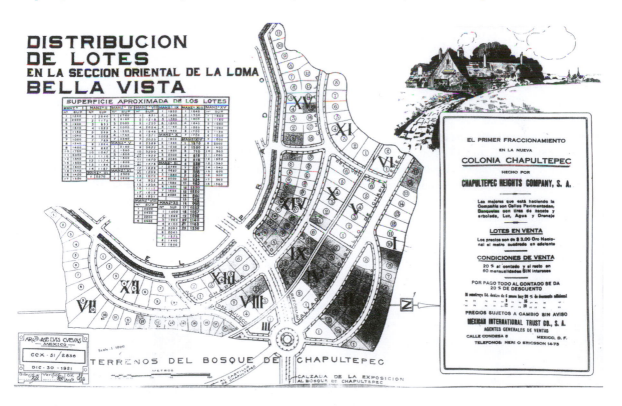

Figure 8.4 *The first 'Garden City': Lomas de Chapultepec. Influenced by the United States, the grid scheme began to give way to curved streets and lots in newly planned suburban subdivisions.*

Source: Lombardo de Ruiz (1996)

The purpose was to create a residential enclave where the wealthy citizens could isolate themselves from the problems of industrialization and, at the same time, engage in a 'green' lifestyle (see Figure 8.4). Influenced by the US, the residential architecture of *Lomas de Chapultepec* adopted the Californian Mission style. For the first time, Mexican architects set aside European models and turned their eyes to North America in search of a modern way of living.

Sadly, *Lomas de Chapultepec* reflected the great inequalities that characterized urban development after the revolution. Although the post-revolutionary governments talked about solving the deficiencies and problems of the poor sections of the city, in fact, they set aside the demands of the working and rural classes and responded more openly to the concerns of the commercial elite – including the old Porfirian entrepreneurs who were involved in these private enterprises (Miranda, 2007). Instead of advocating the common good, local authorities fostered, rather than mitigated, socio-spatial polarization.

Suburbs: 'An ideal place to live'

During the second half of the 20th century Mexico witnessed its 'economic miracle'. The unavailability of goods from the belligerent nations in World War II provided an incentive for governmental policies of import-substitution industrialization that led to a sustained economic growth (Ballent, 1998, p60). In this period, the city became the most important pole of development. Its centrality in the transportation network, its relatively well-skilled workforce, and its larger consumer population promoted the concentration of industries and capital

(Sánchez Ruiz, 1999). For the fist time in its history, the urban expansion spilled over the original boundaries of the city to include adjoining municipalities of the State of Mexico. In a scant three decades, between 1940 and 1970, the population of Mexico City increased 345 per cent, while the metropolitan area grew by 424 per cent (Davis, 1998) (see Table 8.1).

Newly arrived migrants, as well as relocating residents and industries, increasingly established at the urban periphery. There, land-use regulations, including restrictions on sales of previously rural land, were randomly enforced. This offered not only business opportunities, but also lower-priced lands for impoverished families and attractive sites in the western part of the city for high-income residents fleeing the congestion and deterioration of the central area (Rowland and Gordon, 1996).[6] However, the real benefits derived from the import-substitution model were distributed unevenly among the urban spaces. While downtown remained reminiscent of prerevolutionary days, the new suburbs for the affluent benefited from a radiant modernization that only the most privileged groups could enjoy.

One of the most important projects of this period was an exclusive neighbourhood planned and built around the 1950s in the south-west fringe of the city. *Jardines del Pedregal* (the gardens of the stony place) was advertised as the 'ideal place to live'. Formed by 700 large individual plots, it offered the beauty and size of a weekend home without sacrificing the comforts associated with the city. It provided a 'self-contained, self-focused and unconnected subdivision that made it easier for residents to control their own spaces' (Blakely and Snyder, 1999, p8).

Table 8.1 *Demographic growth by urban area 1930–2005*

	Mexico City	Adjoining municipalities of the State de México and Hidalgo	ZMVM (Total)
1930	1,229,576		
1940	1,757,530	13,845	1,771,375
1950	2,923,194	58,881	2,982,075
1960	4,846,497	308,830	5,155,327
1970	6,874,165	1,782,686	8,656,851
1980	8,831,079	4,903,575	13,734,654
1990	8,235,744	6,811,941	15,047,685
2005	8,720,916	10,518,994	19,239,910

Source: CONAPO, 1998

Resembling American suburbs such as Riverside, developed by Frederick Law Olmsted and Calvert Vaux near Chicago, and Llewellyn Park created by Llewellyn Haskell in the outskirts of New York, *Jardines del Pedregal* integrated architecture and nature in an attempt to provide a harmoniously composed refuge for its motorized inhabitants. In this exclusive 'community' a new street pattern based on cul-de-sacs and dead-end streets provided exclusivity and privacy by restricting free circulation and access (see Figure 8.5).

Beyond the street design, Luis Barragán, the architect of the project, built several individual dwellings where backyard gardens played a crucial role (Eggener, 2001). Houses were oriented inwards, turning their back on the roads and making it clear that the domestic sphere was far more relevant than the public arena. The streets became deserted areas where social interactions among neighbours were discouraged, but transportation needs fulfilled. In this sense, while the suburbs indeed satisfied the need for urban development, their physical environment ignored important social goals, such as social integration and community participation.

With *Jardines del Pedregal* and other planned subdivisions located at the edge of the city begins a new housing typology, which has elsewhere been referred to as 'segregated solutions of the urban fabric' because their physical layout diverges from the square-block scheme that had been the norm until the 1950s (Ayala, 1996).

Gated communities: New trends in spatial segregation

During the last two decades of the 20th century, Mexico City has experienced notable transformations. Contrary to past tendencies, demographic growth is occurring in remote parts of the extended urban realm. Of the 20 million residents who live in what is now known as the Metropolitan Zone of the Valley of Mexico (ZMVM), comprised of both the city proper and 59 adjoining municipalities of the State of Mexico, 56 per cent are located outside the city's sphere (Garza, 2000) (see Table 8.1).

In these ever-expanding peripheries, urban development has been notably uneven. The low-income classes have been forced to establish in illegal subdivisions, on land poorly suited for service provision: on the steep, rocky slopes of volcanoes to the south-west and on the desiccated lakes to the east. At the other end of the income spectrum, middle and upper classes have continued their historical exodus to the pristine west side of the metropolitan area, farther from downtown but in the same general direction as old developments. As a result, the ZMVM is still, for the most part, divided by an imaginary line running north to south and separating the rich from the poor.

While the wealthy may continue migrating according to old habits, their residential spaces have

Figure 8.5 *Jardines del Pedregal. The first houses built in this neighbourhood are oriented towards the back. The gardens constituted a prominent feature of the residential space.*

Source: Eggener (2001)

new physical characteristics in response to contemporary social and urban dynamics.

One of the most visible shifts during the last decades is the concern for security. In Mexico City, daily news and conversations between its inhabitants indicate that citizens do not feel properly protected by public institutions. On the contrary, the majority consider that criminality has already overwhelmed the institutions and that delinquency is out of control.

Fear has created new self-protecting behaviour, such as not going out at night, not using jewellery or other visible objects, and not carrying more money than absolutely necessary. The fear of being victimized has led some to stay at home or, when they do go out, to apply certain strategies of surveillance and avoid activities perceived as dangerous.

In this context, residential developments that have physical protections and access-controlled entrances have become the norm rather than the exception. Unlike historical forms of spatial segregation, gated communities of today address the increasing concern for security in the Mexican metropolis. In the past, segregation was not as tightly related to a feeling of insecurity, but rather to convey a certain status. In this sense, one of the features that differentiate new housing schemes from old is the presence of protection devices such as walls, fences, secured entrances, armed personnel and video cameras, all of which seek to restrict access to the gated enclaves (see Figure 8.6).

Along with the fortification of the urban landscape, there are other features that distinguish old from contemporary forms of segregation. One with far-reaching consequences relates to the provision of goods and services inside the gated community. Whereas, in the past, segregation was limited to the residential environment, meaning that seclusion occurred only while physically at home, today it encompasses a large number of activities such as studying, working and exercising.

Everything from recreational amenities such as golf courses, swimming pools and cinemas, to practical services including supermarkets, dry cleaners and hair salons, among many others, have become commonplace in gated communities (see Figure 8.7). This concentration of services in the private residential sphere allows the affluent classes to easily withdraw from other spaces of society. The consequence is a more profound segregation than previously experienced by the city's inhabitants (Duhau, 2001).

When we add to this the lack of a functioning public transportation system, and therefore the need to drive everywhere; the proliferation of corporate office buildings, which require identity cards for access; private health clubs, if your particular gated community does not provide one or is not up to par; and shopping malls where access is often a privilege rather than a right, one can easily see why the 'art of

Figure 8.6 *Restricted control entrances and security devices. Present day gated communities in Mexico City address the increasing concern for security.*

Source: Diana Sheinbaum

Figure 8.7 *Bosque Real Country Club. Bosque Real Country Club is the most important real estate development in 21st century Mexico. Located in the west side of the metropolitan area, this gated community has two golf courses.*

Source: homepage.mac.com/helipilot/PhotoAlbum31.html

living together mediated by the city' has become difficult – and avoidable (Giglia, 2001).

The end result seems to be that as the private sector continues to build these microcosms for the elite, both the need for public spaces and the pressure applied to the government to build them diminishes. It is as if we have fallen into a paradigm where there is 'a curious obligation to produce more urban space yet less city'.

Perhaps even more paradigmatic is that in Mexico City all of this seems to be a very normal and natural response to what is generally accepted as an incredibly inefficient government that is not likely to respond to the needs of its citizens any time soon. Under this reality, those with the means of solving their own problems are going to do so, and those without them will remain dependent on the unfair public provision of public services.

In countries where illegality is the norm, privatization often results in a form of unregulated self-governance as authorities gladly move out of the way while developers and their tenants take on the responsibilities of building roads, providing public lighting, policing the streets and, in general, acquiring services that would ordinarily fall to the municipality. What is alarming is that while in some countries this has become a political and legal debate as citizens complain that they are victims of double taxation, in Mexico this discussion is not taking place because people are used to the government's lack of capability in dealing with the problems of the city. Moreover, their primary concern is not paying for what should be given to them as taxpaying citizens, but rather simply getting the infrastructure and services they require. It is a *de facto* reality where individuals effectively bypass established institutions, which they consider corrupt anyway, and simply get things done. While it is unclear how long society will continue to tolerate this situation, one thing does seem certain: these *ad hoc* solutions bring little relief to the very problems that they are trying to solve and simply perpetuate an ongoing historical process of segregation that has characterized the socio-spatial structure of Mexico City.

Conclusions

There is no doubt that present-day gated communities constitute an urban phenomenon with new physical features and socio-political implications. What were once residential enclaves designed to separate the affluent groups from the poor majority have now become complex microcosms where segregation encompasses different activities and spaces.

However, as we have tried to show, self-segregation has deep historical roots that can even be traced back to the colonial urban grid. In this sense, contemporary gated communities constitute a new link in a process that has historically rationalized social differentiation and exclusion as natural and inevitable (Cabrales, 2002).

In many ways we have inherited a city that has been poorly planned and carelessly designed to benefit the caprice of the few over the needs of the many. There is no doubt that we still are a long way from improving the quality of life for all segments of society and even farther from ensuring the viability of our city and its inhabitants in the future. Therefore, if we are to move towards a more sustainable future and a less divided city we must emphasize the need for long-term public policies and practise interventions based on a new development paradigm, which insists on the fair distribution of resources in society.

Notes

1   This chapter is a post-peer review version of an article published in *Urban Design International*: Sheinbaum, D. (2008) 'Gated communities in Mexico City: An historical perspective', *Urban Design International*, vol 13, no 4, pp241–252, www.palgrave-journals.com/udi/

2   For a comprehensive collection of articles on gated communities from different perspectives, we suggest the web page of the international research network on private urban governance: www.gated-communities.de.

3   Many Spanish towns in the New World had been founded before this time; however, Hernán Cortés was the first to plan the construction of the city in accordance with the royal instructions issued decades ago.

4   *Calpulli* is a social, religious and economic unit formed by a group of families. Each of them had their own lands, autonomous government, army, schools and temples; but at the same time they constituted an administrative jurisdiction of a political entity.

5   In 1813 urban church property accounted for half of the buildings in Mexico City (Morales, 1978, p71).

6   The same process can be traced in different Latin American metropolises. The case of Buenos Aires has been explained in Chapter 7 of this volume.

References

Agostini, C. (2003) *Monuments of Progress: Modernization and Public Health in Mexico City 1876–1910*, UNAM, México

Ayala, E. (1996) *La casa de la ciudad de México: Evolución y transformaciones*, Conaculta, México

Ballent, A. (1998) 'El arte de saber vivir: Modernización del habitar doméstico y cambio urbano, 1940–1970', in García Canclini, N. (ed) *Cultura y comunicación en la ciudad de México*, vol I, Grijalbo, México, pp65–131

Beezley, W., Martin C. and French, W. (1994) *Rituals of Rule, Rituals of Resistance: Public Celebrations and Popular Culture in Mexico*, Scholarly Resources, Wilmington, Delaware

Blakely, E. J. and Snyder, M. G. (1997) *Fortress America: Gated Communities in the United States*, Brookings Institution Press, Washington, DC

Blandy, S., Dixon, J. and Dupuis, A. (2006) 'Theorising power relationships in multi-owned residential developments: unpacking the bundle of rights', *Urban Studies*, vol 43, no 13, pp2365–2383

Bremley, G., Dempsey, N., Power, S. and Brown, C. (2006) 'What is "social sustainability" and how do our existing urban forms perform in nurturing it?', Paper presented at the Sustainable Communities and Green Futures Conference, Bartlett School of Planning, University College London, London

Cabrales, L. F. (ed) (2002) *Latinoamérica: Países abiertos, ciudades cerradas,* Universidad de Guadalajara–UNESCO, Guadalajara

Chen, S. and Webster, C. (2006) 'Homeowners associations, collective action and the costs of private governance', in Atkinson, R. and Blandy, S. (eds) *Gated Communities: International Perspectives*, Routledge New York, NY, pp18–33

CONAPO (1998) *Escenarios demográficos y urbanos de la Zona Metropolitana del Valle de México, 1990–2010, México, 1998,* www.conapo.gob.mx/publicaciones/Otras/zmcm/03.pdf

Cordera, R. and Ziccardi, A. (eds) (2000) *Las políticas sociales de México al fin del milenio: Descentralización, diseño y gestión*, UNAM, México

Davis, D. (1998) 'The social construction of Mexico City: Political conflict and urban development, 1950–1966', *Journal of Urban History*, vol 24, pp364–415

Deans-Smith, S. (2001) 'Review of property and Permissiveness in Bourbon Mexico', *The Historian*, vol 63, no 3, pp619–621, www.encyclopedia.com/doc/1G1-75162026.html

De Gortari, H. (1987) 'Un modelo de urbanización? La ciudad de México de finales del siglo XIX', *Secuencia. Revista Americana de Ciencias Sociales*, vol 8, May–August, pp42–52

Duhau, E. (2001) 'La megaciudad en el siglo XXI. De la modernidad inconclusa a la crisis del espacio público', *Papeles de Población*, vol 30, pp131–161

Eggener, K. (2001) *Luis Barragan's Gardens of El Pedregal*, Princeton Architectural, New York, NY

Fernández, F. (1992) *Años, gente, símbolos y espacio público. Aproximación teórico metodológica a la historia de la ciudad de México desde el análisis del orden y el uso de sus espacios*, Thesis, Maestría en Historia de México, UNAM-FFyL, México

Florescando, E. and Gil, I. (1981) 'La época de las reformas borbónicas y el crecimiento económico, 1750–1808', in Cossío Villegas, D. (ed) *Historia General de México*, COLMEX, México, pp471–568

García Canclini, N. (ed) (1998) *Cultura y comunicación en la ciudad de México*, Grijalbo, México

Garza, G. (ed) (2000) *La Ciudad de México en el fin del segundo milenio*, El Colegio de México-Gobierno del Distrito Federal, México

Giglia, A. (2001) 'Sociabilidad y Megaciudades', *Estudios Sociológicos*, vol XIX, no 57, pp799–821

Giglia, A. (2002) 'Privatización del espacio, autosegregación y participación ciudadana en la Ciudad de México. El caso de las calles cerradas en la zona de Coapa', *Trace* vol 42, pp71–78

González, S. (1993) 'La ciudad de México y la cultura urbana', in Blanco, J. J. and Woldenberg, J. (eds) *México a fines de siglo*, vol I, FCE, México

Grant, J. and Rosen, G. (2007) 'From armed compound to broken arm: The meaning of gates in Israel and Canada', Paper presented at the International Conference on Private Urban Governance: Production of urban spaces, Interactions of public and private actors, Sustainability of cities', 5–8 June, Université Paris, 1 Panthéon-Sorbonne, Paris

Hernández, V. (1981) *Arquitectura doméstica de la ciudad de México 1890–1925*, UNAM, México

Jaiven, A. L. (2003) 'Casas y formas de vida en los alrededores, 1750–1850', in Zárate, V. (ed) *Política, casas y fiestas en el entorno urbano del Distrito Federal, Siglos XVIII–XIX*, Instituto Mora, México, pp77–128

Jiménez, J. (1993) *La traza del poder. Historia de la política y los negocios urbanos en el Distrito Federal: de sus orígenes a la desaparición del Ayuntamiento (1824–1928)*, CODEX Editores, México

Kagan, R. (2000) 'A world without walls: City and town in colonial Spanish America', in Tracy, D. (ed) *City Walls: The Urban Enceinte in Global Perspective*, Cambridge University Press, Cambridge, pp117–152

Kemper, R. and Royce, A. (1979) 'Mexican urbanization since 1821: A macro-historical approach', *Urban Anthropology*, vol 8, no 3/4, pp267–289

Landman, K. (2004) 'The storm that rocks the boat: Analyzing the systemic impact of gated communities on urban sustainability', Paper presented at International Symposium on Territory, Control and Enclosure: The Ecology of Urban Fragmentation, 28 February–3 March 2005, Pretoria, South Africa

Lear, J. (1996) 'Mexico City: Space and class in the Porfirian capital, 1884–1910', *Journal of Urban History*, vol 22, no 4, pp454–492

Le Goix, R. (2007) 'The impact of gated communities on property values: Evidences of changes in real estate markets (Los Angeles, 1980–2000)', Paper presented to CyberGeo, Systemic Impacts and Sustainability of Gated Enclaves in the City, Pretoria, South Africa, 28 February–3 March 2005, article 375, www.cybergeo.eu/index6225.html

Lombardo de Ruiz, S. (1996) *Atlas histórico de la ciudad de México*, Smurfit Carton y Papel, México

Loreto López, R. (ed.) (2001) *Casas, viviendas y hogares en la historia de México*, COLMEX, México

Low, S. (2004) *Behind the Gates: Life, Security and Pursuit of Happiness in Fortress America*, Routledge, London

McKenzie, E. (1994) *Privatopia: Homeowners Associations and the Rise of Residential Private Government*, Yale University Press, New Haven

McKenzie, E. (2003) 'Common-interest housing in the communities of tomorrow', *Housing Policy Debate*, vol 14, no 1–2, pp203–234

Miranda, S. (2007) *Tacubaya: De suburbia veraniego a ciudad*, UNAM-IIH, México

Monnet, J. (2006) 'The geopolitics of visibility: Urban icons in contemporary Mexico city', in Ethington, P. et al (eds) *Atlas of Urban Icons: Studies in Urban Visual History*, *Urban History*, vol 33, p1

Morales, M. D. (1978) 'La expansión de la ciudad de México: El caso de los fraccionamientos', in Moreno Toscazo, A. (ed) *Ciudad de México: Ensayo de construcción de una historia*, SEP-INAH, México

Moreno Toscano, A. (1981) 'El siglo de la conquista', in Cossío Villegas, D. (ed) *Historia General de México*, vol I, COLMEX, México

O'Gorman, E. (1998) 'Reflexiones sobre la traza colonial', in De Gortari, H. and Hernández, R. (eds) *Memoria y encuentros: Lla ciudad de México y el Distrito Federal (1824–1928)*, vol II, Instituto Mora, México

Ortiz, L. (1994) 'Los palacios nobiliarios de la Nueva España, México', Seminario de Cultura Mexicana, México

Perfiles Latinoamericanos (2001) 'La nueva segregación urbana', in *Revista de la Sede Académica de la Facultad Latinoamericana de Ciencias Sociales*, FLACSO, México pp10, 19

Peyroux, E. (2004) 'Residential enclosure and security management: Changing norms of social control and public action in Johannesburg and Windhoek', Paper presented at the International Symposium on Territory, Control and Enclosure: The Ecology of Urban Fragmentation, 28 February–3 March 2005, Pretoria, South Africa

Ramonet, I. (1998) *La tiranía de la comunicación*, Editorial Debate, Madrid, 1998

Roitman, S. (2005) 'Who segregates whom? The analysis of a gated community in Menoza, Argentina', *Housing Studies*, vol 22, no 2, pp303–322

Rowland, A. and Gordon, P. (1996) 'Mexico City: No longer a leviathan', in Gilberth, A. (ed) *The MegaCity in Latin America*, United Nations University Press, New York, pp173–202

Rubial, A. (1998) *La plaza, el palacio y el convento: La ciudad de México en el siglo XVII*, CONACULTA, México

Sabatini, F., Cáceres G. and Cerda, J. (2001) 'Residential segregation pattern changes in main Chilean cities: Scale shifts and increasing malignancy', Paper presented at the International Seminar on Segregation in the City, Lincoln Institute, UK, 26–28 July

Sanchez de Carmona, M. (1989) *Traza y Plaza de la Ciudad de México en el siglo XVI*, UAM-Azcapotzalco/Tilde, México

Sánchez Ruiz, G. (1999) *La Ciudad de México en el Periodo de las Regencias 1929–1997*, UAM-Gobierno del Distrito Federal, México

Socolow, S. (2000) 'Review of property and permissiveness in Bourbon Mexico', *Estudios Interdisciplinarios de América Latina y el Caribe*, vol 11, p2

Svampa, M. (2001) *Los que ganaron: La vida en los countries y barrios privados*, Editorial Biblos, Buenos Aires

Valero de García, A. R. (1991) *Solares y conquistadores: Orígenes de la propiedad en la ciudad de México*, INAH, Buenos Aires

Viqueira, J. P. (1987) *Relajados o reprimidos? Diversiones públicas y vida social en la ciudad de México durante el Siglo de las Luces*, FCE, México

9

Production and Social Sustainability of Private Enclaves in Suburban Landscapes: French and US Long-Term Emergence of Gated Communities and Private Streets[1]

Renaud Le Goix and Delphine Callen

Introduction

This chapter aims to demonstrate that gated communities, although often presented as a recent unsustainable trend of security-oriented urbanism, and which have spread all over the world in the last two decades, are, indeed, a classical and generic form in urban sprawl and the suburban landscape. In attempting this, we apply a theoretical approach that views the private residential community as a *club economy* to analyse the planning, managing practices and social interactions at the local level.

We balance how private communities might be pro-social sustainability tools or, in contrast, may put urban equilibrium (political fragmentation and social interactions) at risk on the suburban edge of sprawling cities. We believe that social sustainability issues connect to the genesis of urban edges' morphologies and require an analysis of the underlying forces that structure them. The following section analyses the long-term trends in the local emergence of private residential governance in order to gain a better understanding of the diffusion of gated communities and how offer, demand and the local nexus of actors interact. Next, we consider how the local adoption of private urban governance models is structured by the

nexus of laws, and planning and residential strategies. More specifically, we analyse appropriation strategies of public space by private enclaves residents, and argue that local policies and discourses of intervening actors are often guided by locally driven interests and rent-seeking strategies that might contradict social equity principles. Finally, we argue that local path dependency truly explains the success stories of gated communities according to local social and political patterns and local institutional milieus.

Considering the nexus of law, as well as the practices of development industries and the layout of neighbourhoods, the findings balance, on the one hand, the strategies of local actors targeting the building of sustainable communities from the viewpoint of owners and entrepreneurs, and, on the other hand, equity principles at a more general level. This demonstrates that common goals of private communities are about getting control over the nearby environment (control over public space, amenities, etc.) and about guaranteeing property values. Nevertheless, field studies and residents' interviews, empirical data describing the political behaviour of gated communities and the social relations of residents reveal path dependencies in the local manifestations of private communities. Whatever the legal context, local actors, residents' strategies, public bodies of governments and entrepreneurs find ways of meeting a continuous demand for local control. This can be met either through private urban governance or through a local body of public government, depending on how local institutional milieus have structured decision-making, fiscal regulation and social exclusion patterns. This demonstrates that the political behaviour and social interactions emanating from private residential areas are eventually familiar and consistent with more casual patterns in a suburban world.

In capitalist cities, markets, speculation and location rent are pre-eminent forces that structure urban space. Thus, the patterns supporting the development of private and gated neighbourhoods seem to be largely characterized by the action of land developers (on the offer side) and a growing desire to control the quality, safety, security and tidiness of the residential environment (on the demand side) (Le Goix and Webster, 2008). In this context, investigating gated communities under the scope of social sustainability requires us to consider the broader context of the *sustainability of communities* and *social equity*. In this chapter, we consider the extent to which gated neighbourhoods are sustainable communities, and analyse the tendency of private streets and gated communities to promote social interaction within communities, demand-side analysis for safety, control over the neighbourhood, and, ultimately, protection of property values. Social equity includes how gated enclaves interact with access to public space, public services and the range of location choices, strategies and constraints of owners and renters. The chapter, furthermore, discusses arguments that have yet been rarely expressed in the literature: the dichotomy between public and private space in private residential enclaves is more apparent than real, and these new 'private residential' spaces are less different, and less unprecedented than is often claimed (Kirby, 2008).

Long-term trends and the emergence of private residential governance in France and the US

Assessing the social sustainability of gated communities requires us to gain a better understanding of how demand and offer for residential private urban governance emerge locally. This, indeed, connects to

social equity in terms of local government body strategies in housing and access to open space versus privatized commons, and how local governments promote equity and spatial justice in a context of suburban growth.

In order to understand the phenomenon of private communities, we must first understand the arguments put forward by current scholars. Since the early 1990s, a discourse has been growing on gated communities or privately governed urban territories. Their rise was initially fastest in the US and Latin America, where the media and academic commentators were quick to describe the phenomenon in terms of security-oriented privatized urbanism (Flusty, 1994; Marcuse, 1997; Davis, 1998; Low, 2001). A popular critique soon followed, warning of the social fragmentation of the city, out-of control urban segregation, secession, etc. (Blakely and Snyder, 1997; Caldeira, 2000; Glasze et al, 2002; Low, 2003). Others view the shift from the 'public' city to urbanization by private enclaves as a 'secession' of the elite and a regressive redistribution of resources and well-being. While the discourse on gated urbanism seemed to spread from American sources, the phenomenon itself had its own local history in every continent and country (Carvalho et al, 1997; Caldeira, 2000; Thuillier, 2005): in China (Giroir, 2006; Webster et al, 2006), South-East Asia and Australia (Burke and Sebaly, 2001); Europe (Glasze, 2003; Billard et al, 2005); Eastern Europe (Lentz, 2006); South Africa (Jürgens and Landman, 2006); and the Arab world (Glasze, 2000; Glasze and Alkhayyal, 2002). Gating may thus be interpreted as a global trend. It is undoubtedly influenced in many ways by US models; but it is developed according to local political, legal and architectural traditions (Glasze et al, 2002; Glasze, 2005).

This section reviews long-term trends in the production of residential area, and how these trends contribute to the local emergence of gated communities. The issue raised connects to the genesis of urban edges' areas, and the underlying forces that structure them. Indeed, private actors contribute to the production of space (e.g. professional territorial management and real-estate developers); local public authorities have key strategies (e.g. control of land use, social selection of residents, and urban sprawl or slow-growth policies); and publicly owned and managed areas tend to disappear, yielding an urbanism in which private residential developments are key features.

As several threads of lineation make gated communities classical features in suburban areas, the following sub-sections analyse the heritage of the legacy of gated enclaves, and push forward the argument that getting a better understanding of the diffusion of gated communities requires correlating them with how public bodies of government manage urban growth.

Lineation of gated communities: Common interest developments (CIDs), exclusivity and fear

The shift from global 'spread' to local 'emergence' as an underlying explanation naturally leads to the study of locally specific antecedents to gated communities (from now on, gated communities). Gated communities have a long history. Private urban governance emerged in 19th-century industrial European cities such as London and Paris, in which the new industrial bourgeoisie sought in privately operated and enclosed suburban neighbourhoods a quiet retreat from the busy city centre (Foldvary, 1994; McKenzie, 1994). Le Parc de Montretout, in Saint-Cloud, France, developed in 1832, probably being the first of its kind (Degoutin, 2004, 2006). In the US, the spread of gated communities has roots in a longstanding ideology of suburban development. One early thread of influence is the romantic suburban utopias and utopian-influenced projects. Haskell's Llewellyn Park was probably the first modern gated community built in the US. It has continuously operated a gatehouse and a private police force since 1854 and introduced private governance of shared amenities based on deed-restrictive covenants that protected the stability and homogeneity of the neighbourhood (Jackson, 1985). A second thread links US modern gated communities to the historical processes that brought common interest developments (CIDs – a form of co-ownership tenure and organization) and exclusionary restrictive covenant laws from Europe to the US. McKenzie (1994) explores the long European history of restrictive covenants and residential associations (observable since 1743 in London). The first homeowners association *per se* was created in the US in 1844 in Boston's Louisburg Square. Llewellyn Park and Roland Park (1891) were the first large privately owned and operated luxury subdivisions, yielding exclusive neighbourhoods. They

established consumer and real-estate developer expectations and legal and organizational approaches that helped to shape contemporary private urban governance in the US. McKenzie (1994, p9) writes:

> … to maintain the private parks, lakes and other amenities of the subdivisions, developers created provisions for common ownership of the land by all residents and private taxation of the owners. To ensure that the land would not be put to other uses by subsequent owners, developers attached 'restrictive covenants' to the deeds.

During the first half of the 20th century, this kind of high-end subdivision became quite common (Mission Hills, Missouri, in 1914; Kansas City Country Club District, Kansas, during the 1930s; and Radburn, New Jersey, in 1928). Along with landscaping and architectural requirements, the idea of social preferences as a commoditized attribute has become common in CIDs. Exclusive lifestyle developments became common by the turn of the 1960s and 1970s, designed as mass consumption real-estate developments, financed by large corporations attracted by potential profits and backed by the government through the Department of Housing and Urban Development (McKenzie, 1994).

Gated communities as generic patterns in suburban sprawl

On a scenic hill, overlooking the Seine River, the Parc de Montretout in Saint-Cloud, France, is a pioneer. The private estate used to be part of the royal domain of Saint-Cloud, and had been a residence for guards and officers. In 1832 the domain was partially dismantled and sold to a private developer, and a homeowner association (l'Assemblée Syndicale des Propriétaires) was incorporated.[2] The first development was planned for 37 properties, and there are today almost 50 distinct units housing about 400 people. 1855 covenants set several restrictions enforced to protect the property values. Housing units were to be built within the three years following the purchase of a lot, and businesses, cafés and ballrooms were prohibited in the development. In 1932, the regulations were amended in order to prevent any lot to be subdivided below a 1000 square metre surface and to restrict the building of non-residential structures.

The development has always been gated (see Figure 9.1); but security was not a pre-eminent goal in the original concept: the restrictive covenants only mention a janitor's booth near the main gate.[3] There is no reference to the gate itself in the covenants, and the walls and gate are physical remainders of the former park enclosure. The gate can be considered as a resilience of former land use: it used to be a gated residence for officers and royal guards.

According to a resident,[4] only one burglary has occurred during five years; but many residents perceive safety concerns as an important issue and rely on the gate to provide more security. This concern seems to be relevant especially among the homeowners who recently moved in. Former residents consider the janitor and the monumental gate as effective enough to deter crime; but some residents (such as Front National's leader Jean-Marie Le Pen and some national and CEOs and top industry executives) requested the installation of electronic devices to control the gate. The implementation of video surveillance at the gate was proposed but declined as illegal: it would have recorded public traffic on a public street for private purposes. Finally, the bucolic landscaping cautiously maintained by the association is regularly disturbed by journalists and TV reporters because of the political activities of the extremist leader in his headquarters.

Montretout was a very early example of a private gated development; but this is not an isolated case in Paris. Many apartment buildings and small individual houses are indeed located in a private street with a private square or in small streets where public traffic is banned. There were (according to a 1977 survey) 1500 *villas* and private streets in Paris (Figure 9.1), operated by property owners associations. The Villa Montmorency in the upper-scale western side of the city (16th district) is one of the archetypal examples of gated residential villas in Paris and was built in 1853 with the completion of the Auteuil Railway (restrictive covenants were set up in 1853; all lots were sold by 1857) (Pinçon and Pinçon-Charlot, 1994, 2001). Although sources are unclear whether the Duchesse de Montmorency or the Comtesse de Boufflers[5] was the last owner, the land used to be a former gated aristocratic property. The villa is composed of 120 luxury units and large estates, and used to be the home of poet A. Gide and philosopher H. Bergson. Security

concerns are far stronger than in Montretout, and the gatekeeper strictly enforces the access restrictions.

Gates and private streets in the early 19th century are not restricted to the upper classes. Working-class villas and small private developments were also built, especially near the south-eastern industrial outskirts of Paris along the Seine River. In Athis (nowadays near Orly Airport), the Villa des Gravilliers was built in 1897 for 75 inhabitants and was the property of a co-operative mutual society of factory employees in Paris. The mutual society built the private street and the fences, and a lottery was organized to designate the future occupants. The residents were given a seven-year lease with an option for purchasing the lot. It must be mentioned that this kind of mutual society closely resembled the utopian socialism that later inspired Howard's Garden City. Usually, the villas are small developments built during the first half of the 20th century, as the property ownership for the working class was favoured by a public policy allowing preferential loans (Laws Ribot and Loucheur).

Some common patterns can be drawn from the examples in Paris. Pre-eminently, the enclosure is often inherited from a former fenced land use. Montretout and Montmorency used to be aristocratic domains, which were fenced. It has also be documented that suburban development in the late 19th and early 20th centuries in Paris partially occurred in former aristocratic forests, properties and hunting domains, some part of them being designed as fenced areas (Bastie, 1964). Montmorency, the large developments of Maison-Lafitte, Le Chesnais, near Saint-Germain-en-Laye Forest, as well as the blue-collar smallest villas on the south-eastern side of Paris were all developed on such former domains. The street patterns of these neighbourhoods also recall the former hunting-trails (*chasses royales*) (Pinçon and Pinçon-Charlot, 1994, 2001).

It is of interest to mention the recent development of small upper- and middle-class neighbourhoods – for example, along the Bièvre Valley, 20km south of Paris, in the municipality of Bièvres. The three gated developments were built between 1985 and 1990, and are located within the walls of the former Parc de la Martinière: when the lots were developed after being sold by the municipality, the development maps fit the original limits of the park, and one of the neighbourhoods even maintained the original wall. This development's purpose was, in accordance with

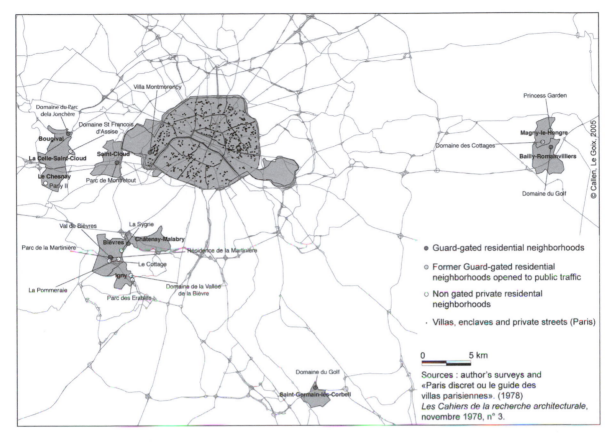

Figure 9.1 *Villas, private streets and gated enclaves in Ile-de-France*

Gated communities and urban growth

municipal authorities, to help finance the maintenance of the domain, the park and the estate. As a consequence, when purchasing the lots, the homeowners were charged a fee to fund the maintenance of the public park (Callen and Le Goix, 2007).

Whatever the historical and cultural context, the enclosure is motivated by the sense of property (private streets of Saint-Louis, Montretout, villas and contemporary gated communities) and their effects on maintenance and tidiness in order to protect the property values. This well-known effect of gating (Newman et al, 1974; Brower, 1992; Webster, 2002) thus contributes in some cases to protect and increase property values (Lacour-Little and Malpezzi, 2001;

Le Goix, 2002, 2007). Such common economic values among club members are not exclusive of high-end development and this sense of property among members has also motivated the gating of private streets in a Paris suburb based on a trade union membership, as previously mentioned about the Villa des Gravilliers.

Whether public authority relies on private urban governance to manage urban growth is still an academic debate. Some empirical researches help to structure the debate in the case of Los Angeles. The alleged guaranty of property values is nevertheless instrumental in enabling public authorities to manage growth with greater fiscal sustainability. Figure 9.2 shows that gating is highly correlated with the pace of urban growth, especially in Orange, San Bernardino and Riverside counties. Rolling Hills (1935) and Bradbury (1938) were the first gated communities in southern California. After World War II, these were accompanied by well-known developments such as Hidden Hills (1950) and the original Leisure World at Seal Beach (1946). Although there were 1700 gated housing units in the Los Angeles area by 1960, the development of enclaves such as Leisure World (1965) and Canyon Lake (1968) resulted in 19,900 gated units

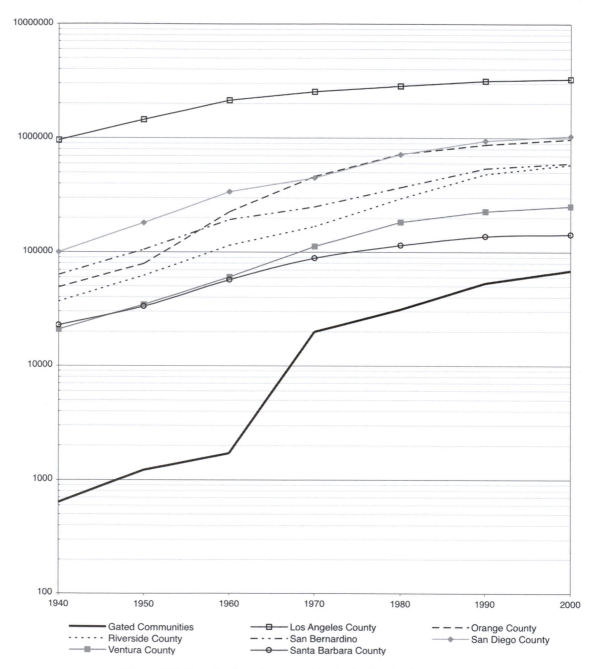

Figure 9.2 *Growth of gated communities in the Los Angeles region: Housing units in 162 gated communities and counties compared (2000)*

Source: 1990 Census, Population and Housing Count 1990 CPH-2-1, 2000 Census, Base de données gated communities

by 1970 (Le Goix, 2003).[6] Since developments after 1970 were smaller, the growth rate decreased: 31,000 gated housing units existed in 1980; 53,000 in 1990; and 80,000 in 2000. In 2000, these units represented approximately 12 per cent of the new homes market in southern California.

Gated communities now represent a significant share of the housing stock in the fastest growing parts of the Los Angeles region, especially in Orange and Riverside counties, where the population has boomed since the 1960s. Since 1990, the growth rate has remained high, averaging 14 per cent between 1990 and 2000. By providing their own security, infrastructure and services, these developments reduce public financial responsibility. As compensation, homeowners are granted exclusive access to their neighbourhoods, a condition that enhances location rent and positively affects property values (Le Goix, 2007). Thus, these developments are instrumental in transferring the cost of urban sprawl from public authorities to private developers and homeowners.

Also, to the extent that gating increases property values, a municipality's property tax revenues also increase. Not only are cities exempt from paying for most of private communities' security, service and infrastructure, but rising property values also increase funds to pay for enhanced public programmes and goods. For instance, in Calabasas (west of Los Angeles), where 30 per cent of the housing stock is locked behind gates, in 2001 the city reinvested 13 per cent of its operational budget in landscaping and leisure centres, such as a public golf course. All of these facilities are within the vicinity of Calabasas Park, the main gated area. This represents a complex synergy in which the municipal government derives fiscal benefit from private enclaves while subsidizing the provision of leisure amenities to enclave residents (Le Goix, 2006).

This may cease to be the case if club residents were able to opt out of certain tax municipal obligations; but even then, they may be willing to pay more for private urban governance than for public urban governance. Until now, courts have rejected requests by gated communities to opt out of municipal taxation (i.e. the double-taxation debate). Some tax rebates have been occasionally granted, but these are exceptions (Kennedy, 1995).

Although some developers are able to maintain profits while producing affordable developments, the vast majority perceive that planning regulations, such as requirements for open space, land dedications, and water systems layout and hook-up fees, are excessive (McKenzie, 2003; Ben-Joseph, 2004). Indeed, private communities proliferate under several interesting dynamics, involving, on the one hand, public governments enlarging their tax base and, on the other, developers seeking to offset the burden of public planning regulations through flexible design within private subdivisions.

Global product versus local actors in the production of gated communities

This section examines how the local adoption of private urban governance models is structured by the nexus of laws, planning and residential strategies. More specifically, we analyse appropriation strategies of public space by private enclaves' designers and residents, often guided by locally driven interests and rent-seeking strategies that might contradict social equity principles.

As mentioned earlier, gating may undoubtedly be interpreted as a global trend, and a large part of the literature has contributed to fostering this idea. It is influenced in many ways by US models; but it is developed according to local political, legal and architectural traditions (Glasze et al, 2002; Glasze, 2005). Furthermore, it has been widely discussed that gated communities proliferate within a climate of growing security concerns. In Argentina, Brazil, the US, Mexico and Europe, gating is associated with a lack of confidence in public law enforcement (Querrien and Lassave, 1999; Caldeira, 2000; Low, 2001). Nevertheless, in different historical and local contexts, gated enclaves have spread according to comparable patterns and have in common the same legal and functional roots.

Gated communities and exclusive lifestyle developments are often considered in Europe as a quite recent trend of security-oriented urbanism imported from the US by international global residents, disregarding the historical gated streets that, for instance, have existed for 150 years, at least in France. Some might argue that heritage street gating of the industrial city cannot be compared to recent mass consumption-oriented large-scale private schemes of the post-industrial era. We nevertheless argue that the rise of private urban governance could not have happened without a local legal and social context, and without urban planning tools, firms and local actors, to support it.

This argument is sustained, first, by the New Urbanism set of theories that has been heavily publicized in the 1990s among city planners and managers. This has, second, contributed to forge a global product that has, indeed, been adapted and targeted towards local markets by both global and local firms. Third, how this local adaptation operates also relies on local strategies of residents and actors, attracted by private urban governance in order to gain local control over nearby public spaces and resources.

Homogenization of planning practices

The gated street model, although already a success among the rich and famous of the golden ghettos during the early 1850s, became popular among land planners and developers in the 1970s. The theory of gating as defensible space was developed by Newman (1972) and the Institute for Community Design Analysis. These practices are now commonly called crime prevention through urban design and are intended to increase safety in residential areas by changing spatial perception, controlling public circulation and increasing private ownership. The erection of street barriers in retrofitted residential neighbourhoods is a way of enforcing public safety and controlling gang activities. Managers and developers have employed these practices in several low-income and public housing subdivisions, such as Mar Vista Gardens and Imperial Courts in south-central Los Angeles (Leavitt and Loukaitou-Sideris, 1994). This set of guidelines became considered as good planning practices when the US Department of Housing and Urban Development released in 1996 a new version of Newman's report (*Creating Defensible Space*). These practices have been exported, by legal and city experts. For instance, dozens of reports and comparative studies (Body-Gendrot, 1998, 2001; Donzelot and Mevel, 2001) have been published in France in order to implement *Defensible Space* in city planning and renewal strategies of decaying public housing (Ocqueteau, 1999).

Protagonists in *Defensible Space* planning usually argue that pre-eminent reasons for gating relate to:

- an enhanced feeling of property by residents and tenants;
- the exclusive use of a private site and amenities in order to prevent any free-riding and unwanted visitor.

Gated enclaves are operated like a club, the members paying for its private services. According to Newman, in Saint-Louis (Missouri), 47 streets have been progressively closed between 1867 (Benton Place) and the early 1920s (University Hills, Portland Place and Westmoreland Place). Built in 1922, University Hills is a 187-unit subdivision with nine manually operated gates, only one of them being opened each day according to a planning-only regulation released among the residents. If entrance is not completely prohibited, through traffic is diverted to other streets. Private streets have been extended to several early suburbs in Saint-Louis. It was reported that residents chose to privatize the streets and gate them in order to locally control zoning and land use and to protect property values. It appeared, furthermore, that the municipality of Saint-Louis was unable to provide the residents with correct infrastructure, thus raising the need for local private arrangements (Lacour-Little and Malpezzi, 2001; Newman et al, 1974). It clearly appears that the exclusiveness is originally designed to protect an infrastructure paid in common by associated private property owners. Defined as a club realm (Webster, 2002; Webster and Lai, 2003; Webster and Glasze, 2006), this association is neither a complete private realm (with complete exclusiveness of property rights) nor completely public (with collective consumption rights and free-riding). In a club, Webster explains that property rights over a local public good (roads and infrastructure) are shared within a group and denied to all external persons. Purchasing a house within a gated community comes along with a required association membership that conditions the use of collective goods and shared amenities included in the development.

The diffusion of reports and comparative studies through urban planning authorities has contributed to popularize private urban governance and enclosure as a powerful model for urban renewal and growth strategies.

Global firms or local developers?

Different intervening actors are commonly considered as playing a major role in the diffusion of residential models, the first of them being the developers. They buy building sites, negotiate with local authorities the layout and development permits of the programme, contract with architects, and promote their products on the market. Traditionally, this sector is considered as one of the most 'national', with local developers working with local producers for a local demand. But in France, global firms appeared and developed at the turn of the 1990s to 2000s.

A survey on real-estate advertising journals[7] shows that in the urban region of Paris, during the early 2000s, these firms and their different branches (Kaufman-and-Broad, Bouygues Immobilier and, more recently, Nexity and Bouwfonds International) represent, depending on the districts, from one tenth to half of the offers of new residential and individual developments. From this point of view, there is no doubt that they have influenced the rise of a standard model of urbanism. The US-based firm Kaufman-and-Broad is commonly considered one of the global firms that participate in the diffusion of an American pattern of security-oriented development, based on community and social homogeneity. Their standardized schemes have standard suburban patterns, standard houses (usually they propose four or six models with different architectures and superficies) and standard sets of services. But the link between the globalization of a few developers and the production of gated enclaves at the local level is not as obvious as it appears at first glance.

A study of the advertising discourse illustrates this view: the trend towards enclosures, either symbolic or concrete, is embodied by the commercial names of every new development. Many schemes are qualified as closed and can be found in almost every suburban area (terminology used being *clos*, *closerie*, *domains* and *villas*). In the Parisian suburban area, between 2000 and 2002, these terms have been found in 15 per cent of new programmes, although actual gated neighbourhoods represented less than 5 per cent of these schemes. Such denominations are used by almost all developers (local as well as international) for their commercial programmes.

Nevertheless, in the Parisian suburban area, the sample of advertisements shows that neither Kaufman nor Bouygues Immobilier has produced any gated community (or any community presented as 'gated' in the ads). Only one closed programme was produced by the Groupe George V (which has since merged with Nexity).

Interestingly, gated residential developments are, indeed, mostly produced by local developers and the enclosure appears as a *niche* market for national or regional developers such as Promogim or Maisons France Confort in the suburban areas or Paris. Moreover, there is a regional specialization for enclosure in France that could be linked to the presence of regional developers specialized in enclosure: Monné Decroix to the south-west in Toulouse, and Merhill in the south near Montpellier (Madore, 2004; Billard et al, 2005).

If the exclusive disposition and the community appear as positive values in the global marketing discourse in Europe, global firms act as if efficiency necessitates that this discourse remains more symbolic than physical. Site exclusivity is, indeed, produced either by a physical enclosure, a symbolic one, or local strategies promoting isolation and privacy.

Valuating public space by design: Enclosures, location and rent-seeking strategies

Beyond a project of social separation, enclosures also promote monopolizing strategies of public places and facilities. Such strategies seek to protect and enhance lifestyle, exclusivity of site rental and control over the local environment. This section reviews some of these settlement strategies that result in an appropriation of public space by design. This provides insights on the following apparent paradox: residents' demand and developers' strategies in designing enclosed neighbourhoods for public leisure facilities and public spaces, blurring the boundaries between private urban governance and publicly owned and managed spaces.

The usage and regulation of rights of way to public areas have produced a rich corpus of court settlements and local usage to illustrate this point. For instance, many gated enclaves were built along a water body and are required to maintain a public right of way along the stream, lake or sea-shore. Large gated enclaves, such as Canyon Lake or Leisure World, actually maintain public right of way along the rivers going though their servitude. In Rincon, a gated community in Santa Barbara County, along the Pacific Ocean, the Rincon Creek streams through the limits of the private gated enclave. The Property Owners' Association (POA) maintains public right of way to the river banks (see Figure 9.3). Many properties also have rights of way on their premises to grant access to the state beach. Although not gated at the origin, the neighbourhood was retrofitted with gates during the 1970s in an attempt to regulate parking and access to the beach (a great surf spot):

> The purpose of the gate was then to settle a private space and to avoid a prescriptive right of way through the community to the beach. Actually, the parking issue was important too: the gate forces the people coming to park on the two parking lots around the gated community, with a direct access to the beach.

In Coto de Caza, a large gated community of Orange County, the right of way issue has turned into an intense local debate. The story has been attentively followed by the *L.A. Times*[8] and clearly shows that residents see the enclosure as a means of preventing non-residents from getting into the premises. In 1998, the Capistrano Unified School District proposed building the first public primary school ever inside a gated community: 20 classrooms and 400 students, mostly – but not exclusively – for children living in the gated community. Asked to do so by local parents, prospective buyers and gated community residents, the developer (Lennar Homes) eventually offered to rent a lot to the district for US$1 a year. In order to accommodate the growing population of a gated community still under development, Lennar Homes also agreed to pay US$500,000 for the school's parking lot and baseball field. This project was, nevertheless, violently rejected by non-residents and some homeowners. The non-resident parents, first, were reluctant to send their children through the gates of a private neighbourhood because of the restrictions of their fundamental freedoms (Kennedy, 1995) and especially their free right of access to school and public facilities. Residents had on their side considered that a public school would have required the POA to deliver permits to pupils, parents and staff in a similar fashion to the permit access to the private school that already existed in Coto de Caza. Some argued that delivering more permits would have created a risk of crime inside the walls; so far, the POA used to deliver during the 1990s an average of 35,000 temporary permits a year. Indeed, opponents actually feared that a public facility located inside a gated

community would have required the POA to leave the gates opened during business hours. Court settlements have, indeed, banned the gating of streets if a public facility (such as the City Hall, Hidden Hills case in 1992) is located within the premises (Ciotti, 1992; Stark, 1998). Citizen groups, such as documented in the 1994 *Citizen's against Gated Enclaves (CAGE) versus Whitley Heights Civic Association* case, have successfully sought to ban the gating of public streets, arguing that gates would have forbidden the free access to a public property, even though the residential association proposed to pay for the cost of gating and street maintenance (Kennedy, 1995). In March 1999, 84 per cent of the 1700 residents voted against the school project in Coto de Caza.

By means of rights of ways, public spaces near gated communities might also be instrumental in valuating gated communities. Near Paris, La Sygrie exemplifies this kind of location strategies (see Figures 9.4 and 9.5). Residents wish to gate the private driveway despite the public right of way going through the domain: the private street is the most convenient walking access for City of Bièvres residents to a public park (Parc Ratel) and municipal sport facilities (tennis courts, kindergarten, gym, city meeting hall). Despite the right of way, city residents walking through the private neighbourhood might feel like trespassers when passing by the 'private street, no walk-thru, residents only' sign posted at the entrance of the subdivision. Residents push for the erection of a gate, which would *de facto* privatize the only convenient access to the newly remodelled park, the alternative access gate being more convenient by car, in contradiction with the walking scale of French street patterns in such suburban village-like communities. The city sued the Homeowners' Association in 2002 in order to guarantee the right of way that has been settled upon in the neighbourhood development permit. Homeowners, nevertheless, profit from this valuable proximity, the public park and facilities being considered as an extension of their own backyard.

Le Parc de la Martinière is another small eight-unit gated subdivision, along the Bièvre riverbank. Although a right of way was defined by the city authority in the development permit during the late 1980s, in order to grant the general public a convenient access to a public park, homeowners have set up an

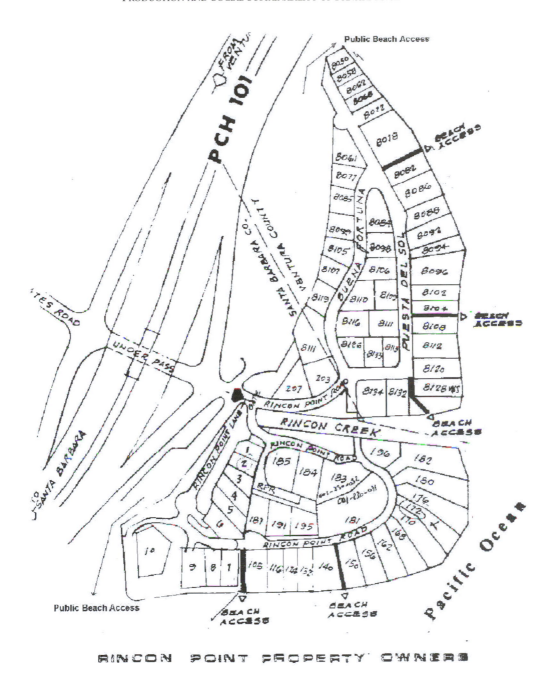

Figure 9.3 *Rincon Point: Rights of way and public access*

Note: This assessor's map mentions several public pathways through the gated community to maintain public access. The beach is open to the general public by pathways near lots 8050 and 10.

Source: Santa Barbara County – Assessor's Office, 2000

automated gate, denying access to the park from the scenic walk along the river. Pedestrians must go around the development, on a narrow and congested road, without any proper pavement to access the public park. In France, planning regulation stipulates that restrictions (such as a public right of way) cease to apply ten years after the development permit is filed, unless public authorities explicitly seek to renew the restrictions. In the present case, the public right of way is now null and void, and the city of Bièvres gave up and never engaged in a legal dispute. Residents of the Parc de la Martinière did not 'privatize' public space; but a nearby public space has been instrumental in a rent-seeking strategy by openly denying public access from the river pathway to the park.

In contrast to common wisdom, there are usually no privatized public facilities inside gated communities. Nevertheless, public space is instrumental in valuating

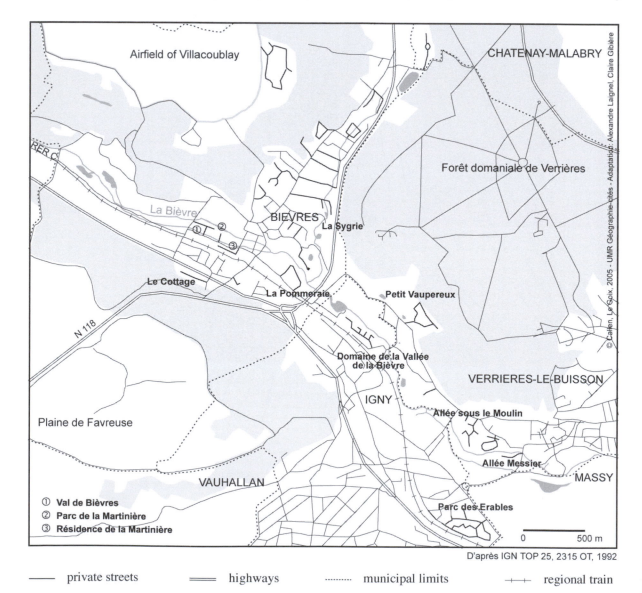

Figure 9.4 *Location of private streets and gated enclaves in Bièvres, Ile-de-France*

Source: Author's Survey, 2002; based on IGN Top 25, 2315 OT, 1992

gated communities. At a local level, private urban governance implies resident-side strategies of appropriation of nearby public facilities and, by doing so, social distinction. Because of this appropriation by design, private communities value public facilities, yielding an appropriation of public areas by members of

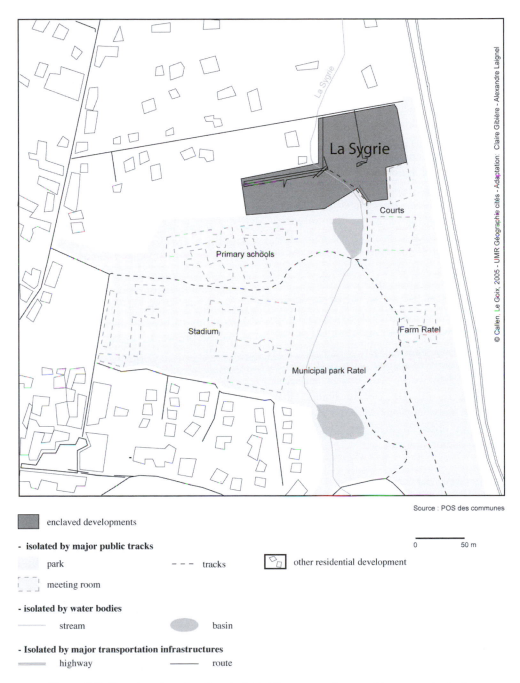

Figure 9.5 *'Location, location, location': Public space and rent-seeking strategies in La Sygrie–Bièvres*

Source: Local Land Use Plans (Plan d'occupation des sols des communes), and Author's survey, 2002

residential clubs. To a certain extent, some examples (such as Rincon and La Sygrie) clearly demonstrate that at a local level, privatization strategies and gated streets are designed to control access to public space.

Local path dependency: Private neighbourhoods, local strategies and institutional milieu

The preceding section sought to demonstrate that gated communities rely more on local developers targeting 'niche' markets and local rent-seeking strategies than on the engineering, designing and financing of housing at a global level. Local patterns have pre-eminent influence on how gated communities and private neighbourhoods are adopted by housing developers, local bodies of governments that authorize them and, lastly, prospective buyers. We argue that local path dependency truly explains the success stories of gated communities according to local social and political patterns and local institutional milieus. We elaborate on empirical evidence from spatial patterns of interactions by residents in gated communities and private streets in order to demonstrate that private residential areas' political and social interactions are eventually familiar and consistent with more casual patterns in a suburban world. Two sets of empirical data are exposed, in the US and in France, that demonstrate how gated enclaves indeed rely on the municipal level in order to make their governance effort sustainable in the long run.

Gated communities as local small-scale governance in the US

By the year 2000, over 15 per cent of the US housing stock was in CIDs and the number of units in these privately governed residential schemes rose from 701,000 in 1970 to 16.3 million in 1998 (McKenzie, 2003, 2005, 2006). The Community Association of America estimated in 2002 that 47 million Americans were living in 231,000 community associations and that 50 per cent of all new homes in major cities belong to community associations (Sanchez and Lang, 2005). Only a proportion – for instance, up to 30 per cent in the region of Los Angeles (Le Goix, 2003) – of these private local government areas are gated.

The breaking down of municipal management into smaller units might in the end deliver a more sustainable urban political economy on the whole, but only at the expense of marginalizing those excluded from the 'club economies', as in *minimal cities* (Miller, 1981). How sustainable this is depends on the wealth redistribution institutions that arise.

The relationships between gated enclaves and public authorities are mostly governed by the fiscal gain that gated communities might produce at almost no cost except general infrastructure (freeways and some public utilities). It has been demonstrated that gated communities are particularly desirable for local governments, especially in unincorporated areas (without municipal government, the county being the only local governing body), where suburbanization, lower densities, growing cost of infrastructures and lower fiscal resources are part of the pre-eminent paradigm (McKenzie, 1994). When developing private neighbourhoods, the homeowner pays for the provision of public services. Indeed, common interest developments are both public actors and private governments. The developer and the Homeowner Association substitute for the public authority and privately provide a public service, such as streets, sidewalks, landscaping and utilities networks (McKenzie, 1994; Kennedy, 1995). But some gated communities also transform into public entities by being incorporating within autonomous cities or taking part in a broader incorporation process. This issue is important in understanding the nature of the new territorial maps built by gated enclaves.

It is a paradox that gated communities, often perceived as a rejection of public governance models, might, indeed, seek to become public actors of their own. The sprawl of gated communities is not, however, to be understood as 'secession' from the public authority, but as a public–private partnership, a local game where the gated community has utility for the public authority, while the Property Owners' Association is granted autonomy in local governance, especially in financing the maintenance of urban infrastructure. But this user-pays paradigm creates a high cost for the homeowner, charged with the property taxes, the district assessment and homeowners' fees. This higher 'entry fee' contributes to the protection of property values but also to socio-spatial selection and segregation. It may then seem paradoxical that gated communities also transform into public entities by being incorporated within autonomous cities or taking part in a broader incorporation process. This issue is important in understanding the nature of the new territorial maps built by gated enclaves.

Le Goix (2006) analysed the recently incorporated Los Angeles area municipalities that are predominantly composed of gated communities: to sum up, incorporations have occurred for two primary reasons.[9] On the one hand, they aim to prevent a potential annexation by a less affluent community looking for an extended tax base (e.g. Rolling Hills and Hidden Hills, or Rancho Mirage and Indian Wells in the Palm Springs area). On the other, they aim to protect local lifestyles, values and planning control (e.g. Leisure World, Canyon Lake, Dana Point and Calabasas). After incorporation, local affairs have been shared with private homeowners' associations, which take charge of road maintenance, security and compliance with land-use regulations and restrictive covenants. These minimal cities also reduce operation costs by contracting with the county and other public agencies to supply public services, such as the police service, water provision, sewers and fire protection (Miller, 1981). Instead of acting as a separate entity, minimal cities are extensions of their homeowners' associations.

By incorporating gated communities as municipal governments of their own, local leaders seek to:

- prevent their upscale fiscal basis from being redistributed in other (poorer) areas, a common goal in incorporation driven by upscale US developments (Miller, 1981);
- legally transfer public resources and assets for the profit of exclusive and enclosed neighbourhoods;
- legally obtain public infrastructure financing within gated areas.

Thus, in some circumstances, fragmentation yields short-term efficiencies at the expense of long-term system disruption with potentially high recovery costs (Le Goix, 2006).

Homeownership inside a gated community is primarily a real-estate investment – offering property security. Second, it offers security of lifestyle. And, third, it is a private attempt to gain local control over a local environment – which adds to the security of property and lifestyle.

Private and gated streets and the significance of the municipal level in France

In the US, gaining local control over the local environment is crucial to understanding the success of gated communities. In Ile-de-France, gated communities have been classical features since the original development of Le Parc de Montretout in 1832. As previously discussed, private streets have been a much longer-term trend, but have never reached the striking amplitude of the phenomenon in the US. The reasons for this containment of gated communities and private streets are not to be sought in morphology (suburban residential developments with lollipops and dead ends are common in France), but rather in local practices by residents.

This discussion elaborates upon a survey conducted in 2002 in 11 private neighbourhoods (four gated and seven non-gated but enclaved private streets) in the Bièvre Valley in south-western Ile-de-France.[10] Located in the upper middle-class urban edge of the 1980s, socio-economic patterns are among the most homogeneous and average 20,000 Euros per year per person. In a greenbelt setting comprised of national forests and farming, this area has been suburbanized during the 1970s and 1980s, accompanying the rise of nearby industrial and high-tech districts of Saclay (nuclear research), Clamart Villacoublay (aerospace, automotive and information technology industries) and Orsay (university research park). The valley has offered a privileged yet protected residential area (see Figure 9.4), efficiently connected to downtown Paris by freeways and regional trains, minutes from Orly Airport (mostly domestic and short-haul flights). The small town environment is an important feature that values the valley: in this close-knit high-density individual housing residential sprawl, the small town centre has its city hall, its marketplace and some basic businesses and grocery stores. Around the traditional town centres, public spaces and promenades along the Bièvre River have recently been remodelled by public authorities by the means of a special district. It is important to mention that residents frequently consider their local life as a village-like idealized setting. This is obviously embodied by local events reviving local heritage, handicrafts and rural celebrations (such as the annual Strawberry Celebration).

The survey aimed to characterize households, their residential strategies both in terms of location and choice for private streets, and their socio-spatial practices at the metropolitan and local levels. Thirty-four variables have been collected, based on confidential answers. A first series of question was designed to characterize lifestyle and lifecycle (age, children, occupation, etc.). A second set of questions describes residents' daily practices and local involvement: memberships in local groups, charities, sports and leisure clubs (at the municipal level or in the neighbourhood); usage of local facilities (municipal meeting hall, public sport facilities); frequent use of parks and forests in the surroundings; and daily trips to work. Finally, information was collected regarding residential strategies, describing both the choice for a

specific house and residential subdivision (qualitative aspects, investment strategies, proximity to families), and the location choice at city level (closeness to work and to friends and families, qualities of city amenities, lifestyle options, etc.). Table 9.1 summarizes the average profile of surveyed residents for relevant variables.

According to a typology of residents based on collected data, four types of answers may be distinguished (see Figure 9.6):[11]

1   A first category of respondents seeks to value *proximity* and *lifestyle*. Respondents in these developments consider that environmental characteristics of the housing lot, as well as its quietness, access to parks and gardens, and perceived security of the investment are pre-eminent aspects of their residential strategy. They have, on average, a good knowledge of the municipal environment and have been well informed of local investment opportunities.

Table 9.1 *Average profile of responses to Bièvre Valley survey (selected variables)*

1 Characterization of households and residents		
Average age	50 to 60 years old	
University degree	66%	40%*
Children per household	2–3	
Persons per household	3–4	2–6*
Owner occupied	95%	66%*
Years in same residency	14.6	

2 Place of work and commuting		
Same *departement* (Essonne – 91)	33%	18%*
Hauts de Seine (92)	20%	
Paris	15%	
Yvelines (78)	15%	
Val-de-Marne (94)	8%	
Other countries in Europe**	6%	
	(5 people)	

3 Local practices	
Club membership with other residents of the private neighbourhood	37%
Membership in a municipal sport/leisure club	43%
Children membership in a municipal sport/leisure facility	42%
Public parks and forests	
1+ weekly trip to Bois de Verrières	66%
1+ weekly trip to river walk and lakes	40%
1+ weekly trip to parks in other municipalities	8%

4 Residential strategies	–
a. Subdivision level	
Quality of the subdivision and environment	79%
Quietness of the subdivision	65%
Buying a home in this subdivision perceived as a secure investment	31%
b Municipal level	
Lifestyle and quality of the built environment	86%
Convenient location to work	41%
Closeness to family network	17%
Quality and efficiency of municipal facilities	7%

Notes: * Comparative information at the municipal level provided where applicable (1999 Census)
**5 people have declared their main place of professional occupation in another European country. This is explained, first, by the proximity with Orly Airport and, second, by the high level of education and responsibilities of some of the residents.

Source: Author's survey, 2002

Proximity to parks and forest clearly count, as well as local social networks. Households with children explain the involvement in local clubs. Finally, data suggests that proximity to relatives in the same municipality has played a role in location strategies.

2   Others have strategies valuating municipal resources and amenities. Respondents in these subdivisions mostly work in the same municipality or district (*departement de l'Essonne*). A location close to work is thus preferable, and respondents subsequently make extensive use of local public resources, making good profit of short distances and commuting time. These characteristics are correlated with a higher level of education than the average profile.

3   A third category of subdivision can be characterized as *pioneers*. Respondents are older than the average profile and have been owners since the origin of the developments. The number of commuters to Paris and south-western industrial and business districts (Les Yvelines) are above average. This well- and long-established residency favours local social networks and acquaintances at the municipal level.

4   A final category is composed of developments where residents may be considered as actors, active in private governance. In these subdivisions, residents are active members of the Property Owners' Association and are characterized by employment in districts that are the furthest away: Hauts-de-Seine (La Défense) or Val-de-Marne. They value the quality of their investment and the 'quality of life' in the valley.

The contrasting strategies suggest that gating is only a weak characterization of the subdivision and does not clearly correlate with residential strategies. Gated districts are found in different categories of the typology; but some common patterns appear. Two gated neighbourhoods are characterized by *pioneer* strategies. In general, residents of gated streets considerably value the local municipal milieu. If they are poorly involved in local clubs and in private governance management, local patterns are structured by closed social networks and nearness to family members. Residents, and their children, also make an extensive use of municipal youth clubs and public gardens and leisure facilities.

But despite these generalities, data shows that respondents' use of local facilities and public spaces is more closely related to educational attainment, age and occupation than the gating structure of the development. Moreover, variance in residential strategies, perception and usage of the local milieu by respondents is mostly determined at the municipal level; the contribution of gated structures seems weak in this regard. In a majority of subdivisions, respondents show strong ties to the municipal level: public facilities, social networks, public parks and closeness to relatives; this clearly demonstrates that sociability cannot be reduced to a hypothetical 'community' created by gates, walls and subdivision limits.

Path dependency and local institutional milieu

Elaborating upon these results, we wish to push further our argument: the significance of the enclosure truly depends on the local context. This local milieu thus explains how gated patterns adapt and correspond to residents' behaviour, social strategies and economic demand. Gated communities are a success in the US, where local governance is structurally weak, in contrast to France, where gated enclaves have been the long-term trend, but have never emerged as a dominant form. The local institutional milieu – the nexus of laws and practices that shape local property markets, development industries and land regulations – create path dependencies in the local manifestation of the global trend towards private cities. They raise and lower the attractiveness of the private urban governance model. For instance, the absence of gated communities in Germany is usually seen as resulting from the absence of legal structuring of horizontal residential co-ownership (Glasze, 2003). In France, the existence of 36,600 municipalities (communes), most of them with 500 to 2000 inhabitants, does not favour the diffusion or invention of gated communities, especially in the outer suburbs, with an average population of 800. Their municipal powers in regulating land use, zoning and allocating resources are very strong and clearly favour social homogeneity of residential suburban schemes. In this context, suburban fragmentation is to be understood as a function of the institutional structure of French municipal government (Charmes, 2005, 2007).

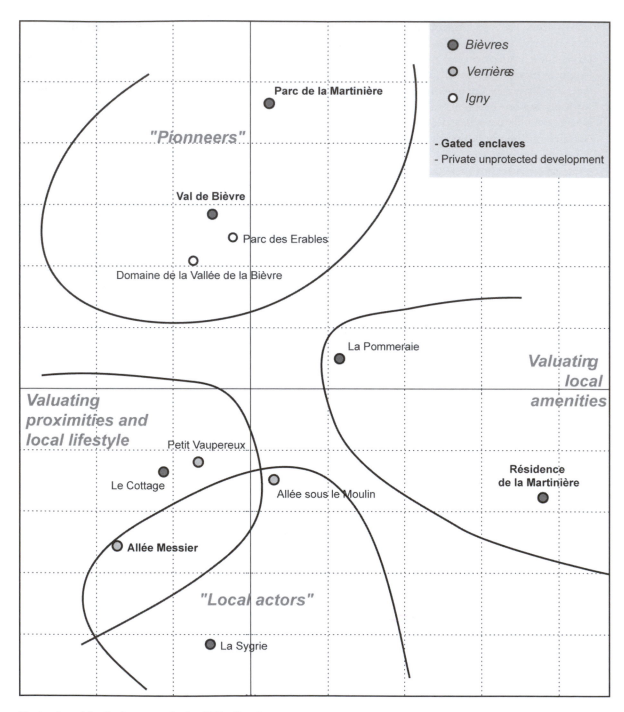

Factor 1 and 2 of a factor analysis. 43% of variance.

Figure 9.6 *Survey results: Private streets residents as local actors (factor analysis)*

Source: Author's survey, 2002

There is less of an institutional gap at the neighbourhood level than in most other European countries and less scope for the creative destruction of public urban governance models. Yet, there is something of a paradox here. Gated communities in France are not a recent innovation. In 1978 a comprehensive survey found that there were 1500 private neighbourhoods (villas) and private streets in the centre of Paris. In France, the 1804 *Code civil* set up a condominium law and regulated property rights, enclosures, rights of ways, contractual agreements; subsequent laws on planned unit developments (1923, 1976, 1986) were derived from this legal framework – every new land subdivision in the country has been required by law to set up restrictive covenants and, in the case of private streets, a Homeowners' Association. Streets can be either public (retrocession) or private. Under France's strong urban municipal culture, these have remained relatively underused and minor elements of the overall urban governance infrastructure (much as town and parish councils have in the UK). In parts of the world where the state is not so successful at delivering civic goods and services or not so minded to do so, the borrowed and adapted French 1804 condominium idea has provided the legal basis for entrepreneurs to supply not just homes but entire neighbourhoods complete with governance structures and private management (private versions of town halls for groups of anything from 200 to 200,000 residents). Co-ownership institutions, such as the French Condominium Law, can, in principle, reproduce many of the features of politically organized municipal government. But that has apparently not been necessary in France, at least partly due to the scale and fiscal design of municipal government units. Because of this path dependency in structuring local suburban governance, the debate over social sustainability of suburban private communities largely derives from the structuring of municipal governance and its redistributive patterns.

Conclusions

The debate over social sustainability of gated communities in a comparative perspective yields balanced conclusions. By means of an exploration of global and local lineation of residential private urban governance, considering gated communities as a global US model of private urbanism yields a simplistic, yet commonly accepted view. An exploration of the historical threads of gated communities connects their diffusion dynamic with suburban growth, whose landscapes are built according to an urban semiotic and a set of regulations made up of exclusivity, community, privacy and local control over land use and amenities. Gated communities have emerged in various forms for different reasons in different places according to local political, legal and architectural traditions.

If a well-known global diffusion of a set of tools has progressively homogenized planning practices (New Urbanism), it may seem a paradox that global developers are not pre-eminent actors in building gated enclaves. Promoters of enclosure are to be found among local smaller developers, whose strategies focus on 'niche' markets. Indeed, it seems that getting a better understanding of the spread of gated communities requires considering the nexus of law, as well as the practices of development industries and the layout of neighbourhoods. This demonstrates that the common goals of private communities are about getting control over the nearby environment (control over public space, amenities, etc.) and guarantee property values. In brief, if local actors target the building of sustainable communities from the owners' point of view, this is often a contradictory goal according to equity principles at a more general level.

However, empirical evidence based on the political behaviour of gated communities and the social relations of residents reveal path dependencies in the local manifestations of private communities. Whatever the legal context, local actors, residents' strategies, public bodies of governments and entrepreneurs find ways of meeting a continuous demand of local control. This can be met either by the means of private urban governance or by a local body of public government, depending on how local institutional milieus have structured decision-making, fiscal regulation and social exclusion patterns. Indeed, French small suburban communes are powerful enough – and oligarchic enough – to exclude undesired populations. Why, then, rely on another level of regulation such as restrictive covenants and private urban governance to reach the same goal of local exclusivity?

Notes

1   Research for this chapter has been sponsored by the French Agence Nationale pour la Recherche (ANR) Research Programme IP4 – Public–Private Interactions

in the Production of Suburban landscapes (2007–2010), which is gratefully acknowledged.

2   Association incorporated on 5 June 1832, according to the deeds, restrictive covenants and regulations recorded by Mr Leroy, notary in Saint Cloud on 28 September 1855. Although substantially amended, these original covenants are still in use today.

3   Article III of 1855 Restrictive Covenants.

4   Anonymous interview in 2000 with the help of S. Degoutin.

5   Contradictory information is provided by the *Nomenclature des Rues de Paris* (Ville de Paris, 2002) and by the *Guide Bleu* (1995).

6   Interestingly, some developments occupied land that was originally fenced and gated. For example, Rolling Hills and Hidden Hills used to be farm and ranching land and were gated to control cattle. Developers kept and reconditioned the former gated entrance of the ranch to make it their own. Canyon Lake used to be a summer camp and trailer park – also a gated land use. It became a 9500-person gated residential development in 1968.

7   The survey in Ile-de-France is based on three major advertising journals in the new housing industry: *Immoneuf*, *Le Guide du Neuf* and *L'indicateur Bertrand*. New enclaved schemes and programmes by international developers have been surveyed in 2000, 2001 and 2002. Among 806 published advertisements, 204 were published by international developers and/or clearly state that the programme is enclaved, gated or is named by a term denoting an enclosure. These first results correspond to the test phase of a large survey currently conducted on residential production between 2000 and 2008 in the Paris greater region. The full survey will be released in 2010. See http://gated.parisgeo.cnrs.fr for further information.

8   See Nguyen (1999) and Seymour et al (1998).

9   Incorporated gated communities include Bradbury and Rolling Hills (1957); Hidden Hills (1961); Canyon Lake (1991); and Leisure World (1999). Enclaves incorporated as part of a new city where a substantial number of single-family housing developments are gated include Dana Point (1989); Calabasas (1991); and Dove Canyon (incorporated with Rancho Santa Margarita in 2000). For details, see Le Goix (2006).

10   On average, 350 housing units and 93 household have been sampled and received the survey. The survey yielded an 80.6 per cent response rate. For methodological review and full results, see Callen and Le Goix (2007).

11   Principal components analysis conducted on 34 variables and 11 subdivisions. The four principal factors account for 72 per cent of total variance. With only 11 individuals, we limit the interpretation to factors 1 and 2 (43 per cent of total variance). See Callen and Le Goix (2007).

References

Bastie, J. (1964) *La croissance de la banlieue parisienne*, Presses Universitaires de France (Publications de la Faculté des Lettres et Sciences Humaines de Paris, Série 'Recherches', Tome XVII), Paris

Ben-Joseph E. (2004) 'Land use and design innovations in private communities', *Land Lines*, vol 16, pp8–12

Billard, G., Chevalier, J. and Madore, F. (2005) *Ville fermée, ville surveillée: La sécurisation des espaces résidentiels en France et en Amérique du Nord*, Presses Universitaires de Rennes (coll. Géographie Sociale), Rennes

Blakely, E. J. and Snyder M. G. (1997) *Fortress America: Gated Communities in the United States*, Brookings Institution Press and Lincoln Institute of Land Policy, Washington, DC, and Cambridge, MA

Body-Gendrot, S. (1998) *Les villes face à l'insécurité: Des ghettos américains aux banlieues françaises*, Bayard Edition, coll. Société, Paris

Body-Gendrot, S. (2001) *Les villes: la fin de la violence?* Presses de Sciences Po, coll. La Bibliothèque du Citoyen, Paris

Brower, T. (1992) 'Communities within the community: Consent, constitutionalism, and other failures of legal theory in residential associations', *Land Use and Environmental Law Journal*, vol 7, no 2, pp203–273

Burke, M. and Sebaly, C. (2001) 'Locking in the Pedestrian? The privatized Streets of Gated Communities', *World Transportation Policy and Practice*, vol 7, no 4, pp67–74

Caldeira, T. P. R. (2000) *City of Walls: Crime, Segregation, and Citizenship in Sao Paulo*, University of California Press, Berkeley, CA

Callen, D. and Le Goix, R. (2007) 'Fermeture et entre-soi dans les enclaves résidentielles', in Saint-Julien, T. and Le Goix, R. (eds) *La métropole parisienne. Centralités, Inégalités, Proximités*, Belin (Collection Mappemonde), Paris, pp209–232

Carvalho, M., Varkki George, R. and Anthony, K. H. (1997) 'Residential satisfaction in *condominios exclusivos* (gate guarded neighborhoods) in Brazil', *Environment and Behavior*, vol 29, no 6, pp734–768

Charmes, E. (2005) *La Vie périurbaine face à la menace des 'gated communities'*, L'Harmattan, Paris

Charmes, E. (2007) *Suburban Fragmentation versus Mobilities: Is Suburbanism Opposed to Urbanism*, Cybergeo, Paris

Ciotti, P. (1992) 'Forbidden city', *Los Angeles Times*, Los Angeles, 9 February, pB3

Davis, M. (1998) *Ecology of Fear: Los Angeles and the Imagination of Disaster*, H. Holt, New York, NY

Degoutin, S. (2004) 'Petite histoire illustrée de la ville privée', *Urbanisme*, no 337, pp39–41

Degoutin, S. (2006) *Prisonniers volontaires du rêve américain*, Editions de la Villette, Paris

Donzelot, J. and Mevel, C. (2001) *La politique de la ville: Une comparaison entre les USA et la France. Mixité sociale et développement communautaire*, Centre de Prospective et de Veille Scientifique (DRAST), PUCA, Paris

Flusty, S. (1994) *Building Paranoia: The Proliferation of Interdictory Space and the Erosion of Spatial Justice*, Los Angeles Forum for Architecture and Urban Design, West Hollywood, CA

Foldvary, F. (1994) *Public Goods and Private Communities: The Market Provision of Social Services*, Edward Elgar, Cheltenham, UK

Giroir, G. (2006) 'The purple jade villas (Beijing): A golden ghetto in red China', in Glasze, G., Webster, C. and Frantz, K. (eds) *Private Cities: Global and Local Perspectives*, Routledge, London, pp142–152

Glasze, G. (2000) 'Les complexes résidentiels fermés au Liban', *Observatoire de la Recherche sur Beyrouth*, no 13, pp6–11

Glasze, G. (2003) 'L'essor global des complexes résidentiels gardés atteint il l'Europe', *Etudes Foncières*, no 101, pp8–13

Glasze, G. (2005) 'Some reflections on the economic and political organisation of private neighbourhoods', *Housing Studies*, vol 20, no 2, pp221–233

Glasze, G. and Alkhayyal, A. (2002) 'Gated housing estates in the Arab world: Case studies in Lebanon and Riyadh, Saudi Arabia', *Environment and Planning B: Planning and Design*, vol 29, no 3, pp321–336

Glasze, G., Frantz, K. and Webster, C. J. (2002) 'The global spread of gated communities', *Environment and Planning B: Planning and Design*, vol 29, no 3, pp315–320

Guide Bleu (1995), Hachette Tourisme, Paris, p900

Jackson, K. T. (1985) *Crabgrass Frontier: The Suburbanization of the United States*, Oxford University Press, Oxford

Jürgens, U. and Landman, K. (2006) 'Gated communities in South Africa', in Glasze, G., Webster, C. and Frantz, K. (eds) *Private Cities: Global and Local Perspectives*, Routledge and Taylor and Francis, London, pp109–126

Kennedy, D. J. (1995) 'Residential associations as state actors: Regulating the impact of gated communities on nonmembers', *Yale Law Journal*, vol 105, no 3, pp761–793

Kirby, A. (2008) 'The production of private space and its implications for urban social relations', *Political Geography*, vol 27, no 1, pp74–95

Lacour-Little, M. and Malpezzi, S. (2001) *Gated Communities and Property Values*, Wells Fargo Home Mortgage and Department of Real Estate and Urban Land Economics, University of Wisconsin, Madison, WI

Leavitt, J. and Loukaitou-Sideris, A. (1994) 'Safe and Secure: Public Housing Residents in Los Angeles Define the Issues', Future Visions of Urban Public Housing, November 1994, Cincinnati, Ohio, pp287–303.

Le Goix, R. (2002) 'Les gated communities en Californie du Sud, un produit immobilier pas tout à fait comme les autres', *L'Espace Géographique*, vol 31, no 4, pp328–344

Le Goix, R. (2003) *Les gated communities aux Etats-Unis: Morceaux de villes ou territoires à part entière* [*Gated Communities within the City in the US: Urban Neighbourhoods or Territories Apart?*], Department of Geography, Université Paris, 1 Panthéon – Sorbonne, Paris

Le Goix, R. (2006) 'Gated communities as predators of public resources: The outcomes of fading boundaries between private management and public authorities in southern California', in Glasze, G., Webster, C. and Frantz, K. (eds) *Private Cities: Global and Local Perspectives*, Routledge and Taylor and Francis, London, pp76–91

Le Goix, R. (2007) *The Impact of Gated Communities on Property Values: Evidences of Changes in Real Estate Markets (Los Angeles, 1980–2000)*, Cybergeo, Paris, France

Le Goix, R. and Webster C. J. (2008) 'Gated communities', *Geography Compass*, vol 2, no 4, pp1189–1214, www.blackwell-compass.com/subject/geography/

Lentz, S. (2006) 'More gates, less community? Guarded housing in Russia', in Glasze, G., Webster, C. and Frantz, K. (eds) *Private Cities: Global and Local Perspectives*, Routledge and Taylor and Francis, London, pp206–221

Low, S. (2001) 'The edge and the center: Gated communities and the discourse of urban fear', *American Anthropologist*, vol 103, no 1, pp45–58

Low, S. (2003) *Behind the Gates: Life, Security, and the Pursuit of Happiness in Fortress America*, Routledge, New York, ppxi, 275

Madore, F. (2004) 'Géographie et modalités de la fermeture des espaces résidentiels en France', *L'Information Géographique*, no 2, pp155–172

Marcuse, P. (1997) 'The ghetto of exclusion and the fortified enclave: New patterns in the United States', *The American Behavioral Scientist*, no 41, pp311–326

McKenzie E. (1994) *Privatopia: Homeowner Associations and the Rise of Residential Private Government*, Yale University Press, London and New Haven, CT

McKenzie, E. (2003) 'Common interest housing in the communities of tomorrow', *Housing Policy Debates*, vol 14, nos 1–2, pp203–234

McKenzie, E. (2005) 'Constructing the Pomerium in Las Vegas: A case study of emerging trends in American gated communities', *Housing Studies*, vol 20, pp187–203

McKenzie, E. (2006) 'The dynamics of privatopia: Private residential governance in the USA', in Glasze, G., Webster, C. and Frantz, K. (eds) *Private Cities: Global and Local Perspectives*, Routledge and Taylor and Francis, London, pp9–30

Miller, G. J. (1981) *Cities by Contract*, MIT Press, Cambridge, MA

Newman, O. (1972) *Defensible Space: Crime Prevention Through Urban Design*, Macmillan, New York, p264

Newman, O., Grandin, D. and Wayno, F. (1974) *The Private Streets of St Louis*, A National Science Foundation study, Institute for Community Design, New York, NY

Nguyen, T. (1999) 'Coto De Caza residents say no to school within gates', *Los Angeles Times*, 4 March Orange County edition, pB1

Ocqueteau, F. (1999) 'Mutations dans le paysage français de la sécurité publique', *Les Annales de la Recherche Urbaine*, no 83/84, pp7–13

Pinçon, M. and Pinçon-Charlot, M. (1994) 'Propriété individuelle et gestion collective: Les lotissements chics', *Les Annales de la Recherche Urbaine*, no 65, pp34–35

Pinçon, M. and Pinçon-Charlot, M. (2001) *Paris Mosaïque*, Calmann-Lévy, Paris

Querrien, A. and Lassave, P. (1999) 'Au risque des espaces publics', *Les Annales de la Recherche Urbaine*, no 83–84, pp3–6

Sanchez, T. and Lang, R. E. (2005) 'Security versus status? A first look at the Census Gated Community Data', *Journal of Planning Education and Research*, vol 24, no 3, pp281–291

Seymour, L., Nguyen, T. and Groves, L. (1998) 'Public school plan rattles Coto De Caza residents', *Los Angeles Times*, 14 December, pB1

Stark, A. (1998) 'America, the gated? (Impact of gated communities in political life)', *Wilson Quarterly*, vol 22, no 1, pp50–58

Thuillier, G. (2005) 'Gated communities in the metropolitan area of Buenos Aires, Argentina: A challenge for town planning', *Housing Studies*, vol 20, no 2, pp255–271

Ville de Paris (2002). Nomenclature officielle des rues de Paris. Ville de Paris www.parius.fr/fr/asp/carto/nomenclature.asp; accessed 2002.

Webster, C. J. (2002) 'Property rights and the public realm: Gates, green belts, and Gemeinschaft', *Environment and Planning B: Planning and Design*, vol 29, no 3, pp397–412

Webster, C. and Glasze, G. (2006) 'Dynamic urban order and the rise of residential clubs', in Glasze, G., Webster, C. and Frantz, K. (eds) *Private Cities: Global and Local Perspectives*, Routledge and Taylor and Francis, London, pp222–236

Webster, C. J. and Lai, L. W. C. (2003) *Property Rights, Planning and Markets: Managing Spontaneous Cities*, Edward Elgar, Cheltenham, UK

Webster, C. J., Wu, F. and Zhao, Y. (2006) 'China's modern walled cities', in Glasze, G., Webster, C. and Frantz, K. (eds) *Private Cities: Global and Local Perspectives*, Routledge and Taylor and Francis, London, pp153–169

10

Barriers and Boundaries: An Exploration of Gatedness in New Zealand

Ann Dupuis and Jennifer Dixon

Introduction

Gated communities are viewed as a relatively new phenomenon in New Zealand. Defined as 'walled or fenced housing developments, to which public access is restricted, characterized by legal agreements which tie the residents to a common code of conduct and (usually) collective responsibility for management' (Atkinson and Blandy, 2005, p178), there are no official New Zealand figures on either the number of gated communities developed or the number of dwelling units within these communities. Similarly, little New Zealand research has been undertaken with people who live in gated communities and the potential implications for both the social and environmental sustainability of gated communities have yet to be identified by local government as issues for consideration.

Over much of the 20th century, New Zealand cities have tended to grow in patterns consistent with a small-scale society that has a fairly recent history of colonization. Urban development was premised largely on the individual ownership of standalone dwellings sited on reasonably large urban sections or lots. As a consequence, sprawl became a feature of the urban landscape, especially in Auckland, New Zealand's largest city,[1] where car reliance and a poorly developed public transport system added to the problem. As a response to these issues and in order to provide a greater choice of housing options in a city characterized by rapid population growth, over the last decade, urban planners have promoted urban intensification. Thus, especially in Auckland, one now sees a proliferation of higher-density dwellings, such as terraced housing, and low- and higher-rise apartments, sanctioned by local authorities in their attempts to ensure intensification. What is interesting to observe is a trend for these developments to be enclosed by walls of various types and for some to have both walls and gates. Real estate agents, in particular, have been keen to promote these developments as gated communities, extolling virtues of exclusivity, security and novelty.

This chapter addresses the theme of this book by demonstrating that in the New Zealand context, while gated communities are recent developments, gates and the enclosure of land by fences, walls or planting have long been part of New Zealand's urban and rural landscapes. Such features have been evident in traditional Maori society, in early colonial settlements of the mid- and late 19th century and in 20th-century suburbs. In order to frame part of our discussion, the chapter uses the comparatively familiar sociological explanatory device of continuity and change in order to trace the various forms and patterns of enclosing land and dwellings evident in various time periods. These different forms of enclosure, in turn, provide a lens through which we can view changes to dominant socio-economic, political and cultural practices over time.

Yet, while it is important to take a historical perspective and move away from the focus on gated communities as unique to the last two or so decades, it would be naive to attempt to draw too tight a connection between various historical forms of enclosures and gates and more recent gated communities. While the forms and functions of enclosures have differed over time, so too have forms of property ownership – a further marker in differentiating gated communities from other forms of enclosure in the built environment. In traditional Maori society, collective ownership of land prevailed; in fact, the concept of ownership brought to New Zealand by the colonizers was not part of a Maori ontology. Maori had no concept of land alienation other than by conquest; but even then a relationship to the land had to be established and the conquered could return and re-establish previous land connections. Colonization, however, saw British law and forms of property ownership set in place, with the vast majority of housing associated with the freehold fee-simple form of property ownership. Recent intensive housing initiatives, including gated communities, signal another significant shift with respect to forms of ownership. Most intensive housing in New Zealand comes under the 1972 Unit Titles Act, which creates the strata titles and is also the legislation through which corporate bodies are established and managed. Under this legislation, while owners have the right to freely sell their own units, the legislation itself involves a form of semi-collective ownership.

The following section of the chapter provides a discussion of the various forms of enclosure of land evident in New Zealand from the time when Maori built *pa*, or fortified villages, through to the forms of enclosure typical of much 20th-century suburban development. The third section draws on research on gated communities undertaken by the authors to show that current forms of gating in New Zealand represent two trends: on the one hand there are examples of gated communities that are much like the typical gated developments in the US and elsewhere; on the other, we identify and present as a typology, an emerging 'kiwi-style'[2] of gatedness, characterized more by gestures towards gated features rather than the more advanced and obvious forms of international gated communities. We follow this with a discussion of the social and environmental sustainability of gated communities in New Zealand.

The continuity of enclosures

Enclosures in traditional Maori society

New Zealand was first settled in the 13th century during an 'era of widespread Polynesian ocean voyaging' (King, 2003, p48). Through adaptation to the new environment over a period of time, these eastern Polynesian arrivals transformed economically and culturally into the New Zealand Maori. Both population increase and the competition for scarce resources led to the growth of tribal organization through the 15th and 16th centuries (Irwin, 1985; King, 2003, p72). It was during this period that *pa*, or fortified and enclosed villages, were first used as sites to withdraw to in times of warfare.

The early ethnologist Elsdon Best (1927) tells us that the Maori word *pa* is both a verb and a noun. As a verb, *pa* means 'to obstruct, to block up'. As a noun, it can be a screen, anything used to obstruct or to block an open space – hence, the application of the word by Maori to describe both their defensive works and fortified villages (Best, 1927, p18). Typically, Maori constructed *pa* on high landforms, such as hilltops, spur and headlands, with the *pa* layout determined by the hill's original shape, although the erection of platforms, ditches, terraces and banks considerably modified natural land forms. On flat land, like plains or valleys, *pa* were often sited on riverbanks where there was a steep fall to the water. Islands too were chosen as *pa* sites. Reflecting the diversity of sites, there was much variation in the external forms that *pa* took. Commonly, however, stockades, as well as trenches and ramparts, were built to protect the sides open to enemy attack. Inside the *pa* was like a village with sleeping huts, stores of *kumara* (a cultivated sweet potato) and other foods with specially erected *pataka* (food storehouses), pits for water or special access to a spring if possible (Best, 1941). According to Best, Captain Cook, the British navigator who sighted New Zealand in 1769, described a *pa* erected on a headland that was defended by ramparts and ditches. Cook estimated that from the top of the rampart to the bottom of the fosse or ditch was a distance of 22 feet. Stockades were erected on the top of the rampart, while those on the outer side of the fosse leaned inward. Cook also noted that the place had been burned, presumably by an attacking force. In Best's opinion, unless attackers used fire or starvation, such fortifications would be well-nigh impenetrable given the type of technology used by pre-European Maori (Best, 1927).

In terms of size, *pa* sites varied greatly, from defended areas of less than 180 square metres to over 55,000 square metres (Walton, 2000) and could accommodate various numbers of people. Thus, some were quite small, accommodating the *whanau* (large family), while others were sufficiently large to accommodate an *iwi* (tribe) of several hundred people. A claim made by the early European missionary, Henry Williams, that there were some 2,000 fighting men in the Whakawhiti *pa* at Waiapu in 1834 suggests that at least some *pa* were very large indeed (Best, 1941).

Traditionally, Maori were hunter gatherers and so did not live in a *pa* all the time. Depending on a variety of factors, including season, weather and the state of relationships with other tribes, they would live in other types of unfortified sites while they were fishing, catching birds and tending gardens (New Zealand Historic Places Trust, undated). The Maori term applied to an unfortified village is *kainga,* which can also mean 'place of residence, home'. Best (1927) notes that, traditionally, Maori communities lived in both forms of village – the *pa* and the *kainga*. Often the *kainga* was sited near a *pa*, making it easy for local people to move themselves, their food and possessions inside the fortification if an enemy approached. It has been suggested that Maori may have lived in open settlements most of the time, only going to the *pa* in times of trouble (New Zealand Historic Places Trust, undated).

Fitting well into the themes of this chapter has been a more recent argument that *pa* fortifications served both defensive and symbolic functions. While *pa* were predominantly built as secure sites protecting against attack in times of war, they were also 'secure places to live and store food, they were residences for important people and centres for learning, crafts and horticulture' (New Zealand Historic Places Trust, undated). Symbolically, therefore, the size and type of *pa* was associated with group identity and the *mana* or status of the tribe and its leaders.

From the colonial to the contemporary: The continuity of 'enclosure'

The first European 'discovery' of New Zealand in 1642 is attributable to the Dutch sea captain Abel Tasman. The earliest sustained interaction between Maori and Europeans, however, was not until the British captain and cartographer James Cook's first visit to New Zealand in 1769. European commercial interests in the latter part of the 18th century and early 19th century centred around sealing, whaling and timber, with close economic connections between New Zealand and

Australian settlements. It was during this period that Maori entered into trade with European merchants and acquired muskets. Christian evangelizing in New Zealand began in 1814, and thereafter missionaries of various faiths brought not only Christianity but also literacy.

At the time of its annexation as a British Crown Colony in 1840, the population of New Zealand was estimated to be 117,000: 115,000 Maori and 2000 Europeans. By 1906, the total population was just over 936,000 (Neville, 1979). Late 19th-century New Zealand was fundamentally a frontier rural society; but small settlements and then towns and cities developed, often reflecting characteristics of the religion and place of origin of the early settlers. Social class distinctions intensified over time too (Pearson and Thorns, 1983) and were reflected in the size, quality and other features of both urban and rural housing.

European dwellings in 19th-century colonial New Zealand were frequently enclosed. While the large sheep runs of the South Island went largely unfenced (although ridge lines and rivers provided natural boundaries), the landed gentry who owned these properties lived in Victorian-styled antipodean mansions that, while not enclosed, certainly were characterized by the elegance of the gates and sweeping drives that led up to these houses. More modest rural dwellings of this period were fully enclosed in order to ensure that both people and animals were either kept out or kept in. Urban dwellings were also enclosed. During the early colonial period, housing in small and growing settlements was often close to farmland, so gorse and blackberry hedges, or stone or wooden fences were practical measures to keep animals from wandering onto property (Salmond, 1986, p110). The general enclosure pattern for middle- and upper middle-class dwellings was 6 feet high fences, hedges or shrubbery along the sides and rear boundaries of a section. For the street boundary, barriers tended to be lower and more fancy paling fences were common, as were rather grand-style gates. Even working-class homes, while often sited very close to or on the street, were on sites enclosed by either paling or wire fences. Photographs of 19th-century houses show that fences not only marked the particular urban form that had developed in colonial New Zealand, but were also a marker of socio-economic levels (see, for example, Salmond, 1986).

By the early years of the 20th century, an important purpose of the fences and hedges used as boundary markers was to separate out components of the garden within. According to Leach (2000, p85), this represented the preoccupation of the time in ensuring a division between public and private areas, mirroring issues of both class and privacy important in, first, Victorian and then, later, Edwardian society. Leach (2000) further describes the importance of screening the front door from sight from the road for the privacy of middle- and upper middle-class callers. By the post-World War I period, tall hedges and other such screens were no longer common and front garden areas, while still fenced, were opened up to the street. Despite the adoption in New Zealand of such housing designs as the American-inspired bungalow, New Zealand did not follow the common practice seen in many American suburbs of the 'continuous communal front lawn' (Leach, 2000, p85).

Privacy also seemed to drive the continued tradition of fencing urban sections in the post-World War II period. As housing styles changed to incorporate patios, terraces and decks with access from external sliding doors, and much greater use was made of outdoor spaces for family recreation, the desire for privacy continued to be met by urban sections separated off by 6 feet high fences on three sides and a lower fence or planting at the street frontage. Until about the 1960s, urban sections, or lots, tended to be generous in size. By the 1960s, the quarter acre section had become the norm for urban New Zealanders. Into the latter years of the 20th century, as section sizes decreased, fences were built of more diverse materials, but were still the norm for New Zealand's suburban houses although, as housing designs changed, gates were no longer mandatory. The important point underpinning this brief sketch of the history of New Zealand dwellings is that enclosures of various forms and gates have been ubiquitous.

Change: Contemporary gated communities in New Zealand

So far we have argued that fences and gates have been common features of New Zealand's built environment, both historically and throughout the expansive suburban development that occurred in the post-World War II period. However, gated communities of the last decade represent not only a different built form, but also a new form of ownership. With respect to the built form, our research has delineated two trends pertaining to contemporary gatedness. The first is the design of gated communities; the second trend is the emergence

of a 'kiwi-style' of gatedness which we present in a later sub-section as a typology of gatedness.

Trend 1: International influences in gated communities

The built environment of a city is an expression of (indeed, some might say even a celebration of) particular values held by communities who have shaped its development – social, religious, political and environmental. The identity of a city is influenced by place, space and the economic and cultural activities of its people. What is evident in Auckland is that there is little expression of cultural differences in the city's built environment that reflect elements of Maori, Pacific people's or even Pakeha cultural and aesthetic values. The architectural design of most intensive housing developments, including gated communities, demonstrates an uncritical uptake of architectural identity mostly drawn from Europe and the US.

Typical examples of exotic influences on local design can be seen in many gated communities in the Auckland region and take the form of weak gestures towards Tuscan or mission-type influences. These gated communities sit as individual architectural projects in various urban residential landscapes as ubiquitous, could-be-anywhere nondescripts. Often they were inaugurated in a context of promise and hype, but demonstrate little reference to sustainability or sustainable design principles. Mostly constructed in greenfield sites during the last decade, many of the gated communities are car dependent, with some façades showing signs of deterioration. Since the construction of some of these developments, there has been a significant shift in the expectations of communities for higher-quality intensive developments, and the emergence of a more sophisticated planning regime that is better equipped to address urban design issues. Nonetheless, a legacy of derivative and mixed-quality gated communities remains, affirming the necessity to ensure architectural design that is much more attuned to this country's location in the South Pacific.

Trend 2: Kiwi-style gatedness

Contemporary gatedness is not, however, a unitary phenomenon. Unlike the more extreme examples of gated communities seen in such cities as Johannesburg and Buenos Aries, a much less obtrusive, more low-key 'kiwi' form of gatedness is emerging. In order to capture aspects of this style, we undertook an analysis of a range of intensive housing developments in the Auckland region. From this we developed our 'typology of gated forms' (Dixon and Dupuis, 2003), an eightfold classification of gatedness that identified the following features:

- physical barriers: walls, gates, doors, trees/hedges/greenery, speed bumps;
- technological barriers: surveillance cameras and videos, security alarms, access via swipe card or the intercom;
- 'manned' surveillance: e.g. security patrols and the 'front desk' barrier;
- signs: neighbourhood watch signs, 'private property', 'no trespassing', 'beware of dog', 'be respectful of private residence', 'no parking', 'tow away', 'residents only' parking, road paint and road markings;
- design features: narrowing or partly obscured entrances, change in colour, texture of roading, walls, doors, gates with no handles or levers;
- natural surveillance: being observed by residents;
- implicit signals: closed, unmarked doors and gates; and
- retro-gating: where gates have been erected some time after the original construction of the development.

Consideration of the above typology led us to make the following observations about gatedness in medium- and higher-density housing in Auckland:

- Many of the forms of gatedness observed could be described as 'symbolic' forms of gatedness, designed to act as a deterrent, rather than as a barrier, to access. For example, many gated communities have walls that could easily be climbed, making access to buildings or grounds a possibility.
- Forms of gatedness occur across a range of socio-economic levels and quality of housing involved.
- Gatedness is generally more apparent when the enclosed housing is close to public streets or walkways. Gatedness in developments in suburban areas tends to be less obvious than it is in more urban sites.

- Gatedness in public areas appears to be aimed at restricting car access and car parking as much as it is aimed at deterring people.
- In some instances, the erection of fences, walls or other barriers is an attempt to create privacy, rather than safety or security.
- Smooth surfaces on doors, gates and garage doors, with no visible handles or levers, give a very 'inaccessible' message. While this might also be about design and/or style, the message of inaccessibility comes through strongly.
- Associated with the previous point is a 'sterile' type of look that denotes a sense of privacy and has the effect of deterring outsiders.
- Gates have been erected as a later addition by residents, some still allowing access by pedestrians.

Gated communities and sustainability

This section addresses some dimensions of sustainability with respect to gated communities. Sustainability can, of course, be defined in many ways. Nonetheless, while we do not intend to traverse the myriad of definitions, concepts of 'sustainable development', 'sustainability' and 'sustainable design' are increasingly influencing local planning and building practices. Drivers for this change are coming from government policy directives through legislation, the adoption of new technologies and practices, and the recognition of the need to develop adaptive responses in urban management given the rate and extent of global environmental change. Increasingly, too, attention is being paid to social sustainability alongside economic and environmental considerations. We take up the notions of security and community as two indicators of social sustainability. We note that these comprise elements within a working definition of social sustainability developed by Bramley et al (2006). We conclude the section with reference to some environmental features of gated communities.

The ensuing discussion on sustainability makes reference to a small-scale study of gated communities undertaken by the authors. North Shore City was chosen as the location for the research as it contained a significant supply of greenfield land for residential development and had already attracted a number of these developments. North Shore is New Zealand's fourth largest city with a

Figure 10.1 *A typology of gatedness in New Zealand*
Source: Sav Schulman

population of 220,300 (North Shore City, 2006), and one of the four cities that make up the Auckland region. Until this research, explanations for the emergence of gated developments in Auckland had been largely based on supposition and conjecture, which drew on international literature. The intention of our study, therefore, was to provide some solid locally derived data regarding the incidence of gated developments in a specific area and the views of people who were involved in these developments in various capacities.

The study had two components. The first was a mapping exercise aimed at ascertaining the location of all the gated developments on Auckland's North Shore. As no records of gated developments were held by the North Shore City Council (NSCC), their location was identified in a number of ways. Information on some sites came from existing knowledge bases, like statutory planning maps, while information on others was elicited from real estate agents. A total of 17 gated developments were located, visited and photographed. The largest development comprised 180 units, while the smallest had four units. The oldest gated development was built in 1993; but the majority were constructed from the period of 1997 onwards. Seven developments were located on sites subject to redevelopment, while ten were on sites that had previously been undeveloped; seven of these were greenfield developments.

The second component of the research comprised interviews with 25 residents living in gated developments, 5 developers and 2 NSCC staff. All interviews with residents took place at their homes and all but one resident were owner occupiers. Interviews were held in ten different gated communities selected because they covered gated communities of different sizes, and dwellings of different quality, age and dwelling type. All of the gated communities visited for interviews had vehicle entry gates that required a sensor of some type (e.g. remote, keypad and intercom) to allow the gate to be opened. Some, but not all, also had pedestrian gates with security sensors. Other developments had pedestrian gates that were not secure or had no pedestrian gate at all. Some developments had apartments or units fronting onto the road with their own secured individual front gate.

The interviews were qualitative in style with open-ended questions. Topics covered in the resident interviews included reasons for living in a gated community; previous experience of gated living; expectations around gated living; issues and problems; cooperation and decision-making among residents; relationships with the wider neighbourhood; living again in a gated community; and perceptions around exclusivity. Developer interviews focused on such questions as: why they chose to build gated communities; why purchasers liked gates; the future for gated communities; their experiences of building gated communities; issues for residents, neighbours and local authorities; and governance arrangements. Interviews with NSCC officials covered such issues as their general views of gated communities; gatedness and environmental sustainability; the implications for local government of increasing private governance issues and service provision; and associated concerns such as traffic flows.

Security and social sustainability

The interviews with gated community residents provided us with some puzzling findings. Given the novelty of gated communities in New Zealand and the extent to which gates are used as an advertising tool promoting increased security, the expectation was that gated community residents would have made an unambiguous choice of living in a gated community because of the security factor associated with gates. A surprising finding reported by most interviewees, however, was that the presence of gates had very little bearing on their initial reason for choosing to live in their gated community. Instead, we were told that residents had based their decision to move to a gated community on such factors as location (including proximity to amenities, arterial routes for ease of transport or closeness to family members), design, low maintenance and convenience:

Interviewer: Why did you choose to live here?

Resident: Because of the location and the view.

Resident: We've always had big houses, big gardens, that sort of thing. But now we're enjoying the convenience. You can pull your car right up to the door, 2m to carry the groceries and things. It's really, really convenient. If you want to go away for the weekend, just lock the door and away you go.

In four instances (in four separate developments) interviewees had even bought their units directly off the plans without realizing they were buying into a gated community:

> Resident: When we decided to come here we didn't know there were going to be gates. We didn't even think about it. It was more that we were downsizing and the curtains needed changing.

When discussing the positive features of gated community living, many residents claimed that what they liked most was the lifestyle associated with living in an apartment or unit, making frequent references to not having to mow lawns, do the garden, clean the pool or do any external painting:

> Resident: I think there is within the community at large a group of people who prefer the lifestyle reasons – lifestyle, security – whatever, but certainly prefer that their disposable time is not devoted to maintaining a home.

Some residents did, however, comment on security, but as a contributing rather than a main factor, shaping their initial decision to live in a gated community:

> Interviewer: Why did you choose to live here?
>
> Resident: Primarily it runs across probably three or four issues. One is location – just the physical location – close to [a main centre]. Secondly it's secure – so because we travel a lot security was an issue. It's low maintenance from an owner's perspective, so there's a collective maintenance of the premises and, in our case, there's no lawns to mow or gardens as such and then probably just the style of it. Both our unit and the physical environment fit our lifestyle – so it's strongly for lifestyle and location considerations. This was a choice that supported our lifestyle rather than *prima facie* security as such.

The finding that gates were not the major driver in people's initial decisions to buy and live in gated communities was in direct contradiction to a view that came through strongly in the developer interviews: that purchasers perceived gated communities as providing greater security. Adding to the puzzle was the finding that, despite gates not being a significant driver initially, once residents had experienced living in a gated community, gates took on much greater importance. The sense of security that the gates gave those we interviewed, along with more minor advantages such as a lack of door-to-door salespeople, appeared to significantly increase their likelihood of living in a gated community again, if they moved house in the future:

> Interviewer: If you had had a wish list [when you bought], would the gated feature have been in the first five or ten on your list?
>
> Resident: No.
>
> Interviewer: How about now that you're here – is it important to you?
>
> Resident: I think we'd definitely look for it again. We'd certainly look at – for a private dwelling – putting gates in. I spend a few weeks away from home on work and [my wife] really appreciates the security of it. She still doesn't like me going away, but feels a lot more comfortable here than in previous places we've lived at.
>
> Interviewer: How much of a factor were the gates when you bought?
>
> Resident: Minimal.
>
> Interviewer: And how important is it to you now that you're here?
>
> Resident: It's quite important now – it's a good, secure feeling.
>
> Interviewer: So if you were to shift again you'd look at gates again and would they come in the top five or ten on your wish list?
>
> Resident: Easily in the top five – yeah.
>
> Interviewer: Would you do it all again? Would you live in another place like this?
>
> Resident: Oh yes – definitely.
>
> Interviewer: And if you had to move, how far up on your list would gates be?
>
> Resident: Higher than they were when we came here. We didn't realize the benefits so much until we came into the community here. It's all very well to think you're going to have gates and how nice that's going to be – you don't have a sense of just how important it is until you've got them – it's quite lovely. We do have individual burglar alarms. So there's that two-phase security. I think in the changing world of today where it's become a lot more violent – there seems to be a lot more burglaries – we – I certainly have a

greater sense of security here and I'd certainly like to think that that's what we'll do in the future if we do build another house or we do move from here. It'll be really important to me to have that sense of security.

The findings reported on above led us to a consideration of the 'orthodox' explanations for why people choose to live in gated communities: security, lifestyle and elitism (Blakely and Snyder, 1995); and the concern over class-based urban segregation and exclusion strategies (Low, 2003); or simply that they might represent a new fashion in urban living copied from overseas. At one level, we cannot discount that gatedness may be nothing more than the latest urban fad to hit New Zealand. Fashion provides a logical explanation too in that it could explain why gated communities are becoming more common on Auckland's North Shore, a high socio-economic area, whose inhabitants tend to be well travelled and knowledgeable about international trends (see Glasze et al, 2006). Moreover, the interview material with developers confirmed that they had taken on board many of the features observed in gated communities in Australia's Gold Coast area of Queensland when building gated communities in New Zealand.

With respect to the explanation of exclusivity, we again draw on interviewee responses on whether outsiders might perceive their gated community as exclusive. Some residents claimed that it had never occurred to them that living in a gated community could be viewed that way by outsiders. Others responded that they could see how outsiders might view it as exclusive, but that they did not personally see living in a gated community that way. Some mentioned that their present home was no more exclusive or any different from previous homes they had lived in, which were not part of gated communities. Others commented that they regarded particular suburbs in Auckland as more exclusive than the gated community they lived in. So neither fashion nor exclusivity provides a fully satisfactory basis for exploring the conundrum around security, exposed in our interview data.

Our concern remained that orthodox explanations for the rise of gated communities were still firmly rooted within a modernist paradigm, either strongly anchored in an individualistic psychologically oriented perspective, a technocratic planning approach to the urban, or a concern with the development of both class- and ethnicity-based urban enclaves (Marcuse, 1997a, 1997b). What such explanations fail to do is tap into a more sociological viewpoint, framed around issues of fear and risk that better appreciate the late modern nature of contemporary society and the issues and concerns concomitant to this epoch (Beck, 1992; Giddens, 2000). Such work, we think, allows for an explanation of the conceptual disjuncture with respect to security that was made clear in the resident interviews.

The question remained as to why our research showed that while residents said initially that gates were not important in their decision to live in their gated community, they all noted they would choose to live in a gated community again should they move house. The major reason given was the increased sense of security they felt living in a gated community. We ask: security from what? What prompted that response? After all, the connotations of security in North Shore City are very different from, for example, security in South African cities with the transformation of the apartheid city to the post-apartheid city; 'without doubt, [therefore], the fear of crime plays a significant role in the drive for neighbourhood closure' (Jurgens and Landman, 2006, p118). The North Shore has low crime rates and its population has high levels of skills, education and income. A national set of indicators rates North Shore City schools the highest of any urban area in New Zealand and the city enjoys a higher than average rate of homeownership (Enterprise North Shore, undated). Statistically, North Shore City is a very safe place in which to live. What, then, does security mean to the residents who live in these North Shore gated communities? More importantly, why is security even deemed to be an issue in an area such as the North Shore?

In our view, the recourse to notions of security on the part of residents has less to do with any daily reality of crime, a statistically unlikely experience for most North Shore residents, and more to do with the pervasive sense of fear that has come to be associated with urban living in late modernity. The concept we have drawn on in our attempt to explain the conundrum discussed above is that of 'derivative fear' which comes from Zygmunt Bauman's 2006 text *Liquid Fear*. In his explanation of the concept, Bauman describes derivative fear as a 'sort of "second degree" fear, a fear, so to speak, socially and culturally "recycled'" (Bauman, 2006, p3). Derivative fear, he continues, guides human behaviour 'whether or not a menace is immediately present'. It is a 'steady frame of mind' depicted as 'the sentiment of being *susceptible* to danger; a feeling of insecurity … and vulnerability' (Bauman, 2006, p3).

Bauman goes on to explain that the derivative fears are of three kinds: those that threaten the body and possessions; others of a more general nature that threaten the social order, such as insecurity over employment, income, old age or disability; and those that threaten 'one's place in the world' – for example, one's identity. For the purposes of this discussion, the derivative fears most apt are of the first kind – those that threaten the body and possessions. A key point that Bauman then makes is that of the 'decoupling' of derivative fear from the dangers that may cause it (Bauman, 2006, pp3–4). Derivative fear, in this sense, can then be experienced and, as a consequence, shifted across any range of possible concerns that may, or may not, have a rational basis or a statistical likelihood of occurring. In describing how derivative fear operates, Bauman (2006, p4) writes:

> Most fearsome is the ubiquity of fears; they may leak out of any nook or cranny of our homes and our planet. From dark streets and from brightly lit television screens. From our bedrooms and our kitchens. From our workplaces and from the underground train we take to get there and back. From people we meet and people whom we failed to notice.

It is here that Bauman makes an important move in his argument when he claims that despite the ubiquity of fear, we do not live in constant fear all day, every day. This is because we have 'more than enough shrewd stratagems … supported with all sorts of clever gadgets obligingly offered by the shops to ensure that we do not live in a constant state of fear' (Bauman, 2006, p5). Here we argue that gates could be one of Bauman's 'clever gadgets' that are employed in order to allay the amorphous fears of late modernity.

This still leaves the question of what it is that effects the change in people with respect to their attitude to gates after they have lived behind them for some time. While it might simply be that familiarity breeds not contempt but attachment, it is not, for example, the attachment we might have to an old but comfortable pair of shoes. It is one that is bred in the waters of the social currents of late modernity and links to the deep unease, disquietude and insecurities that are intrinsic to our times.

Community and social sustainability

In this sub-section we focus on community within gated communities, the element of social sustainability we describe as 'getting on' with one another. This can pose something of a problem when it comes to co-owners negotiating with each other around common property issues and with property professionals allied to corporate bodies in various ways. In the New Zealand context, the problem of getting on can be even more acute as most New Zealanders, growing up in detached houses on separate sections, have had little experience of living closely together in intensive urban environments such as gated communities and consequently lack the understanding of what it means to rub shoulders with one another in close proximity. While most New Zealanders are used to next-door neighbours, they are not used to them on shared stairways, or having them live above or below, or on the other side of the wall. Nevertheless, as one resident observed, a sense of community can develop in gated situations:

> Interviewer: Is there a sense of community [in the development]?
>
> Resident: Yes there's quite a good sense of community. We have four Korean families and they interact, I guess, amongst themselves. And then there's three kiwi families and we have a lot to do with these people who are Korean. Not so much for the people up the drive because you don't really see them – only just occasionally in the drive and just wave and say hello. But we've quite often been over there for drinks and down there and they've come here and everyone generally gets invited – but not everyone comes.

The interview data with gated community residents showed that despite the positive views of gated community living, one topic that residents expressed reservations about was the extent to which a sense of 'community' was engendered within their gated communities. The data suggest that gates in themselves do not appear either to create or increase a sense of community. Somewhat ironically, they may, however, have an indirect effect on community building in that gates broke down in all the gated communities our interviewees lived in, so residents needed to interact with one another over making joint decisions regarding the repair and maintenance of the community's gates, although any cooperative activities such as group working bees in commonly owned gardens or body corporate meetings could also help to create a sense of community. Any of these activities might equally bring about a rise in tension within the community and among residents if there are opposing views about how such activities should be managed:

Interviewer: Have there been any issues, good or bad, that have related to living in a gated community?

Resident: I think the difficulty that I've found is that we've had a number of working bees for the gardens and the fence – exterior fence and once the house – the apartments were painted [so] the exterior fence needed to be done and to do the fence there was only me and the fellow next door doing it. So that was a long hard day and then with the gardening there was only him and I and one of the owners of one of the other apartments from the front here that helped in the gardens. So I've actually put forward for the minutes of the next AGM [annual general meeting] that we'll bill an hourly rate for those that don't attend working bees because it's – they're just taking advantage – they've got a nice looking property that has its market value upgraded at the expense of us. So, yeah, a bit of bitterness there.

Interviewer: Do you put that down to that owner/renter mix or the issue of whether you own or rent?

Resident: A little bit. I know it's a time thing for a lot of people, but everybody in both instances was given over a month's notice. To me I think it's ignorance because the rented apartments by foreigners are owned by foreigners and I think they just take advantage. If it was coming out of their pocket they might decide that a bit of labour is preferable.

A few interviewees could say that they felt a sense of community and, as the following interview excerpts indicate, put that down to individual personalities:

Interviewer: Is there any sense of community?

Resident: Not entirely. I think units and blocks like this can have two effects – either you become close with your neighbours or you become a little insulated and that just

depends on who you are and what kind of person you are and whether you're willing to talk to your neighbours – I tend to keep my eye out and watch what's going on if I'm home.

Interviewer: Do you think perhaps the gates have provided more of a community feel?

Resident: No – I think that's something that we make. That's not something that a gated community gives us – I think that's something that we do. We're a bit social.

The interview data also suggest that there is a strong connection between the design and layout of the dwellings within gated communities and the extent of interaction among the residents:

Interviewer: You've mentioned that you know everyone [in the development] – do you think perhaps the gates have provided a little bit more of a community feel?

Resident: It'd be very hard to measure, but I think it'd be there anyway [the community feel] just because of the layout – it's the layout. On this side [external to the development] we don't really know anybody because trees block them off.

Interviewer: Do you feel part of the community … within this development?

Resident: Yes [hesitantly] – but it's limited – because of the design there isn't any – there's no daily interaction. Yes we see people – but mainly when people are moving across the property rather than living – because of the adjacency of living. In some communities you're forced if you like because of the egress – the way in which you can access it. But here we're not. It's pretty independent living within this facility.

The issue of living an independent lifestyle while still within a gated community was a dominant theme in the interviews. As one resident commented:

Resident: People are interested – they're not disengaged but it's hard to describe. It might sound strange, but people are very independent because you are not looking in on anyone. It's not like other developments. You've got a pretty motivated group here and they engage when it's necessary to. But beyond that – really there's no interaction, there's no hassle.

I think the main challenge here is that because there's no onsite management, it just doesn't qualify for it in terms of quantum – I think getting other owners interested in the physical property has been the challenge.

It's never frustrated us, but it's simply because people live so independently and many people travel as we do, or are away regularly you could say. That's been the only issue here… Security isn't really the issue – it's more about just maintenance in the property and garden maintenance.

Environmental sustainability

In New Zealand, as elsewhere, the urban planning agenda has been dominated by the rhetoric of sustainability. The advent of the Sustainable Development Programme of Action in 2003 (DPMC) and the launch of the Urban Design Protocol in 2005 (Ministry for the Environment, 2005) were important signals from government in highlighting the need to improve design quality and sustainability of urban form. In addition, the 2002 Local Government Act requires local authorities to address sustainable development as a key goal in their overall planning frameworks. Increasing effort in both funded research programmes and public policy formulation is focusing on the implementation of sustainable practices in urban development in order to improve the sustainability of New Zealand cities.

Two issues exemplify mixed approaches to the adoption of sustainability principles in gated communities. First, the construction and management of commonly owned infrastructure (such as swales and rain gardens) on gated and non-gated sites is becoming increasingly common, particularly in those countries where water-sensitive sustainable practices are being encouraged by national and local governments (Dixon and van Roon, 2006). The provision of features for storm-water management and water recycling are becoming the norm in many new residential developments as local authorities seek innovative ways of increasing the efficiency of water use and managing both quality and quantity of storm water more effectively at source, rather than pursuing traditional 'end-of-pipe' solutions.

One such example is found in a major gated community on Auckland's North Shore. This development incorporated provision for several swales, rain gardens, underground storm-water tanks and a storm-water pond, although some modification was made following the consenting process. These features are being managed by the body corporate which is required to meet the conditions governing environmental

management of the site by the NSCC. However, practices vary between cities. In another example, despite its location in a city where there is a particularly strong commitment to sustainability principles, the inclusion of extensive impermeable surfaces on the whole development site denied opportunities for more innovative approaches to storm-water management.

Second, there are issues around architectural design and layout. Gated communities tend to comprise a mixture of standalone and low-rise terraced housing, which is usually homogenous in nature. Some reflect elements of sustainability policies. For example, they are located close to public transport nodes, intended to promote urban intensification and reduce car dependency. Others, of course, are developed in greenfield locations where public transport provision is not as extensive as in more built-up areas and residents are required to use cars to access employment and other services.

Council officers interviewed for this research commented on both positive and negative aspects of gated communities. The officers observed that gated communities can provide good opportunities for comprehensive design outcomes in terms of privacy, indoor/outdoor flows, the inclusion of solar power, reuse of water and so on with cheaper installation costs. The inclusion of gates also helps to define whether communal facilities (such as tennis courts and pools) are public or private, and provide security in areas that receive extensive public use, such as popular beaches. On the other hand, connectivity with existing neighbourhoods and reserves can be a problem in large gated communities, particularly where there are few access points which reduce the number of bus routes. High walls and fences, a feature of gated communities, can also contribute to a loss of oversight of a street or road. Traffic congestion can develop in developments which have been gated post-design and construction, and rubbish collection is problematic if facilities are not located close to gates for pick-ups. There can also be arguments by developers for exemption from required development contributions where they are providing facilities onsite for residents.

Conclusions

This chapter has explored the phenomenon of gatedness and enclosures in New Zealand from both a historical and contemporary perspective. Using the explanatory device of continuity and change, it has demonstrated that gates and enclosures in various guises have long been part of urban and rural landscapes. What has changed across the time periods discussed, however, have been the functions served by gates and enclosures and the forms of landownership involved. In traditional Maori settings, *pa*, or fortified villages, were enclosed by stockades and variously accompanied by ramparts and ditches, designed to ward off the onslaught of tribal enemies. In 19th-century colonial New Zealand, the standalone housing which dominated in urban areas was invariably enclosed on all sides, with the quality and type of fencing materials frequently signifying the social class of the occupants. In 20th-century New Zealand suburbs, the practice of ensuring that standalone housing was enclosed continued. Our examination of the functions and forms of enclosures and gates over these periods shows that, to a greater or lesser extent, security, privacy and exclusivity have all been influential in shaping the built form.

Currently, there is a change taking place in building codes and planning requirements for residential housing in New Zealand. Strongly influenced by an agenda that reflects global environmental concerns, these local responses are underpinned by notions of sustainable development. Gated communities, as part and parcel of any new housing development, will inevitably be part of this shift and thus will reflect many more elements of sustainability in their design and construction than is occurring now. In addition, a forthcoming review of the 1972 Unit Titles Act is likely to make a number of changes that will improve the operation and management of corporate bodies, with specific references to issues of rule change, the funding of long-term maintenance and opportunities for dispute resolution. This major overhaul of the act should also go some way to improving the social sustainability of gated communities.

Over the last decade or so, with the implementation of urban policies aimed at addressing urban sprawl, intensive housing developments have become increasingly common in New Zealand. A proportion of these are gated communities. While some owe much to international styles and design, also observable is a lower key kiwi-style of gatedness which incorporates only some of the components of international mainstream gated communities. As of yet, however, the incidence of gated communities in New Zealand is not high. There are very few gated communities of any major scale that can compare with what can be observed overseas. Many New Zealand gated communities are relatively small and as such do not pose much of a threat to the way in which neighbourhoods are connected. It could even be argued that the small gated communities, observable in Auckland suburbs, are not intrinsically very different from the detached, enclosed standalone housing that characterizes New Zealand suburban landscapes. Yet, the potential still remains for larger purpose-built gated communities to be erected on greenfield sites on the periphery of large urban centres. Given that the current economic downturn has already scuttled some major development proposals in various parts of the country, in the short to medium term, it is unlikely that we will see significant growth in the number of large-scale gated communities in New Zealand.

Notes

1   New Zealand has a population of nearly 4.285 million people, approximately one third of whom live in the greater Auckland area (Statistics New Zealand, 2008).
2   The kiwi is a nocturnal flightless bird native to New Zealand. It is frequently used as a national symbol and the term is a nickname applied to New Zealanders and used by New Zealanders themselves.

References

Atkinson, R. and Blandy, S. (2005) 'Introduction: International perspectives on the new enclavism and the rise of gated communities', *Housing Studies*, vol 20, no 2, pp177–186

Bauman, Z. (2006) *Liquid Fear*, Polity Press, Cambridge

Beck, U. (1992) *Risk Society: Towards a New Modernity*, Sage, London

Best, E. (1927) *The Pa Maori*, Board of Maori Ethnological Research for the Dominion Museum, Wellington, New Zealand

Best, E. (1941) *The Maori: Volume 1*, Board of Maori Ethnological Research for the Author and on Behalf of the Polynesian Society, Wellington, New Zealand

Blakely, E. J. and Snyder, M. (1995) 'Fortress America: Gated and walled communities in the United States', Working paper for Lincoln Institute of Land Policy, US

Bramley, G., Dempsey, N., Power, S., and Brown, C. (2006) 'What is "social sustainability" and how do our existing urban forms perform in nuturing it?', Paper presented at the Planning Research Conference, University College London, London, April

Department of Prime Minister and Cabinet (2003) *Sustainable Development for New Zealand Programme of Action*, Department of the Prime Minister and Cabinet, Wellington, New Zealand

Dixon, J. and Dupuis, A. (2003) '"gatedness" and governance: Residential intensification in Auckland, New Zealand', Paper presented at the international Conference on Gated Communities: Building Social Divisions or Safer Communities?, Department of Urban Studies, University of Glasgow, Scotland, 18–19 September

Dixon, J. and van Roon, M. (2006) 'Private governance of low impact design features: A comparative investigation of issues', Paper presented at the International Sustainable Development Research Conference, Hong Kong, 6–8 April

Enterprise North Shore (undated) *North Shore City*, www.ens.org.nz, accessed 3 June 2008

Giddens, A. (2000) *Runaway World*, Routledge, New York, NY

Glasze, G., Webster, C. and Frantz, K. (2006) 'Introduction', in Glasze, G., Webster, C. and Frantz, K. (eds) *Private Cities: Global and Local Perspectives*, Routledge, Abingdon, pp1–8

Irwin, G. (1985) *Land, Pā and Polity: A Study Based on the Maori Fortifications of Pouto*, New Zealand Archaeological Association, Auckland, New Zealand

Jurgens, U. and Landman, K. (2006) 'Gated communities in South Africa', in Glasze, G., Webster, C. and Frantz, K. (eds) *Private Cities: Global and Local Perspectives*, Routledge, Abingdon, pp109–126

King, M. (2003) *The Penguin History of New Zealand*, Penguin Books, Auckland, New Zealand

Leach, H. (2000) 'The European house and garden', in Brookes, B. (ed) *At Home in New Zealand*, Bridget Williams Books, Wellington, New Zealand

Low, S. (2003) *Behind the Gates: Life, Security and the Pursuit of Happiness in Fortress America*, Routledge, New York, NY

Marcuse, P. (1997a) 'The ghetto of exclusion and the fortified enclave – new patterns in the United States', *American Behavioral Scientist*, vol 41, no 3, pp311–326

Marcuse, P. (1997b) 'The enclave, the citadel, and the ghetto – what has changed in the post-Fordist US city?', *Urban Affairs Review*, vol 33, no 2, pp228–264

Ministry for the Environment (2005) *New Zealand Urban Design Protocol*, Ministry for the Environment, Wellington, New Zealand

Neville, R. (1979) 'Trends and sources', in Neville, R. and O'Neill, C. (eds) *The Population of New Zealand*, Longman Paul, Auckland, New Zealand

New Zealand Historic Places Trust (undated) *Archaeological Remains of Pa*, www.historic.org.nz/heritage/archsites_pa.htm

North Shore City (2006) 'About North Shore City', www.northshorecity.govt.nz/about_the_city/population_and_statistics.htm, accessed 1 August 2008

Pearson, D. and Thorns, D. (1983) *Eclipse of Equality*, George Allen and Unwin, Sydney, Australia

Salmond, J. (1986) *Old New Zealand Houses*, Reed Methuen, Auckland, New Zealand

Statistics New Zealand (2008) *Hot off the Press: Subnational Population Estimates: At 30 June 2008*, www/stats.govt.nz, accessed 1 October 2008

Walton, A. (2000) *Archaeology of the Taranaki-Wanganui Region*, Department of Conservation, Wellington, New Zealand

11

Afterword

Ola Uduku and Samer Bagaeen

Introduction

Gated communities, it can be seen from the preceding chapters, have a myriad of different interpretations and uses. The global spread of the chapters within this volume has pulled together an international survey of types and forms. The majority of the book's chapters give a historical overview to the context in which the gated communities have operated (and continue to operate) in each country reviewed.

There seems to be little discrepancy in the fundamental objectives of today's gated communities: the need for security and/or exclusivity. How this is achieved today appears to be modelled on the definitions discussed in the Foreword: the condominium/club exclusivity of the affluent gated estate, versus the pragmatic response to high crime levels in cities such as Lagos and Johannesburg, which has also resulted in lower middle-class and poorer neighbourhoods clubbing together to construct makeshift metal booms and pay 'security' to guard streets and neighbourhoods from external crime.

The evolution and development of gated communities, however, have a more variegated spread across the countries examined in this volume. The African contributors, Uduku and Landsman, acknowledge strong continuing links in urban areas with traditional forms of living and aspirations towards living in exclusive 'security'-controlled enclaves, which have become the pattern in most major cities (see Chapters 5 and 6). The historical debt that these current developments owe to earlier African 'quasi-urban' locations, such as the ruins of Great Zimbabwe, in Zimbabwe, and more historic urban archaeological cities, such as the ancient kingdoms of Benin and Kano in Nigeria, is evident. The more recent socio-economic

and political situations in each country have led to different routes of evolution to the high-level security regimes employed to help counter serious and violent urban crime.

In Latin America, the class politics and urban growth of cities in the 20th century have had a different influence on city formation and, subsequently, the formulation of gated enclaves. The proximity of the subcontinent to mainland US also had an influence in the development of these 'West Coast'-style enclaves, which have become a ubiquitous part of urban live in these countries. Roitman, Giglio and Sheinbaum give their different descriptions on the 'specifics' of gated community evolution in their differently analysed countries (see Chapters 7 and 8).

China comes from an equally different traditional history of 'forbidden' walled cities and earlier enclaves for foreigners, which were still quite common until the commencement of World War II. J. G. Ballard (2008), in his autobiographical memoir, describes how he viewed China as a young boy prior to the outbreak of war. Its current rapid urbanization has led to a reinterpretation of the contemporary gated community, which has evolved from its historic adaptation of traditional forms of communal residence, residential segregation, social stratification and structural conditions, including state control over land and its continual intervention in the construction of housing.

European (French) and American gated communities are further scrutinized by Le Goix and Callen who, like Tomba, highlight the importance of local institutional and building traditions in shaping gated suburbs (see Chapters 9 and 4, respectively). They particularly highlight the role played by the local smaller developer whose strategy focuses on niche markets where ideas of sustainability are sold in tandem with ideas of exclusivity rather than integration. Whatever the context, they argue, local actors, residents' strategies, public bodies of governments and entrepreneurs find ways of meeting what is deemed to be a continuous demand for local control, which can then be met either by means of private urban governance or by a local body of the public government, depending on institutional and social exclusion patterns.

Landman's take on South Africa, with reference to large-scale socio-spatial engineering that goes as far back as 1656 when the Dutch settled in the Cape, is that gated places, in some cases, were the direct result of gated mindsets based on a logic of difference (social space) that manifested themselves in separated spaces in the built environment (physical space) (see Chapter 6).

Reflections on key themes

What can we make of this analysis? Sardar's polemic critique on the nature of gated communities gives an extreme reading of the situation, in which 'no good' can come of the capitalist project of exclusion in which countries, globally, are now engaged (see Chapter 2). That said, we do, however, feel that the purpose of the book has been to give alternative readings in order to enable us to use a different range of lenses to appreciate this global phenomenon, its different evolution in different contexts, and, most importantly, to consider what sustainability issues 'global' gating presents. Uduku (see Chapter 5), like Dupuis and Dixon (see Chapter 10), highlights strong influences of global agendas that reflect international environmental concerns underpinned by notions of sustainable development.

The contribution of this book to this field of knowledge lies in examining how, historically, cultures and traditions have managed the public and the private, both as systems of values and responses to these in the built environment. In the Foreword, Sassen argued that a key aspect of this paradigm shift lies in moving the debate on gated communities forward from the familiar notion of the gated community to a more generic notion of urban gating. The remaining chapters take this position on board in their exploration, with Bagaeen (see Chapter 3) looking at how changes in laws and local customs have shaped traditional built environments over the years to take on board desires for safety and security and, sometimes, the need to be

different and to be seen, or not (as the case may be) as different. In New Zealand, Dupuis and Dixon (Chapter 10) argue that what has changed over time was not the functions served by gates and enclosures, but the forms of landownership involved.

Initially maintaining the notion of the 'gated community', the chapters have shown that gated communities are not necessarily a new form of housing but a product of time, institutional prowess, and sometimes change.

In China, the gated community grew out of adapting traditional forms of communal residence, residential segregation, social stratification and structural conditions, including state control over land and its continual intervention in the construction of housing. As a residential form, it provided the new elites with enough autonomy to participate in the market, while asking them to participate in legitimating the regime. Tomba (see Chapter 4) has shown that by empowering management companies and developers, local administrations were able to contain conflict emerging from the privatization of space, while preventing consumers' anger from threatening political legitimacy, social order and authority. As a residential form, gating provided the new elites with enough autonomy to participate in the market while asking them to participate in legitimating the regime.

Good access to services appears to be an attraction of suburban urban gating in Argentina. This is, of course, at odds with recent research by Barmley and his colleagues in the Sustainable Urban Form Consortium (Jenks and Jones, 2009), who find that access to services is better at higher densities as opposed to suburban low density. It is these services that give shape to what Sheinbaum (see Chapter 8) calls 'self-segregated complex microcosms' that constitute a new form in a long process over time which has historically rationalized social differentiation and exclusion as natural and inevitable. Uduku, in her study of Lagos (Chapter 5), also explored successful attributes of gating, highlighting its future potential as a sustainable micro-community model when sustainable energy sourcing becomes affordable and available at the micro level.

Conclusions

From the preceding chapters and the analysis of their key themes by the contributing authors, it is clear that in response to Sardar's polemic (Chapter 2), there can be benefits to be gained from urban gating. In addition, the issue of sustainability remains crucial to the success of contemporary gated communities.

Sustainability takes on a new life in many emerging and developing countries. Gated communities in many of these situations create for their residents self-sustaining enclaves with services such as electricity and pipe-borne water delivered to residents by communally owned power generators and boreholes. These communities, therefore, are both self-selecting and exclusive in their membership; but importantly, they are also self-sustaining and autonomous to local authorities or national services provision.

The historic context, as explicated by all contributors, to the gated communities cannot be divorced either from the reading and understanding of contemporary gated communities. Indeed, history, it seems, relates directly to the evolution and development of today's gated enclaves – whether or not it is publicly acknowledged. As Landman points out, sometimes the authorities remain 'closed' or gated within their own realization of the influence of history on today's contemporary evolution of urban gated communities (see Chapter 6).

Historic case studies of gated communities lie outside the remit of the book; but it is useful to note that aside from the known anthropological background to gated/fortified communities, in more recent times the history of the original ghettos in Eastern Europe, and also internment camps used by some countries before and during the World Wars were in themselves examples of authoritarian-controlled gated or secured environments with a more political than necessary socio-economic or particularly high-security imperative.

The emergence of 'densification' as a strategy for achieving urban sustainability in cities is also likely to impact positively upon gated communities who are less based on suburbia, the traditional West Coast American design, and more based on the more dense inner-city gated 'mews', 'close', and other urban typologies found in the UK and other parts of Western Europe. Inner-city gated enclaves are already ubiquitous in London and other large cities in the UK such as Liverpool and Glasgow.

In terms of tenure, the idea of the gated 'community' also has pragmatic benefits. Self-selecting communities of interest, such as are found amongst gated developments, do develop deeper ties at the local level and tenure is longer than is the case in non-gated residential areas. The need to make this a force for good and positive development and not the 'gated minds' enclave phenomenon described by Landman (Chapter 6) is imperative.

So, are gated communities a good thing? Despite the preceding discussion providing a 'positive' viewing of the gated community environment, the overwhelming view in academe and in practice is less convinced. We know that for many the jury remains out, but hope that this volume has contributed through its various authors and commentators a range of challenging views that can engage with the ongoing debate. This is both a continuing research project and discussion that will absorb us in the years to come.

References

Ballard, J. G. (2008) *Miracles of Life*, HarperCollins, London, Chapter 5, pp59–60

Jenks, M. and Jones, C. (eds) (2009) *Dimensions of the Sustainable City*, Springer, London

Index